W9-BZI-527

DATE DUE

JUL 1 0 2002	
DEC 0 2 2002 AUG 1 3 2009	
JUN 1 6 2011	
MAY 1 4 2016	
JUL 3 0 2017	

BRODART   Cat. No. 23-221

Student Companion to

Zora Neale HURSTON

Student Companion to
Zora Neale HURSTON

Josie P. Campbell

Student Companions to Classic Writers

Greenwood Press
Westport, Connecticut • London

Library of Congress Cataloging-in-Publication Data

Campbell, Josie P.
    Student companion to Zora Neale Hurston / Josie P. Campbell.
        p.   cm.—(Student companions to classic writers, ISSN 1522–7979)
    Includes bibliographical references and index.
    ISBN 0–313–30904–3 (alk. paper)
    1. Hurston, Zora Neale—Criticism and interpretation—Handbooks, manuals, etc.
    2. Women and literature—United States—History—20th century.   3. African
    Americans in literature.   4. Folklore in literature.   I. Title.   II. Series.
    PS3515.U789Z64   2001
    813′.52—dc21   2001030154

British Library Cataloguing in Publication Data is available.

Copyright © 2001 by Josie P. Campbell

All rights reserved. No portion of this book may be
reproduced, by any process or technique, without the
express written consent of the publisher.

Library of Congress Catalog Card Number: 2001030154
ISBN: 0–313–30904–3
ISSN: 1522–7979

First published in 2001

Greenwood Press, 88 Post Road West, Westport, CT 06881
An imprint of Greenwood Publishing Group, Inc.
www.greenwood.com

Printed in the United States of America

The paper used in this book complies with the
Permanent Paper Standard issued by the National
Information Standards Organization (Z39.48–1984).

10 9 8 7 6 5 4 3 2 1

Cover portrait of Zora Neale Hurston reproduced from the collection of the Library of Congress.

AUSTIN COMMUNITY COLLEGE
LIBRARY SERVICES

To
my daughters

Contents

Series Foreword

This series has been designed to meet the needs of students and general readers for accessible literary criticism on the American and world writers most frequently studied and read in the secondary school, community college, and four-year college classrooms. Unlike other works of literary criticism that are written for the specialist and graduate student, or that feature a variety of reprinted scholarly essays on sometimes obscure aspects of the writer's work, the Student Companions to Classic Writers series is carefully crafted to examine each writer's major works fully and in a systematic way, at the level of the nonspecialist and general reader. The objective is to enable the reader to gain a deeper understanding of the work and to apply critical thinking skills to the act of reading. The proven format for the volumes in this series was developed by an advisory board of teachers and librarians for a successful series published by Greenwood Press, Critical Companions to Popular Contemporary Writers. Responding to their request for easy-to-use and yet challenging literary criticism for students and adult library patrons, Greenwood Press developed a systematic format that is not intimidating but helps the reader to develop the ability to analyze literature.

How does this work? Each volume in the Student Companions to Classic Writers series is written by a subject specialist, an academic who understands students' needs for basic and yet challenging examination of the writer's canon. Each volume begins with a biographical chapter, drawn from published sources, biographies, and autobiographies, that relates the writer's life to his or her work. The next chapter examines the writer's literary heritage, tracing the literary influences of other writers on that writer and explaining and discussing the literary genres into which the writer's work falls. Each of the following chapters examines a major work by the writer, those works most frequently read and studied by high school and college students. Depending on the writer's canon, generally between four and eight major works are examined, each in an individual chapter. The discussion of each work is organized into separate sections on plot development, character development, and major themes. Literary devices and style, narrative point of view, and historical setting are also discussed in turn if pertinent to the work. Each chapter concludes with an alternate critical perspective from which to read the work, such as a psychological or feminist criticism. The critical theory is defined briefly in easy, comprehensible language for the student. Looking at the literature from the point of view of a particular critical approach will help the reader to understand and apply critical theory to the act of reading and analyzing literature.

Of particular value in each volume is the bibliography, which includes a complete bibliography of the writer's works, a selected bibliography of biographical and critical works suitable for students, and lists of reviews of each work examined in the companion, all of which will be helpful to readers, teachers, and librarians who would like to consult additional sources.

As a source of literary criticism for the student or for the general reader, this series will help the reader to gain understanding of the writer's work and skill in critical reading.

Acknowledgments

I owe a debt of gratitude to Barbara A. Murphy, my extraordinary administrative assistant, who assisted and helped me with all of the computer work on this manuscript.

I am also deeply indebted to Professor Bruce A. Rosenberg, Brown University, who taught me to read more sensitively and whose book, *The Art of the American Folk Preacher*, provided me with so many valuable insights.

I am also indebted to the remarkable work of the last ten years by Hurston scholars; their work often led the way to my own reading of Hurston.

1

The Life of Zora Neale Hurston

Although there seems to be a great deal of information about Zora Neale Hurston's life, sifting through it remains a challenge. In her autobiography, *Dust Tracks on a Road* (1942), Hurston is coyly vague about her own birth date. She claims to have "heard" that she was born in January in Eatonville, Florida, but she is also careful not to be precise about the year. Indeed, Hurston, who admits in *Dust Tracks* that she is a word-changer, manipulates personal dates, events, and places throughout her life. The important fact, however, is that Zora Hurston was born between 1891 and 1903—she refers to various dates during this time span—in Notasulga, Alabama, where her father grew up—not in Eatonville, as she claimed (Lowe 98). Her parents were John Hurston and Lucy Ann Potts. Lucy Potts (1865–1904) was the dark daughter of a relatively well-off landowner; she became a country schoolteacher before becoming the wife of John Hurston. John (1861–1917) was a mulatto, the son of a black woman and a white man, probably her owner. He was an itinerant carpenter, a Baptist preacher, and eventually the mayor of Eatonville. He also became the moderator of the South Florida Baptist Association. Zora was the sixth of eight children. They lived in a large house, with plenty to eat from their large garden. Zora and her siblings apparently had a happy childhood, at least until their mother died in 1904.

Not only was their home life nurturing, but so too was the town of Eatonville, a "Negro" town, run by Blacks—mayor, town council, and other municipal officers. It was the first Negro town to be incorporated and the first to be organized and self-governed by Blacks in America (Howard 13). In Eatonville, Zora lived the folklife she would later study as an anthropologist. Everyone knew the Hurstons, and they knew everyone in the town. She grew up listening to the stories told by men on the porch of Joe Clarke's store; later she would include the porch with its "lying" sessions in *Dust Tracks* and *Their Eyes Were Watching God*. She attended a local school in Eatonville and read such works as Grimm's Fairy Tales, Greek and Roman myths, Norse Tales, Kipling's Jungle Books—and most certainly the Bible.

When Lucy Potts died in 1904, John Hurston remarried almost immediately. He and his second wife sent Zora, even though she was underaged, to Jacksonville, Florida, to attend school with a brother and sister. Zora would later write that it was in Jacksonville she learned she was "colored." Because her father failed to pay the school, Zora returned to Eatonville, where she and her younger siblings were generally neglected by her stepmother and father. In order to make her own way in the world, Zora, at fourteen, began to work at various jobs: as a maid for white folks, as a doctor's receptionist, even as a maid for her brother and his family. She became a sort of wardrobe girl for a singer in a Gilbert and Sullivan repertory company. All the while she continued to read voraciously. Eventually she ended up in Baltimore, Maryland, where she took waitressing jobs and attended night school at Morgan Academy, a high school that later became Morgan State University. She spent two years there, finishing in 1918, and went to work in Washington, D.C., in the G Street Barber Shop, run by a black man but catering only to Whites. Zora entered Howard University in the fall of 1918, although she attended Howard Prep first (1918–1919) in order to prepare herself for the most prestigious black university in the country (Howard 16–17).

Hurston remained at Howard studying with such people as the black poet Georgia Johnson and Alain Locke, who would later become a potent force in the Harlem Renaissance. At Howard, Hurston published her first short story, "John Redding Goes to Sea," in *Stylus*, the literary club's magazine. As a result of this story, Charles Spurgeon Johnson, who had just founded *Opportunity Magazine*, contacted Hurston for more work to publish; she sent him the short story "Drenched in Light," followed by the story "Spunk" and a play, "Color Struck." Because of the power of these works, Johnson urged Hurston to come to New York to make a name for herself. Later, Hurston would give Johnson credit for pretty much single-handedly starting the Harlem Renaissance (*Dust Tracks* 176).

Hurston had already dropped out of Howard because of illness and for lack of money. She went to New York in 1925, virtually penniless, and was taken in by Charles Johnson and his wife.

While Hurston had been at Howard University, she met and fell in love with Herbert Sheen, a fellow student. In 1921, Sheen had moved to New York where he formed a jazz band; he would eventually enter the University of Chicago and become a doctor. Hurston and Sheen married in 1927 and divorced in 1931, most likely because Hurston believed that her marriage interfered with her own work and career. Sheen would later tell Robert Hemenway, Hurston's biographer, that Zora's "career doomed the marriage," leading to a subsequent, friendly divorce (Hemenway 94).

When Hurston arrived in New York, she could not have arrived at a more propitious time. The Harlem Renaissance was in full swing, flourishing from the beginning of the 1920s until the onset of the Great Depression in 1934. Harlem itself occupied a little less than two square miles of northern Manhattan. Although it was the poorest and perhaps the most crowded section of New York, it was the most livable of the ethnic ghettos. Certainly it was far better than the lower East Side, with its smoke and filth. Harlem had broad avenues, flanked by trees, and the brick and brownstone buildings of the early German and Dutch settlers. Those settlers were gone now, their places taken by people from the South, Africa, and the West Indies. Within the area known as Harlem was an incredible assortment of writers, painters, sculptors, musicians, and politicians—all of whom were engaged in energetic activity unrivaled anywhere in the United States. Such people as the black poets Langston Hughes and Countee Cullen mixed with European royalty and Broadway performers. The great musicians Fletcher Henderson, Jimmie Lunceford, and King Oliver played in the Savoy Ballroom, which held some four thousand people. "At the Savoy Ballroom, social, racial, and economic problems fade away to nothingness" (*Amsterdam News*, quoted in obituary, Moe Gale, *New York Times*, September 3, 1964). After all, stylish white crowds from "downtown" took the "A" train north to dance at the Savoy or to go to the Cotton Club to hear Cab Calloway, Duke Ellington, and Louis Armstrong play (Watson 4).

Writers such as Hurston, Hughes, Cullen, Claude McKay, and Jean Toomer were not the first African-American writers, of course, but they were among the first to be conscious of themselves as *black* writers who believed that the bridge between the white and black races depended upon the arts. Moreover, they were proud of their black heritage, with its roots in Africa and a black folk tradition. Not only did the artists of this period make their own way, but they established a cultural tradition for those black writers and artists who followed: such writers as James Baldwin, Alice Walker, and Toni Morrison, for example, and musicians like Charlie Parker and Wynton Marsalis. W.E.B. Du Bois, with whom Hurston would study, was one of the major black intellectual leaders of the early twentieth century. He wrote the classic *The Souls of Black Folks*, a collection of essays still studied at universities today, and founded *The Crisis: A Record of the Darker Races* in 1910. The magazine, sponsored by the National Association for the Advancement of Colored People (NAACP), became the bible for the Harlem Renaissance. Du Bois was a sociologist, but he sent out a call for a "renaissance of American Negro literature" ("Negro Writers" 298–99). Zora Neale Hurston was one of those talented Blacks who answered Du Bois' call.

If *The Crisis* sounded a battle call for a New Negro Movement, *Opportunity: A Journal of Negro Life* delivered what its title promised: an opportunity for Blacks to publish their works. Whereas *The Crisis* might be seen as the political arm of the Renaissance, *Opportunity* was its cultural arm. Sponsored by the National Urban League, the magazine was edited by Dr. Charles S. Johnson, who saw literature as a "great liaison between the races" (quoted in Bontemps 238). At the first *Opportunity* awards dinner in 1925, Hurston won second prize for her short story "Spunk" and met one of the judges, Fannie Hurst, a white novelist (Howard 19). Hurst hired Zora as her secretary but soon fired her because Hurston was not much good in the area of "clerking." Hurston was good at entertaining, however, and Fannie Hurst retained her as a chauffeur and a sort of black pet who could entertain Hurst and her guests with oral tales and folk songs. At the awards dinner, Hurston also met Annie Nathan Meyer, a novelist and a founder of Barnard College; she arranged for Hurston to attend Barnard on a scholarship. Hurston entered Barnard in the fall of 1925 and graduated with a B.A. in 1928. While at Barnard, she studied mainly English, political science, history, and geology, as well as the fine arts, economics, and anthropology. During her studies of anthropology, she wrote a term paper which came to the attention of Dr. Franz Boas, then a professor at Columbia. Boas took immediate notice of Hurston, hiring her on as an apprentice, and training her as an anthropologist.

Robert Hemenway, Hurston's biographer, notes that anthropology gave her the analytical tools she needed to understand her cultural roots. As Hurston grew up in Florida, she had, in fact, been living black folk life; as an anthropologist, she came to recognize the deep emotional resonance of her culture. In particular, she began to understand the richness and multilayered meanings of the oral tradition that was—and still is—the heart and soul of black people. The creativity and imagination of black language and storytelling were also to be at the heart of Hurston's own work (Hemenway 21–22).

In February 1927, Hurston began her research of folklore in the South and was singularly unsuccessful in collecting material because she was considered the academic outsider by the people she interviewed. She learned very quickly that she had to return to her people as one of them, speaking their language, living, eating, and playing with them. Later, she wrote an article for Boas on Cudjo Lewis, a survivor of the last slave ship known to deliver Africans to the United States. Although she did indeed interview Lewis, Hurston used materials of others for her so-called "original" essay (Howard 21). Hurston's later fieldwork, however, was highly original; she soon became (and remains) one of the most noted folklorists in this country. She also came to the attention of Mrs. Charlotte Osgood Mason, an extremely wealthy white New Yorker. Where Hurston collected folk stories, Mrs. Mason collected African-American writers and artists, becoming their patron. Mason was known as a sort of fairy godmother to black artists, among whom Hurston was one. Mason interested herself in what she called the "primitivism" of Indian and African art, and she looked for such primitivism in the artists she collected. Langston Hughes, who accepted for a time Mason's patronage, finally objected to the subservient role he had to play for "Godmother" Mason, as she wanted to be called. Hurston was willing to play such a role in return for the small amounts of money Mason doled out to her for her research; at the same time, there is evidence that Hurston chafed as much as Hughes under Mason's control (*Dust Tracks*, especially 144–45). Hurston worked for Mason (there is no other way of describing the relationship) from 1927 through 1931, although Mason did extend some money to Hurston until the fall of 1932 (Howard 22–23). In return, Mason determined what materials Hurston could and could not publish in her books—a hard contract, indeed.

Hurston's fieldwork put her in touch with all kinds of people, from the lumber camps to the jook joints (saloons and dance halls). Along the way, she was able to collect the incredibly rich heritage of her people, not merely the folklore but the work songs as well. She attended storytelling contests and lying sessions, and she researched Hoodoo (voodoo, as white Americans called it) in New Orleans. Indeed, she participated in Hoodoo rituals themselves. Material from this research would find its way into Hurston's first novel, *Jonah's Gourd Vine*.

Materials from Hurston's fieldwork also found their way into such dramatized versions as *Spunk*, *The Great Day*, and *Color Struck* (Speisman 34–46) and into what she called a "story book," *Mules and Men* (1935). She came to believe that the folk stories and the music she had collected could be better presented upon the stage. In the early 1930s, Hurston set about writing dramatic sketches and revues for the stage, including *Fast and Furious* (1931); the revue lasted only a week. She eventually hired her own troupe of performers and arranged a show called *The Great Day*, which dramatized a single day in a railroad work camp. Although the show opened to critical acclaim in January 1932, it failed at the box office, and Hurston had to disband her theatrical troupe. Hurston went to work for the Creative Literature Department at Rollins College at Winter Park, Florida, where she was supposed to produce a program of Negro Art. This venture also proved unsuccessful, especially when Hurston's concert group performed for audiences which excluded Blacks. She returned to New York but was plagued by intestinal illness.

Eventually she returned to Eatonville, Florida, her home base. Here she began a collaboration with Langston Hughes on a play, *Mule Bone*. The collaboration was unsuccessful, leading to a rift in their longtime friendship (Howard 28–31). Ironically, the original title of the play was "The Bone of Contention"; as Robert Hemenway points out, the play proved true to this title much more than its writers ever anticipated (136–58).

In 1934, Lippincott published Hurston's first novel, *Jonah's Gourd Vine*. Once *Jonah* was accepted, Lippincott also agreed to publish an expanded version of *Mules and Men*, a collection of African-American folk tales. In some ways, *Mules and Men* is similar to a novel with the collector of the tales (Hurston) as the narrator/protagonist. John Lowe, in his book on Hurston, *Jump at the Sun*, points out that the first line of *Mules* echoes the first line of Psalm 122: "I was glad when they said unto me, Let us go into the house of the Lord." Hurston writes "I was glad when somebody told me, 'You may go and collect Negro folk-lore' " (Lowe 85). In *Mules*, then, Hurston becomes the "one" who will enter the temple of black folklore culture (85–86). Hurston not only signifies on the Bible in *Mules*, that is, turning it to her own literary uses, she continues to do so in *Jonah*, in *Moses, Man of the Mountain*, and in her unpublished "Herod the Great." The critic, John Lowe, among others, notes that Hurston's habit of "appropriating, mimicking, reshaping, and parodying 'sacral' utterances—those of preachers, prophets, and God himself—[begins] on a large scale in *Jonah*" (86).

Jonah's Gourd Vine is based loosely on the life of Hurston's preacher-father, John Hurston, and his marriage to Lucy Ann Potts. In the novel, she tells the story of a man's flaws as well as of his greatness in preaching the word of God. The novel is also a love story that is doomed to a large extent by the inability of the protagonist, John Buddy Pearson, to recognize his own failings and weaknesses. As a result, Pearson attempts to run from his wife, his God, and from himself.

The publication of *Jonah* led to further publications of short stories and plays. None of these publications, however, alleviated the financial difficulties that plagued Hurston all of her life. In the fall of 1935, she accepted a position with the WPA (Works Project Administration) Federal Theater Project. During the time that she worked on this project, she wrote and produced a number of short plays; she also received a Guggenheim Fellowship to collect folklore in the West Indies. She resigned her WPA job and left for the Caribbean. Out of her time there, she collected material for her second book on folklore, *Tell My Horse* (1938), a study of voodoo and life in Haiti and Jamaica.

Somehow in the midst of all of this work, Hurston had found time to fall in love with a cast member of her play, *The Great Day*. This love affair was destined to end, but out of it came one of Hurston's most well-known novels, arguably one of her best, *Their Eyes Were Watching God* (1937). In this novel, Hurston captures not only the intensity of desire, but the wellspring of love that helps to shape the identity of the protagonist, Janie.

Again, to make money, Hurston found herself working for the Florida Federal Writers Project, and in 1938 became the editor of the Florida volume of the American Guide series (Howard 38). During this time, she worked hard to complete work on *The Florida Negro*, containing "the true history and present status of the black American experience" (Hemenway 252). Although the work was completed, the book was never published. Much of the material, however, found its way into Hurston's last published novel, *Seraph on the Suwanee*.

Hurston taught for a short time at the North Carolina College for Negroes at Durham. Although she was hired to organize a drama program, she never produced any plays, complaining that the college never funded her work appropriately. She did, however, find time to work with Paul Green, a noted playwright in the drama department at the University of North Carolina at Chapel Hill. She also was writing her third novel, *Moses, Man of the Mountain*, which was published by Lippincott in November 1939. Since its publication, *Moses* has received mixed reviews, perhaps summed up by Robert Hemenway, who calls it both a masterpiece and a "noble failure" (170, 215). John Lowe recognizes the novel's power and significance, noting that the novel "comments eloquently on the history of slavery that the Israelites and African Americans had in common, but [the novel] also encompasses group dynamics, the problem of racial leadership, sibling rivalry, father-son relations, people's connection to God, and the sacral quality of life" (205).

During the time Hurston worked on various WPA projects, she met and married Albert Price III. She remained married only a short time from June 1939 until February 1940, when Hurston sued him for divorce. Price countersued her, charging that she had practiced voodoo or black magic against him. Although they reconciled for a brief time, the divorce became final in 1942. In the winter of 1940–1941, Lippincott suggested to Hurston that she write her autobiography. Although she claimed that she did not want to write the book, she had most of it written by July 1941. She wrote a good deal of it in California, at the home of a wealthy friend, Katherine Mershon. Hurston had to revise her manuscript, *Dust Tracks on a Road*, after the Japanese attack on Pearl Harbor. A number of her comments in the book, considered anti-American, were deleted as irrelevant to her biography. While busy with the revisions, Hurston worked as a story consultant for Paramount Studios from October 1941 until January 1942 (Howard 41). *Dust Tracks on a Road* was not published until November 1942.

The autobiography proved far more successful than *Moses*. Ironically, given the comments Lippincott deleted from the book, *Dust Tracks* won the

Anisfield-Wolf Award for "the best book on race relations and for the best volume in the general field of fiction, poetry, or biography which . . . will aid in the sympathetic understanding and constructive treatment of race relations" (quoted in Howard 41). A number of critics charged that Hurston simply wrote what a white reading audience wanted to see; in short, Hurston had "sold out" her race in order to publish and make money. Today, however, *Dust Tracks* may be read as a "kind of 'figural anthropology' of the self" (Lionnet-McCumber 242). Hurston attempts in this work to present herself as a protagonist of her own life, as of course she is. At the same time, Hurston recreates herself, in many ways constructing a fictional persona that mediates between Hurston the author and Hurston the character in *Dust Tracks*.

In 1942, Hurston moved to Daytona Beach, where she bought a houseboat she called the *Wanago*. The name aptly describes Hurston's own wanderlust in her life, a fact she discusses rather fully in *Dust Tracks*. In Florida, she became fast friends with Marjorie Kinnan Rawlings, a Florida novelist, who wrote *Cross Creek*. To a certain extent, Rawlings and Hurston were kindred spirits; they both loved the South, its people, and especially its natural landscape.

By the spring of 1944, Hurston was back in New York City working on a script for a musical comedy, "Polk County." She and her coauthor, Dorothy Waring, expected to have the musical produced in the fall of 1944; indeed, so confident was Hurston that she moved her houseboat, berthing it in Manhattan. Unfortunately, nothing came of the project. In May of 1947, Hurston switched to Scribner's as her publisher, and in 1948, Scribner's published Hurston's last novel, *Seraph on the Suwanee*.

Seraph was a shock to many readers, for Hurston had written a novel about Whites, a novel in which Blacks for the most part remain peripheral characters. Even though the reviews for the novel were mostly positive, some readers believed that Hurston was simply selling out to white readers, giving them what they wanted to read. Robert Bone read the novel as "assimilationist," a novel that panders in its own way to white readers (169). Robert Hemenway finds Hurston turning her back on her source of creativity in her writing; instead of focusing on the black people and their lives, she gives up a celebration of black folk life for a kind of soap opera about hard-scrabbling white Florida crackers (307). Hurston's last published novel is highly experimental, rich in its realistic depictions of people and place, and in its use of language and humor.

Plagued by her own uneasiness over the novel, Hurston wrote to Rawlings that, although she had tried to do her best in the novel, she felt that she had not succeeded (Howard 46–47). By this time, Hurston was once again in New York City. On September 13, 1948, she was arrested by the police for sexually molesting a ten-year-old boy. Although the charges were subsequently dropped— Hurston was in Honduras conducting anthropological exploration at the time of the alleged crime, and the boy was proved to be mentally disturbed—various newspapers picked up the story and ran it. Black newspapers had a field day with the story. Hurston felt betrayed by her own people and vowed to leave New York forever (Howard 48–49). She returned to Florida, where she went to work as a maid for some white people. Even that fact was destined to end up in the newspapers when her employer discovered that her maid was a famous black writer.

Hurston continued to write essays, as well as short stories, while she lived in Florida. In 1950–1951, she moved to Eau Gallie to live in a one-room cabin and to continue to write. She lived there five years, suffering bouts of illness from a recurring gallbladder infection and various intestinal diseases. She had very little money, as usual. Hurston's final major writing project was her work on Herod the Great. Although she attempted to interest various publishers, she was unable to secure its publication; the manuscript is part of the Hurston Collection at the University of Florida.

Hurston continued to work at a variety of short-lived jobs near the end of her life. In 1959, she was both obese and unwell, suffering from high blood pressure, as well as other illnesses. She suffered a stroke and was forced to enter the Saint Lucie County Welfare Home. Zora Neale Hurston died of hypertensive heart disease on January 28, 1960. Her family and friends paid for her funeral service. She was buried in a segregated cemetery, ironically called the Garden of Heavenly Rest. Her grave remained unmarked—and thus unknown—until the novelist Alice Walker searched for and uncovered it. The grave marker, erected by Walker, that now takes notice of Hurston reads:

ZORA NEALE HURSTON
"A GENIUS OF THE SOUTH"
NOVELIST   FOLKLORIST
ANTHROPOLOGIST
1901   1960
("Looking for Zora" in Bloom 107)

No headstone, of course, can sum up a life. Zora Neale Hurston's life surpassed anything she ever wrote, but we are privileged to have that writing as testimony to a life full of courage, extraordinary talent—of genius, as Walker put it—and love, not only for her people but for the world's people. In *Dust Tracks* Hurston writes about herself: "The stuff of my being is matter, ever changing, ever moving, but never lost" (226). She was right, of course, as she so often was. We remain grateful that through her work, Zora Neale Hurston is not lost to us and to future generations of readers.

Zora Neale Hurston's Fiction: An Overview

Zora Neale Hurston's fiction, especially her novels, leads us to examine ourselves in relation to the world around us. Without exaggeration, her novels enlarge both our minds and our hearts. Hurston, however, would not make such a claim; instead, she would keep moving towards some goal to be reached, some project to be started. Her anxious restlessness about herself and her work makes her a very contemporary writer, a modernist who tried to enlarge the very notion of what it is to be American. She wrote about traditional subjects—love and loss, displacement and home, failure and triumph—at the same time she attempted to redefine our notion of American culture. In her autobiography, itself a fiction that contained truths, she wrote: "Well, that is the way things stand up to now. I can look back and see sharp shadows, high lights, and smudgy inbetweens." She went on to write the famous line about being in "Sorrow's kitchen" as well as being on the "peaky mountain," with a harp in one hand, a sword in the other (*Dust Tracks* 227). Nothing sums up more fully the story of her life, and of America, than her sense of great contrasts and of great hope. Her novels—and her short stories—offer us the same vital contrasts and the same struggle to reconcile the harp and the sword.

All of her novels, as John Lowe has so astutely observed, are comedies in a "cosmic" sense (passim). That is to say that the comedy is a matter of life and death, with death finally always being outwitted through love, through generosity, through imagination, and perhaps most of all, through the act of storytelling itself. Hurston grew up hearing stories from her immediate family and from her extended family, the people of Eatonville, Florida. She listened to and remembered the ritual storytelling on the porch of Joe Clarke's store. All of these stories, plus the many that she collected in her anthropological work, became sources for her own imaginative use and recreation of them.

Telling and retelling stories has always been a way of keeping people and their culture alive. For Hurston, born black in a predominantly white world, stories are a way of becoming alive as well; not only does she become alive through her story work, but she can give her people life. In addition, through these stories, Hurston hopes to cross the color divide in the United States, as she quickens the breath of both black and white readers. Lowe points out that Hurston is like the African "griot," the oral historian/poet/musician, bringing all of these talents into play in her writing (5). Griots were also known as "praise-singers," Lowe writes, and the term is particularly apt for Hurston (5). In *Jonah's Gourd Vine*, for example, we hear the great and ancient drum of Africa at the funeral of John Buddy Pearson. The drum repeats the rhythm of death—O-go-doe—but we also hear the angelic singers around the throne of God, welcoming John Buddy home.

The strong oral cadences of Hurston's fiction have their own music. Her use of language has its roots not only in the black oral tradition but in black music as well: in the black spirituals Hurston heard as she grew up, in the blues of Ethel Waters, and in the jazz of the jook joints she visited. In Hurston's fiction we do not simply hear the talk of characters, we hear their song. Most of all, we hear the distinctive voice of the praise-singer herself.

PLOT DEVELOPMENT

Hurston's plots are straightforwardly chronological. They often deal with the protagonist's journey to an awareness of the self and the surrounding world. To a certain extent, the form of the plot is that of the *Bildungsroman*, which deals with the growth of the major—as well as occasionally secondary—characters. In *Jonah's Gourd Vine*, for example, John Buddy Pearson discovers his weakness is vanity, but it takes him a lifetime to learn this. Janie Crawford, in *Their Eyes Were Watching God*, is both young and innocent at the beginning of the novel; through her experiences with life, and especially with marriage, she grows to understand who she is.

The characters fall from unknowing into experiences that push them into knowing themselves in relation to others. Each time, for example, that Janie finds herself in a relationship with a man, she discovers more about herself. With Tea Cake, she is able to continue to grow and finally *be* herself. Even Moses, in *Moses, Man of the Mountain*, finds out who he is in relationship to his

God. For Hurston, plot always seems to arise out of character and situation. Even in *Dust Tracks on a Road*, the autobiographical plot comes out of Hurston's character as well as the situations in which she finds herself. Not surprisingly, the past and the roots of Hurston's characters play a significant role. John Buddy, Janie Crawford, Arvay (in *Seraph on the Suwanee*), and Moses come to understand who they are by examining their roots; Hurston spent her life studying her own cultural roots. Hurston, who had read many of the ancient Greek, Roman, Norse, and African myths recognized that the great life plot had to do with origins and the discovery of the individual self.

In each of Hurston's novels, and in her autobiography, the plot revolves around the major character's quest to discover the self. The account of origins becomes a part of the totality of the protagonist's life and his or her interrelation with others. Each of Hurston's plots always seems grounded in the present even as it looks backward to the past and forward into the future. At the end of *Their Eyes Were Watching God*, Tea Cake is dead, but not dead as long as Janie remembers him. Life for Janie is not over but beginning, even as she remembers the past. Moses goes up the mountain and takes a long look into the past but then sees into the future of his people. Similarly, John Buddy is both dead and not dead, as he arrives home to the delight of God. Moreover his people do not let him die, remembering him with the ancient rhythms of the great African drum. Arvay awakens on board the boat her husband has named for her to a new day dawning and to new life. In each case, the plots are not so much those of resolution as they are of *becoming*.

Although it is easy to say that Hurston's plots are simple, they are complicated by her use of fictions within fictions. The stories told within the major plot may seem unrelated, told for the sake of relating a tale. This is never the case. For example, in *Their Eyes*, the story of Matt Bonner's yellow mule is directly related to Janie's grandmother's tale about black women being the mule of the world's work. In addition, the mule is also associated with Janie's first husband, Logan Killicks and his mule. Indeed, Logan plans to hitch Janie up to her own mule to plow his acreage, thus fulfilling the grandmother's tale. Moreover, Janie herself is "yellow," that is, biracial. Matt Bonner's mule is bought by Jody Starks, Janie's second husband, making it seem that she will not escape the black woman's role her grandmother desired the girl to escape.

The stories within stories are often comic, but they can in no way be seen as some sort of "comic relief" from the main stories themselves. Like Shakespeare, Hurston uses these inner stories to comment on the main action, to expand upon it, and to focus our attention on major issues and themes. Thus, these seemingly digressive stories, like the one of Matt Bonner's mule, always bring us back to the main plot. In this sense, Hurston's writing is close to that of William Faulkner, who used similar techniques in his novels. More than Faulkner, however, Hurston's plots, with their fictions within fictions, seem close to jazz piano, where one hand beats out the main rhythm, as the other improvises around the melodic line. Toni Morrison today practices similar improvisations; indeed her novel, *Jazz*, makes use of this musical structure.

CHARACTER DEVELOPMENT

Hurston's minor characters are often humorous, as is Matt Bonner with his mule. They frequently are also obsessive, as is Logan Killicks, in *Their Eyes*, a man who cannot forget about his land and his mule long enough to pay attention to the young girl he has married. Similarly, Jody Starks becomes so obsessed with being a great man that he forgets to demonstrate any love he may once have felt for Janie. Peripheral characters often comment on the past, as does Janie's grandmother, who reflects on her hard life of near slavery, and on her daughter Leafy's rape. The grandmother cannot forget the past and so unwittingly attempts to bind her granddaughter to it. In *Jonah*, Lucy Potts' mother cannot forgive her daughter for marrying a man who not only is "yaller," or biracial, but who also comes from a lower class of Blacks, tenant farmers. Lucy's mother comments on both class and race prejudices of Blacks themselves. White characters, except for Arvay Henson and Jim Meserve of *Seraph on the Suwanee*, generally are kept in the background. Nevertheless, the prejudices of Whites are evident in *Jonah* when John Buddy goes to work on a former plantation. The white owner of the tenant farm on which John Buddy grew up demonstrates the harsh cruelty of Whites whose tenants were often worse off, if possible, than slaves. Even the Washburns in *Their Eyes*, although well-meaning, are insensitive to the lives of their black workers.

Hurston's major characters are not only heroic, often fighting great odds, but they also demonstrate growth. From John Buddy in *Jonah* to Arvay Henson in *Seraph*, Hurston's protagonists are always in a state of "becoming." They become capable of looking inside themselves in order to discover their place in the world around them. Often they struggle against what they will become. Such is the case with Moses, who never wants to be the leader of his people. Indeed, he is not at all sure who his people are. Arvay Henson fights against the passion and love that she feels for Jim Meserve, but in the end discovers that such passion and love are in large part who she is. Her reconciliation with Meserve leads Arvay into the morning of a new day. Perhaps Janie Crawford demonstrates the growth of the individual that is so important to Hurston's characters and to her own life. At the end of *Their Eyes*, we find in the diurnal round of time always a beginning, not just for Janie, but also for the listeners of her story—for her best friend Pheoby and for us as well.

SETTING

Hurston's fictional world contains, for the most part, those places with which she is most familiar: Florida, in particular the town of Eatonville (*Jonah* and *Their Eyes*), as well as the coast of Florida (*Seraph*), and New York City, particularly Harlem ("Story in Harlem Slang," "Book of Harlem," and "Harlem Slanguage," for example). *Moses*, of course, is set outside the United States; it is the story of the Exodus, the mass migration of the Jews out of Egypt into the promised land of Jerusalem. This novel, however, also retells the story of the mass exodus of African Americans from the South to the North, the journey Hurston herself took when she left Eatonville for Washington D.C., eventually working her way to Harlem.

Eatonville is probably the single most important geographic landmark in Hurston's fiction. It was the town where she grew up; her father, John Hurston, served as mayor of the all-black town. Eatonville was not merely the black part of a white town, but it was organized and operated by Blacks, self-governed by Blacks. John Hurston attained some prominence in the town, not merely as the mayor, but as a carpenter and a Baptist preacher who became moderator of the South Florida Baptist Association. His wife, Lucy Potts Hurston, had been a country schoolteacher. In this environment, Zora Neale Hurston was able to thrive. She grew up hearing stories told on the porch of Joe Clarke's store; both the stories and the porch would be immortalized in Zora's fiction. The town of Eatonville figures prominently in *Jonah*; it is where John Buddy Pearson rises to prominence and where he meets his downfall. The town is also the main setting, aside from the muck, in *Their Eyes*. Janie Crawford travels there with her second husband, Jody Starks, where he becomes a self-made man—a "big" man, as he likes to think. As he grows "big" in the community, he loses Janie's love and eventually his life.

Hurston creates and uses setting as if she were filming a movie, often beginning with a broad long-distance shot of the community and then moving into houses and rooms with spatially tight, close camera work. Architectural space and detail are important to Hurston's use of setting. For example, in *Jonah*, John Buddy grows up in little more than a hovel, the space allotted to his mother and stepfather, Ned Crittenden, a tenant farmer. The house itself is deteriorating as rapidly as the family it contains. The broken-down house, as well as its broken furniture, represents the broken family relationships. The squalor of the Crittenden house repeats itself in the meanness of the stepfather's temper. Contrasted with John Buddy's family house is Alf Pearson's plantation, with its huge white house and clean small houses for his plantation workers. There is no mistaking that Pearson's plantation is a former slave plantation, and in many ways, the place suggests remnants of slavery days. In comparison,

Pearson's plantation seems enlightened compared to the tenant farming that Crittenden does. Neither setting, however, ultimately is desirable; in both cases, Blacks slave over the white man's work just as they did in pre-Civil War days.

The Potts' house by comparison seems a veritable paradise. Lucy Potts' father, who has worked hard all of his life, has managed to acquire land and a decent house. Even here, however, Hurston uses architectural space and detail to skewer middle-class pretensions. Moreover, the acquisitions of the Potts family, even their placement of "things," seem little more than outward manifestations of their pride and vanity. Lucy's mother disowns her daughter for running off and marrying a "yaller," biracial man. She sees John Buddy himself as a commodity, ill-produced by the Crittendens who still serve the white man.

Often architectural space suggests the materialism of the characters who inhabit it. Logan Killicks has a parlor with an organ in it, but we never see Janie Crawford and Logan in it, nor do we ever hear music in that house (*Their Eyes*). Jody Starks' store becomes far more important than his wife; she merely serves as a decorative ornament both in the store and in their house. Indeed, the Starks' house is very much like the white plantation house of former slave-owners (*Their Eyes*). On the other hand, Janie and Tea Cake, her third husband, place little value on things; Tea Cake owns only a guitar. Their house on the muck belongs to the owner of the farm.

In *Seraph on the Suwanee*, the grander the Meserve house becomes, the more Jim and Arvay Henson Meserve's marriage falters. In their house, kitchen, living room, and bedroom are crucial, both materializing and grounding what turns out to be a soap operish story. The Henson house in Sawley serves to reinforce the narrowness of the lives of the family that inhabits it; finally the house self-destructs as a result of the mean-spiritedness of the family. The house is taken over at the end literally by rats and by Arvay's "rat" of a sister and brother-in-law. Ultimately, Arvay must torch the Henson house in order to preserve her own self-integrity.

Hurston uses houses, with the things they contain, as symbolic representations of politics and of historical events, particularly those events having to do with slavery, tenant farming, and racial prejudice. Houses and buildings also demonstrate important links to character, family, and human relations. These dwellings, however, are always temporary; the Crittenden house threatens to fall down; Arvay torches her family homestead. Paradoxically, houses do not necessarily provide protection against a cruel world; instead, they often reveal the contingencies of the world.

In addition to the use of geographical and architectural space, Hurston also uses nature to delineate character and human relations. We see this especially in *Moses*, where the protagonist truly is a man of the mountain. The often rock-hardness of Moses seems fitting as he climbs the mountain to talk with

God and, finally, to talk with the wise old lizard that resides there. As Hurston wrote about Moses, many could climb mountains and bring back laws to the people, "But who can talk with God face to face?" ("Author's Introduction," *Moses* xxiii).

In *Jonah*, John Buddy was at one with nature, leaping from rocks and swimming the Notasulga River, crossing over the river that separated him from Lucy Potts and a far different life from that with the Crittendens. On the Pearson plantation, the woods afford Blacks a space in which to hold their festivals, to sing their songs, and dance their dances, away from prying white eyes. John Pearson is in awe of the industrialization that is enticing Blacks from their agrarian roots; the train that takes so many of the Blacks to the North and supposed freedom is also the train that ironically kills John Buddy.

Janie Crawford also feels at home with nature. Her sensual experience under the pear tree, with its white blossoms and pollen-bearing bees, provides Janie with a vision of potential love between a man and woman. In that vision, she sees that a giving and taking are necessary. Logan Killicks and Jody Starks see nature as something to exploit. Logan tills his acreage in order to acquire more. He sacrificed his first wife to work on the farm and plans to do the same with Janie. Starks, too, clears the land to build houses and roads. He, like Killicks, is interested in acquisitions, things that will make him a "big" man in the town of Eatonville. And, like Killicks, Starks is willing to sacrifice Janie for the sake of aggrandizement and power. Only with Tea Cake does Janie find fulfillment of the vision she experienced as a teenager under the pear tree. Nature is not necessarily benign, however. The hurricane that strikes on the muck kills many and indirectly kills even Tea Cake. Yet Tea Cake is absorbed into Nature, linked with the seeds he leaves Janie. The seeds are linked to the cycle of the seasons, to life itself, just as Tea Cake is. At the end of *Their Eyes*, Janie looks out of the window of her house to see and feel Tea Cake alive in the cosmos itself.

Hurston herself felt at home in the natural world, especially in Florida. She wrote in her autobiography that Harlem had become like hell to her, where people betrayed one another and exhibited envy and viciousness. She never seemed to stay in urban areas very long, always returning to a more rural setting. When she lived on her houseboat off the coast of Florida, she felt that she had truly come home. Arvay, in *Seraph*, always believes that Sawley, her hometown, is the ideal place, where people are naturally good. When Arvay moves with her husband Jim to Citrabelle, Florida, she finds a rich and beautiful world of wonderfully bright flowers, a world of scent and color. Yet, she also finds this world too "easy," as she puts it; people don't have to work hard enough to appreciate what they get. To be sure, Arvay is right to suspect the natural world; no matter how beautiful on the surface, it is not paradise. She discovers this when a rattlesnake wraps itself around Jim, threatening his very life. At the end of *Seraph*, Arvay learns the dangers of the ocean, but she also learns of love and of life. The dawn brings more than a new day; the dawn brings to Arvay the knowledge that, if one is willing to take risks, life itself is full of new beginnings.

HURSTON'S BODY OF WORK

Zora Neale Hurston's works, especially her novels, demonstrate a remarkable facility with narrative and with dialogue. Her plots repeat the age-old story of characters who seek to discover who they are and their place in the world around them. Often the characters are unaware of their quest—John Buddy Pearson in *Jonah* does not realize his journeying until the last day of his life. This fact, however, does not minimize the importance of the journey. The titles of Hurston's novels suggest her understanding that such journeying is spiritual. In addition, Hurston's novels deal with the political issues that faced the United States during her day: the racism of Jim Crow laws, the cruelties of tenant farming, the grinding poverty of many Blacks, the lynching of black men, for examples. Hurston was not afraid to comment on class and racial prejudices of Blacks themselves: Lucy Potts' family who despise John Buddy as an "over-the-creek nigger"; Mrs. Turner who looks down on Tea Cake as being too black for Janie Crawford, who is light-skinned; and Miriam, who despairs that Moses has brought the dark Zipporah to be Queen over all the other, lighter-complected women.

Hurston's first novel, *Jonah's Gourd Vine*, makes use of these issues. At the opening of the novel, John Buddy Pearson is a young boy, a teenager, who seeks to have a better life. His story is a love story in many ways and deals with his courtship of and marriage with Lucy Potts. In this novel are many issues of family deterioration and betrayal, but there are also issues of growth and self-discovery.

Their Eyes Were Watching God has become Hurston's best-known novel and perhaps her most critically acclaimed. In this novel, Hurston demonstrates a sure gift for storytelling. The framed narrative, which begins in the present and ends there, contains Janie Crawford's quest to become herself. Hurston also uses in this novel stories within stories, such as the tale of Matt Bonner's mule. This tale comments not only on such issues as materialism and charity, for example, but also indirectly comments on the actions of various characters in the novel, in particular Logan Killicks and Jody Starks.

The skills developed in Hurston's first two novels are repeated in *Moses, Man of the Mountain*, perhaps her most ambitious novel. She does nothing less than to recreate the myth of the biblical Moses, the leader of the Jews out of Egypt, into a leader of Blacks, taking them out of bondage into the promised land. In many ways, *Moses* is Hurston's most polemic novel in which the politics of power are explored from a variety of points of view.

Following *Moses* was *Dust Tracks on a Road*, Hurston's autobiography. Although the work is obviously not fiction, it nevertheless uses many of the same techniques that Hurston incorporates in her novels. Hurston looks at herself as a character, one who follows the same plot as her fictional characters, John Buddy and Janie Crawford, for example. The character Zora is also journeying, moving from the South to the North, seeking education and a better life. As polemic and even more controversial than *Moses*, *Dust Tracks* takes a hard look at racism and injustice in the United States.

Hurston's last published novel, *Seraph on the Suwanee*, is perhaps her most experimental. The major characters, Arvay Henson and Jim Meserve, are white, yet their story follows the same narrative curve as Hurston's other novels. The novel uses the romance formula to explore both male and female relationships as well as marriage. In addition, *Seraph* also looks at barriers of class and race in this country.

MAJOR THEMES

There are numerous social issues that Hurston deals with in her fiction, but these should not be confused with major themes. Issues change from novel to novel, but Hurston's themes recur in her fictional works. The social issues she raises are many; they include rape, violence, religion, racism, class, gender, feminism, poverty, and materialism. In a number of ways, Hurston is similar to the poet Walt Whitman. Both writers loved their country and rejoiced at its great potential. At the same time, they saw the devastating consequences of the denial of opportunities for all Americans, no matter their color, sex, class, or beliefs. For Whitman and Hurston, the critical juncture in U.S. history occurred over slavery; both knew that the Civil War had in many ways resolved nothing of the so-called "race problem."

Hurston's themes are almost always connected to shared human experiences. They most often have to do with an awareness of the self. In addition, Hurston deals with love and betrayal, loss and regain in the relationships between men and women, from John Buddy and Lucy Potts to Arvay Henson and Jim Meserve. In all four of her novels, Hurston explores the relationship between the individual and his or her God. Janie Crawford sees God in her vision of the world from under the pear tree; Moses goes to the mountain to talk with God about leading his people out of slavery. In Hurston's novels—as in Whitman's poems—God is often to be found in nature. The relationship between God and African Americans, as Hurston points out, is both personal and communal.

For Hurston, as well as a great many American writers, one of the major conflicts for her characters arises out of a desire to be part of the community without being stifled by it. Flight from the community and return to it recurs over and over in her novels. In this, Hurston writes in the tradition of Mark Twain or Sherwood Anderson. At the same time, as a black writer, Hurston recognizes the value of community in ways that Twain and Anderson never could.

Only because of her enormous energy and white fascination with "Negro" art in the 1920s could Hurston pursue a career in anthropology and writing. Even so, she was unable to count on her writing to make a decent living for any length of time. She wrote in *Dust Tracks* that poverty smelled like death because she had observed near-destitution first hand. Poverty was like "[d]ead dreams dropping off the heart like leaves in a dry season and rotting around the feet" (87). She goes on to say that "[p]eople can be slaveships in shoes." From her growing-up years in the South, she found the wellspring of her creativity as well as an almost obsessive need to document black culture. Hurston was well aware that the southern values and rituals of her people were being eroded at an increasing rate, and thus she devoted a great deal of her life to documenting the life she had heard, seen, and lived. She did this in her great anthropological works, *Mules and Men* (1935) and *Tell My Horse* (1938), in many of her short stories, as well as in her novels.

Hurston never left the South in her ability to use the language of southern Blacks and Whites and to tell their stories. At the same time, she was able to sustain a vision of this country—indeed the world—that saw all peoples as brothers and sisters. Her influence on contemporary African American writers has been enormous. One need only read Alice Walker's *The Third Life of Grange Copeland* or *The Color Purple* to discover traces of Hurston's voice; indeed, *The Color Purple* is Walker's homage to Hurston. Anyone reading Toni Morrison's *The Bluest Eye* finds many of Hurston's themes revisited. Even *Jazz*, one of Morrison's most experimental novels, owes a great debt to Hurston and her own experiments with novelistic forms.

We are not grateful to Zora Neale Hurston, however, for the influence she has had on later novelists. We are grateful because she was not afraid to explore who we are as a people, to reveal to us not only how far we had come in our treatment of one another but how far we have to go.

3

The Short Fiction

Zora Neale Hurston's early short stories rehearse characters, themes, and actions that are more fully developed later in her novels. For example, her first short story, "John Redding Goes to Sea" (published in Howard University's *Stylus* in 1921 when Hurston was a student) makes use of male-female conflict. John Redding wants to see the wide world (much like Hurston herself), while his mother wants to see him married and "settled down" near her. The story itself lacks the energy and deft use of language that Hurston will later develop, but the narrative includes clear touches of irony, especially at its closing. The father-son relationship, poignantly presented, will be developed more fully in *Moses, Man of the Mountain*. John Redding's wife and mother also bear a striking resemblance to Moses' wife Zipporah, as well as his mother-in-law, both of whom wish that their menfolk stayed at home a great deal more than they do.

All of Hurston's short stories are closely connected to African-American folk life, to its language, its rituals, and its culture. Of the stories she wrote, "Drenched in Light" (1924), "Sweat" (1926), and "The Gilded Six-Bits" (1933) are perhaps the most anthologized, and for good reason. All three demonstrate Hurston's talents as a writer and storyteller.

"DRENCHED IN LIGHT" (1924)

"Drenched in Light" was Hurston's first professionally published work, appearing in the Urban League's magazine *Opportunity: A Journal of Negro Life*. It established Hurston as a writer and brought her to the attention of Fannie Hurst and Annie Nathan Meyer; Hurst later employed Hurston, and Meyer provided her with a scholarship to Barnard College (Howard 57–58). "Drenched in Light" is a story about Isis Watts, an eleven-year-old black girl who seems to be the alter ego of Hurston herself. Isis not only has a vivid imagination, but she also has an overabundance of energy. She has both talent and self-confidence, a girl who seeks to express herself to other people. She brims with curiosity about the world around her and beyond.

The story takes place in Florida and deals with the life of Isis, who lives with her Grandma Potts. Grandma is modeled after Hurston's own grandmother, who was strict, puritanically so, believing that her less-restrained granddaughter would be either lynched or sent directly to hell. Indeed, the town in which Isis lives turns out to be Eatonville, Hurston's hometown, and many of the events in the short story are built on Hurston's memories of her own childhood. Isis demonstrates the desire for distant horizons in the same fashion as Hurston did in her childhood: by sitting on a fence post and watching, searching the horizon.

PLOT DEVELOPMENT

The plot of "Drenched in Light" is simple, depicting one day when Isis escaped the clutches of her grandmother. As Isis and her brother watch their grandmother sleep, Isis sees long gray hairs growing out of Grandma Potts' chin. Isis decides that she will do a good deed by shaving her grandmother. She grabs her father's razor, and with mug, brush, and washbasin, brother Joel lathers Grandma with great gobs of soap. Isis, holding the razor above her grandmother, stands by. Unfortunately Grandma awakens and sees Isis with the razor ready—so Grandma thinks—to cut her throat (a clever and comic revision of the stereotypical black man with a razor, ready to cut someone's throat [Lowe 64]). Of course Grandma jumps up out of her chair and dashes out of the house screaming. Isis, who fears being punished, hides under the house to contemplate the sure whipping she expects, but becomes distracted by the band of the Grand United Order of Odd Fellows, who parade by the house enroute to a barbecue and log-rolling contest to be held to raise money for a new hall. The distraction for Isis pulls her towards the carnival.

She takes time, however, to run into the house to ransack her grandmother's trunk for a red tablecloth, a substitute for a Spanish shawl. Isis wraps the cloth around her and heads for the carnival where she intends to dance for the spectators. This she does, drawing a crowd around her. The red tablecloth is further enhanced by a daisy behind Isis' ear, and by the smell of lemon extract in place of perfume. As Isis dances in front of a crowd, her grandmother discovers her and cries out that her granddaughter is wearing the table cloth just bought in Orlando (22). When Isis sees and hears her grandmother, she runs into the woods and follows a creek, despairing over the second whipping she now expects.

In her despair, Isis imagines drowning herself in the creek. Her thoughts are interrupted by a couple who had seen her dance at the carnival and stop to ask her the directions to Maitland, the nearest town populated by Whites, and the Park Hotel. Isis promptly gives those directions and is invited to ride beside the driver of a grand car. In the rear of the car sits a white couple, the woman obviously enthralled with the vibrant, imaginative Isis, the man, bored and disdainful. Inspired by the two of them—and the car, as well—Isis proceeds to tell them of her dreams of trips to the horizon, of gowns that trail on the ground, of gold shoes, of a white horse, and of her adventurous, heroic fights against monsters and dragons.

As the car glides past Isis' house, Grandma Potts catches a glimpse of her and cries out, "You Isie-e! . . . Come heah *dis instunt*" (24). The woman, Helen, tells her driver to stop and let Isis out. As Grandma approaches, with switches in hand to whip Isis, Helen defends her. In fact, she pays five dollars for Grandma's tablecloth, which had cost only one dollar. As Helen says, the little girl "loves laughter," and asks if she can take her to the hotel to dance in the red tablecloth for her. Grandma agrees that Isis may go, and Isis, in her joy, dances a few steps right there. Grandma wants to clean Isis and comb her hair, but Helen tells her not to bother, that she likes the child as she is. Moreover, she believes Isis would not like being "combed and scrubbed" (25). As Isis gets into the car, she snuggles up to Helen and asks if she wants a song. The man with Helen tells her that she has been "adopted" (25). The woman pulls the child closer and says that she hopes so; hungrily, Helen desires to have the "sunshine" of Isis "soak into [her] soul" (25) because she so much needs it.

This brief story is interesting for a number of reasons, not least of all for the autobiographical details, of course. Hurston's own grandmother was extraordinarily strict with her. Then, too, the story recapitulates Hurston's own rebelliousness against traditional adult authority and the traditional roles required of women. Isis, because she is a girl, is required to do the dishes and to work in the house. Her grandmother punishes her if she whistles or sits in a brazen fashion, with legs spread apart or crossed. In addition, it is a story about dreams and imagination, which in this case are fulfilled on this one day in Isis' life.

CHARACTER DEVELOPMENT

Even though the characters are merely sketched, we seem to discover a great deal about them. Grandma is the strong arm and force in the family. There seems to be no mother present; although a father lives there, as evidenced by the shaving paraphernalia, he is absent. Grandma's word is law, backed by a hickory switch. Her job, as she sees it, is to restrain Isis' energy and/or redirect it into the proper work and behavior required of girls and women. But there is more to Grandma than this; she comes from the tradition of slavery, which had inflicted upon her the very same sorts of restraints. As soon as Grandma meets Helen, the black woman becomes obsequious. When Helen asks to take Isis to the hotel to dance, Grandma says: "Oh, yessum, yessum. . . . Everything's alright, sho' she kin go, yessum" (25). Those three "yessum" responses in so short a sentence speak volumes. Grandma warns the child to behave with "de white folks" (25). At the same time, Grandma is also proud of Isis for her talents. Grandma Potts shows up not only in Hurston's autobiography, *Dust Tracks*, but also in *Jonah* and in a much expanded version, as Nanny in *Their Eyes Were Watching God*.

Even Helen, whose role, though important, is minor, becomes more fully realized upon reflection. Helen recognizes talent, warmth, and vitality in the little brown girl even though she lacks those qualities herself. Like some of the white women in Hurston's life—Fannie Hurst and Godmother Mason—Helen hopes to be able to garner some of Isis' "light," the energy or life force of the child. Helen purchases the "light" for five dollars, if only to light up her own drab life momentarily. The white man, Harry, who is with her remains aloof, even harsh, but allows Helen her desire. Isis' "sunshine" is needed to fill up Helen's empty soul, which, as far as Hurston is concerned, undoubtedly represents the souls of many white folks.

And what of Isis, who is so eager to show off her talents, in a sense to be bought? Her very name, Isis, tells us much. Isis was the ancient Egyptian goddess who wandered the world in search of her brother Osiris, the god of fertility and the companion of Thoth, god of death and writing. The Osiris myth in which Isis functions as a high priestess has to do with memory, imagination, and immortality; whatever else Isis is, she is a link between two worlds, of the living and the dead. Isis, the fictional child of Hurston's imagination, represents the significance of her own African–American memories, not just for herself, but as a bridge between Blacks and Whites. Like Hurston, Isis desires the praise and financial backing of a white audience, but Hurston also desired the praise of the black community. We should not forget that Grandma represents the older generation of the black community, nor should we forget her pride in the talent, the spunk, and the vitality of the new, young Black who stands before her.

THEMATIC ISSUES

The themes of "Drenched in Light" are complex for such a short story. There is, first of all, the conflict between youth and authority. Isis rebels against her grandmother's strict control by running off to the carnival. In addition, Isis' flamboyant and dramatic dance for the crowd runs counter to her grandmother's rules about being a lady. The grandmother's desire for control, however, remains evenly counterbalanced by love for her granddaughter. At the same time, Hurston reveals the difficulties of a whole generation of Blacks expressing love for their families. Blacks of Grandmother's age knew the folly of showing love for their slave children who could be taken away by Whites at any time.

Hurston's second theme seems to be the impoverishment of white souls such as those of Helen and Harry. Although Harry is unaware of his coldness, Helen recognizes her own emptiness. Hurston suggests that only the vitality and creativity of Blacks can assuage the soul-weariness of Whites. In black artistry—and one supposes Hurston is thinking of her own talents here—lies the possibility of healing, perhaps eliminating racial divisions.

"SWEAT" (1926)

"Sweat" was published two years after "Drenched in Light" and rehearses some of the bitterness of marriage to be found in *Jonah* and especially *Their Eyes*.

PLOT DEVELOPMENT

The story is set in Florida, and the action takes place on the outskirts of a town very much like Eatonville, Hurston's hometown. Delia and Sykes Jones have been married for fifteen years, but their marriage went wrong very early. Although they seemingly married for love, it does not take long for love to disappear, at least on the part of Sykes. Two months after their wedding, Sykes gives his wife a brutal beating, and he begins a series of relationships with a variety of townswomen. His current companion is Bertha, an exceedingly fat woman, talked about by the townsmen as worthless in looks and character.

While Delia tolerates Sykes' running around with women, she stays home, doing white folks' laundry in order to earn a living. She has in fact worked hard to buy a home for herself and Sykes, a home he now wants to give to Bertha. It is unclear how much Sykes works, but whatever money he has made, he has spent on himself and his womanizing. When Sykes decides that he wants to be rid of Delia for good so that he can marry Bertha, he capitalizes on his wife's fear of snakes, basically to get her to leave but, since that does not work, eventually to kill her, body and soul.

The story opens with Sykes throwing his snake of a bullwhip into the room to scare Delia. When she admonishes him, reminding him that she is mortally afraid of snakes, he responds that he knows how much snakes frighten her.

"That's how come Ah done it," he says (74), doubling over in laughter and slapping his thigh. Delia decides to ignore Sykes and to continue her work. Somehow this angers Sykes even more, who kicks her carefully organized pile of laundry about the room. He accuses Delia of being a hypocrite, someone who attends church on Sunday and comes home to wash white folks' clothes, thus breaking the Sabbath. This is too much for Delia, who has apparently maintained a meek demeanor for most of her fifteen years of marriage. She lashes out at Sykes, saying he has gone too far. Not only has she been married for fifteen years, but also she has taken in laundry for all of those years—in order to have a house for the two of them and to support them. "Sweat, sweat, sweat! Work and sweat, cry and sweat, pray and sweat!" (75). In short, her sweat has not only provided the roof over their heads, it has also provided food for them. Sykes has contributed little. Later, as she reflects upon this moment, she realizes she took love with her into the marriage; Sykes had only brought a desire for the flesh (75).

But Sykes, too, reflects upon his marriage and decides that in order to be rid of Delia and marry Bertha, he must take more drastic measures. He brings home a rattlesnake, which he pens in a box near the back door. Delia of course is terror-stricken. She attempts unsuccessfully to get Sykes to remove the snake. Even the village people learn of this snake and come by to see it, wondering how Sykes ever managed to capture a six-foot rattler. Although the townsfolk believe the rattler should be killed, no one does anything about it. Delia continues to ask Sykes to remove the rattler, just as he continues to refuse her request. Finally, Delia looks him in the eye and says, "Ah hates you, Sykes. . . . Ah hates you tuh de same degree dat Ah useter love yuh" (81). Indeed, she says that she hates him like a "suck-egg dog." The image is not merely colorful but right on target, since Sykes' behavior mimics the male dog that forever chases the female dog. Sykes is thus dog-like in his preying on women. When she tells him to leave the house, Sykes is taken aback in his amazement. Although he threatens her, Sykes does leave and does not return that night.

Because the next day is Sunday, Delia goes to church and stays for the night service, the "love feast," a service of prayer and singing, in which people become filled with the spirit of God, a spirit that overflows into love for others. When Delia makes her way home, it is dark, so dark in fact that she takes the last match to light the kerosene lamp. As she goes into the bedroom to sort clothes for the laundry she would do the next day, she realizes that Sykes has placed the snake in the hamper of clothes in order to kill her. In her fear, she runs from the house, taking the lamp with her, and into the barn. The wind blows out the light, and Delia climbs up onto the hay, "gibbering" in her terror.

Icy calm follows her terror, however, as she realizes that the snake is somewhere in the house and that Sykes is likely to return and stumble over it. She could warn him but instead rationalizes that she has done the best she could, that "Gawd knows" whatever might happen is not her fault. She falls asleep as the night moves toward dawn and Sykes returns to the house. Delia steals to the house and hunkers down under the bedroom window. As she hears the whirring of the rattler, she thinks "Dat ol' scratch is woke up now!" (84).

But Sykes hears nothing as he searches for a match to get some light in the kitchen. When Sykes finally hears the snake, he calls for light, but it is too late. He thought the snake would be too sick from striking Delia to strike him, but he is wrong. The snake strikes again and again. Delia, who remains outside, hears her husband's cries, sounds that are like a "maddened chimpanzee, a stricken gorilla" (84). Finally, amid screams of terror, Sykes manages to kill the snake, but it does him little good. He calls his wife's name over and over, but she does not move at first. When she finally enters the house, the sun is up, and she finds him on his hands and knees. Only one eye is open, and his neck is swollen. Delia is well aware that Sykes, through that one open eye, can see the tubs for the laundry and the lamp. He knows, then, that she could have warned him and did not. She knows, as well, that to go for a doctor in Orlando is too great a distance.

At the love service on Sunday, Delia had sung, with the other parishioners, the song about Jordan, the river Christians cross into Paradise. The Jordan water, "black an' col," which may chill the body but not "de soul" (83). For Sykes, that water, the cold Jordan, creeps up to extinguish his open eye and him forever (85).

CHARACTER DEVELOPMENT

In "Sweat," Hurston again exhibits her talents for characterization. As she did in "Drenched in Light," she also makes wonderful use of black language and idioms, switching effortlessly from the "standard" English of the narrator to the vivid language of the townspeople, Sykes, and Delia.

Although Delia and Sykes marry for love—at least she did—the marriage can not hold together. Sykes turns away from her to other women and spends whatever money he earns on self-indulgent living. Delia's response is to retreat into her religion and to accept her situation meekly, that is until Sykes brings home the rattlesnake. Only her obsessive fear of snakes causes her to turn against Sykes, and once she declares her hatred for him, there is no turning back. Readers are sympathetic toward Delia because she works so hard and suffers so much. In addition, the townspeople agree that she is a fine woman; moreover, when Sykes first married her, Delia was a good-looking woman. His treatment of her has destroyed her beauty as well as her spirit. The townspeople, the men on the porch of the store in town, function as a communal chorus, prefiguring the townspeople in *Their Eyes*. Joe Clarke, who runs the store, remarks that nothing can turn Sykes into a decent man; he has chewed his wife like a piece of sugarcane, sucking all the juice and sweetness out of her and then discarding her. Joe will become Jody Starks, who attempts to do the same with his wife Janie in *Their Eyes*.

Delia's religion is a significant part of her life; she even changes her church so that she does not have to take the sacraments with Sykes. Indeed, one of the ironies of the story is that she rejects Sykes right after having attended her church's love feast, a service that emphasizes love for one another and redemption. Instead of Delia's forgiveness of Sykes, she turns away from him, refusing to warn or save him from the rattler. As readers, however, we have compassion for Delia and understand her failure to warn Sykes.

Sykes Jones is a bully, brutally beating his wife and turning to other women for consolation and flattery. He claims to like fat women, and the townsmen, who discuss Sykes, say that he has always liked them. As the critic John Lowe points out, Hurston recasts jokes in the black community about some men's desire for heavy women, providing us with a variation on the classic blues expression about "Big fat momma[s] wid de meat shakin' on huh bones / Evahtime she wiggles, skinny woman los' huh home" (quoted in Lowe 73). Because Delia is independent of him—she has worked to support both of them and managed to buy a house—Sykes' sense of his masculinity is threatened. We have little compassion for someone so brutal and clearly mean-spirited, who deliberately sets out to kill his wife in order to gain her property to give to another woman. Because the townspeople see through Sykes for what he is, no-good and mean, we tend to view him in the same way. The fact that Sykes acquires a snake to kill Delia, and is in turn killed by the rattler, is a neat bit of poetic justice; one might go so far as to say that Sykes kills himself out of his own meanness.

In contrast to Sykes, Delia elicits our sympathy. An independent woman with a strong work ethic, her desire for love and companionship with someone who will reciprocate is commendable. She does not seek Sykes' death; she reacts to his devious plan to kill her. Indeed, his plan to eliminate her seems to paralyze Delia as much as the snake itself.

THEMATIC ISSUES

Clearly Hurston wants her readers to pay attention to the theme of male domination of women. In particular, she focuses on the inordinate pride, the *hubris*, of the male and his abusive treatment of women in order to feed that pride.

There are also allusions to racism brought out in Sykes' hatred of seeing his wife wash the dirty clothes of white folk. Although he despises her job, one that can be traced back to slave days, at the same time he seems incapable of providing the means for her to quit. Ironically, Delia's laundry tubs alert Sykes to the fact that his wife might have saved him from the rattler's bite.

Delia's strength as a woman, as well as her ability to work to support herself as well as her husband despite his infidelity and brutality, seems only to make Sykes more anxious about his manhood. Her religion and her fear of snakes become interwoven in Hurston's use of the snake as both a religious and a phallic symbol. Just as the snake represented the evil of self-pride in the Garden of Eden, so the snake represents evil in the hands of Sykes. He uses the bullwhip, which resembles a snake, to brutalize Delia, and he does it purposefully, even laughing about it. With the rattler, Sykes raises the level of his hatred to psychological and physical death. The snake comes to represent all that is evil about a twisted masculinity.

The end of "Sweat" is bitterly ironic, since the snake presumably bites Sykes on the marital bed. Sykes calls for light, but it is far too late for him to see the light about himself and his relationship to Delia. He is lost in the darkness; what is left for him is the coldness of death itself. Hurston provides an excruciating pun at the end of the story, as death creeps up to "extinguish that eye" or "I" that was once Sykes. The erasure is total.

"THE GILDED SIX-BITS" (1933)

"The Gilded Six-Bits" was the last short story published before Hurston wrote her first novel, *Jonah's Gourd Vine*. The story has greater characterization and generally more depth than most of her earlier stories. "The Gilded Six-Bits" is the most frequently anthologized of all of Hurston's short stories.

PLOT DEVELOPMENT

The story is set in Eatonville; like "Sweat," "The Gilded Six-Bits" is about a marriage but tells a tale the reverse of the earlier story. Missie May and Joe Banks have a wonderful, caring marriage, but one that has not been tested. As Lillie Howard points out, the story falls naturally into three parts, each of which centers around the marriage of a young couple. The first part concerns the youthful joy and passion of the couple; the second part has to do with the test of the marriage and its near demise; and the third with its recreation as a richer and deeper relationship.

The story begins with Missie May and Joe as a carefree young couple who have a wonderful home. The opening line of the story, "It was a Negro yard around a Negro house in a Negro settlement" (86), makes clear that Blacks had caring and loving marriages, just as Whites did. In this story, Hurston also does more with setting than she does in her earlier works. She describes the yard, raked not only clean but with a pattern made by the rake. Freshly and fancily cut newspaper lines the kitchen shelves. There are bottles stuck along the walk, in a communal art form that one can still see in certain black communities, a remnant of African survivalism that has to do with marking one's lodging (Lowe 75). Joe works in the fertilizer factory (apparently the only industry in town), and Missie May keeps the house and yard smartly clean and decorated out of simple things. She cooks Joe's favorite foods to demonstrate her love for him. In addition, they fill their house with laughter, games, and play. Every Saturday afternoon, Joe brings home his pay, nine silver dollars. He announces his presence by throwing each one in the doorway and then hiding in the shrubbery in the yard. "Nobody ain't gointer be chunkin' money at me and Ah not do 'em nothin,'" Missie May always responds, pretending anger, as she runs about the yard trying to find Joe. Once she catches him, she immediately tries to get what he has in his pockets—always some candy kisses. This kind of joking play reveals their creative love for each other, a kind of ritualized, yet spontaneous and ever-fresh joy. Joe refers to their game as a "play-fight" (88).

Hurston pays a great deal of attention to the details of Missie May and Joe's dinner, the communion between them. There is the clean red and white checked tablecloth, the buttermilk in the pitcher, with its drops of butter, churned by Missie May (88). The hot fried fish, crackling bread (a thin corn bread, with cracklings—crisply cooked ham or pork rinds), the ham and string beans, the new potatoes, and the spicy potato pudding. The details of this meal not only represent Missie May's love for Joe, but they convey to us a sort of deliciousness about their relationship.

To show his thanks, Joe decides to take Missie May to the ice cream parlor for a treat. He tells his wife about the owner of the parlor, one Mr. Otis D. Slemmons, a city man who has apparently moved from one place to another—Memphis, Chicago, and so forth (89). As Joe describes Slemmons, it becomes clear that Joe, at least, finds this man impressive—in his dress, his manner, and most of all in his money. Missie May is not so readily convinced and assumes he is certainly no better a man than Joe. But Joe insists that though Slemmons may have a fat belly, it only makes him look like a "rich" white man. To be a rich man means to have a big belly (89). Indeed, Joe himself wishes that he had such a belly, that is, that he was rich. As Missie points out to him, Henry Ford and Rockefeller are not fat, but none of this matters; she loves Joe as he is. Joe, however, does not let his fascination with Slemmons rest. Slemmons' five-dollar gold piece, and his ten-dollar gold piece on his watch chain, as well as his gold teeth, tell everything about the man; as Joe says, he wishes the ten-dollar gold piece was his (90). What makes this money so wonderful, according to Joe, is that Slemmons got all of it from women.

Missie May does not forget this story or Joe's desire to be like Slemmons with his gold. She wants Joe to have gold, if it will make him happy. Perhaps he will find some, she tells him, and then he could wear it without women having to give it to him. Joe reminds her that he is happy with the way he is, especially as her husband. But Missie is not so sure—and as readers, perhaps we are not so sure, either; Joe spends an awful lot of time singing the praises of Slemmons, and wishing he had the portly man's gold piece.

One night, because of unforeseen circumstances at the fertilizer factory, Joe gets off work early. As he walks home, he sees the moon, which makes him long for a boy child with Missie. When he arrives home, he notices a light in the bedroom and decides to enter the house through the kitchen, stopping to wash the fertilizer dust from him before slipping into bed with Missie Mae. He knocks over some dishes, however, which crash to the floor, causing Missie to make a scared gasp. He rushes into the bedroom to reassure Missie and discovers a man's legs working to get his pants on. Joe hears Missie sobbing and Slemmons pleading for Joe not to kill him. Ironically, he offers Joe gold (93). As Slemmons attempts to leave, Joe grabs at him with his left hand, while he hits him with his right, knocking the man into the kitchen. Slemmons runs out of the kitchen door, and Joe is left holding his golden watch charm. Missie Mae continues to sob, as Joe laughs and puts the gold charm into his pocket.

No longer do Missie and Joe have a happy home. Joe remains polite and kind, yet cold. There are no more games and no more silver dollars. The only coin in Joe's pockets is the yellow coin, "like a monster," waiting to destroy Missie, she thinks. One night, when Joe returns from work, he asks Missie to give him a back rub because his back hurts; three months have passed, and for Missie, even touching Joe seems strange. That night for the first time since Slemmons was whipped out of the house, Missie and Joe make love. The next morning, when Missie makes the bed, she finds the gold piece of money underneath her pillow. She discovers that it is not a gold piece, after all, but a gilded half-dollar. She believes that Joe has paid her, just as he would a prostitute, for a night of love. Missie puts the money into his Sunday pants pocket and leaves. However, she meets Joe's mother, and, rather than admit to her that she has left Joe, Missie returns home. She determines that Joe will have to leave her.

Although Joe never mentions either the incident with Slemmons or the gilded piece put back in his pocket, about every ten days, after he comes home, he asks for his back to be "rubbed" (96). Missie is soon pregnant and has a baby boy, who looks just like Joe. Even his mother tells Joe that the child looks just like him. Although he asks every day for a week how Missie is, he says nothing about the child. On Saturday, he goes to Orlando to buy staples for the house, but he also buys bananas and apples. Finally he goes to the candy store, where the clerk greets him, saying he has not seen Joe in a long time. Joe throws the gilded coin on the counter and buys some molasses kisses for Missie. He tells the clerk he got the coin off a "stray nigger" who came through Eatonville, who tried to fool people that his watch charm and stickpin were gold. When the clerk asks if Joe had been fooled, he answers no, that he had knocked him down and taken the charm from him. When the clerk suggests that he buy some chocolate bars with the money, in addition to the kisses, Joe says that all he wants are kisses. He adds that he has a little boy now, and maybe he can suck on one of the kisses.

As Joe leaves the store, the clerk, obviously white, turns to another customer and says how much he wishes he could be like these "darkies" who laugh (98). Nothing ever seems to worry them. When Joe returns to Eatonville, he throws his silver coins into the house—fifteen times. Although Missie cannot yet run to the door, she moves as fast as she can. The last line of the story is Missie's, and it echoes her line early on: "Ah hear you chunkin' money in mah do'way. You wait till Ah got mah strength back and Ah'm gointer fix you for dat" (98).

CHARACTER DEVELOPMENT

The characters in "The Gilded Six-Bits" have a richness and depth that they lack in Hurston's earlier stories. For all that Missie May is naïve, she is also loving, caring, and playful. Missie May is a young woman who has lived her life in circumscribed circumstances, in a rural community in the South. No wonder then, that she gives herself to Slemmons in order to make her husband happy, and to shower him with riches. Doing so, she believes, will prevent some other woman—or women—from giving Joe the gold he seems so ardently to desire.

At the same time, Missie May is much more than the young, childlike girl her name suggests. Her care of her house makes readers aware of the self-dignity she has. In addition, she is a proud woman, too proud to run and hide from Joe, and yet not too proud to reenter the playful game between them at the end of the story.

Joe, as well as Missie, is naïve. He stands in awe of Slemmons, who takes Joe in by city-slickness. Yet Joe, like Missie, reveals his capacity for love and forgiveness. And like Missie, he grows in stature by the story's end. Joe's physical desire for Missie serves as minor motivation in his full return to her and his new son. Joe fully engages himself with his family, however, because he *cares* deeply for his wife and son. He reenters his marriage creatively, knowing that play is an essential part of enduring love. Joe can be forgiven the small lie he tells the clerk that he saw through Slemmons' act.

Slemmons, of course, is meant to be contrasted with Joe. Unlike the country boy Joe, Slemmons is a city con-man. He is a fast talker, as fake as his so-called gold piece. In addition, he preys on vulnerable innocents like Joe and Missie May.

The characterization, as well as the plotting, of "The Gilded Six-Bits" is also enriched by its ironies and its use of images. Joe's laughter, for example, after he finds Slemmons in his bed, comes not because he finds humor in the situation but arises out of Joe's need to strengthen himself in the face of his wife's infidelity. At the same time, however, the scene *is* funny as we watch Slemmons struggling to get into his pants before the irate husband who bars the door. It is too easy to read the scene as a domestic mini-tragedy, even a cliché; for Joe and Missie, not only time but eternity stands still. A "howling wind," the wind of chaos before time begins, sweeps through Joe's heart. Even the gilded coin becomes a source of irony. After a period of abstinence, when Joe finally returns to Missie's bed, he leaves the coin he so much admired and she so much wanted him to have under her pillow. The gilded half-dollar not only reveals Slemmons' fakery, but also pays Missie doubly. The usual two-bit payment to a prostitute is itself literally doubled, Missie's pay for sleeping with both Slemmons and Joe (Lowe 77). In addition, the breakdown in the fertilizer factory exposes the breakdown of Joe and Missie's marriage. At the same time, however, the breakdown at the factory makes it possible for the marriage to become stronger in its love. Even the clerk's voice at the end of the story reveals the deft, sure writing of Hurston at this time. The wonderful use of dramatic irony in the clerk's unawareness and his blind misreading of Blacks reminds us of Shakespeare's use of such irony, in which the audience knows so much more than the speaker in his ignorance.

THEMATIC ISSUES

Thematically, "The Gilded Six-Bits" suggests that urban areas hold out a promise that is itself perhaps gilded. In the early part of the century, Blacks by the thousands were flocking to cities in the hope of a new and better life. Indeed, during the Harlem Renaissance, Blacks moved to New York, just as Hurston did, to get ahead. Slemmons comes from "spots and places," such as Memphis, Chicago, and so on. At the end of the story, when the clerk asks Joe where he has been, he ironically answers that he has been "round in spots and places" (97). Yet, as readers discover with Slemmons, his promise is fake, even vicious. Once Slemmons is uncovered (literally, it turns out), Joe and Missie are thrown back upon their own strengths. Hurston suggests that out of their rural background comes the strength required to rebuild their marriage. The birth of their child is not simply procreative, but re-creative as well.

Also significant in this story is the use of play, which seems essential for the health and well-being of Missie and Joe. At the beginning of the tale, Missie and Joe's lives are enriched by play, and at the end they return to such play, albeit wiser and stronger about its meanings. As Lillie Howard points out, four out of five stories Hurston published between 1924 and 1933 deal with marriage (70–71). Marital relations becomes one of Hurston's major themes, not only in her short stories but in her novels as well: *Jonah, Their Eyes, Moses,* and *Seraph* all deal with marriage, both its problems and its joys. Even in her autobiography, *Dust Tracks,* Hurston considers not only the marriage of her parents, but the potential and the problems of her own.

Hurston's short stories demonstrate a sure command of plot development, as well as of narrative voice, especially in her use of black vernacular. In addition, she demonstrates the often subtle dynamics among a group of characters from her hometown of Eatonville. Even "The Eatonville Anthology" (1926), based on her anthropological studies of the people who lived there, contains stories within stories. Many of the character sketches in the "Anthology" concern people who show up in her novels: the pleading woman in *Their Eyes*; Jim Merchant in *Seraph,* for examples.

LATER SHORT STORIES

Her later stories are also of interest because they demonstrate Hurston's concern with such issues as black migration to the cities, justice, and cultural diversity. Her "Story in Harlem Slang" (1942), in which two young black men vie with each other to get a black girl to buy them a meal, shows the deferred dreams of Blacks who migrated to northern cities in order to have a better life. The end of the story exposes not only the ruse of the men, but their failure to make a decent living in the North. At the end of the story, Jelly, one of the male characters, is barely cognizant of what is happening around him, as he thinks about what he left behind in Alabama: "those full, hot meals he had left back in Alabama to seek wealth and splendor in Harlem without working" (133).

In "The Conscience of the Court" (1950), Hurston tells the story of a poor, black domestic servant, Laura Lee, who is taken to court for aggravated assault. Clement Beasley, who appears to suffer from numerous fractures of the body, testifies that he loaned $600 to Mrs. Celestine Clairborne, Laura's employer. When the loan was not repaid, Beasley attempts to take Mrs. Clairborne's furniture, only to be stopped by her black maid, Laura. She has no attorney but defends herself admirably by telling a story of love and loyalty to Mrs. Clairborne and by exposing Beasley as a fraud and confidence man. The court fully exonerates her and congratulates her for her integrity and steadfastness. Laura Lee would have gone to prison for Mrs. Clairborne, who borrowed the $600 from Beasley in order to provide a funeral for Laura's deceased husband.

Such a brief summary hardly does justice to this story, which essentially deals with moral issues and justice.

One of the most interesting stories is "High John De Conquer" (1943), published during World War II. John is the famous black figure of myth, a trickster who helps the powerless. John takes on both heaven and hell and seems to triumph in both places. He is the figure who laughs, and with laughter overcomes trials and adversity. For Blacks, John De Conquer represents joy and life itself. As a hero, he leads black people to understand that what is significant is inside of them, in their souls, their laughter, and their imagination. Hurston begins this story by saying that perhaps "now," in this time of war and trial, "we used-to-be black African folks, can be of some help to our brothers and sisters who have always been white" (139). Although Blacks are still black "ethnologically speaking . . . nationally and culturally, [they] are as white as the next one" (139). It is difficult to imagine this being written by a black author, even today.

Hurston goes on to tell white America that Blacks offer them "our hope-bringer, High John de Conquer" whose sign was a "laugh" and whose "singing-symbol was a drum-beat" (139). High John taught black folks about freedom so that they knew about it one hundred years before it came (142). Although John has plenty of "scrapes and tight squeezes" (144), he manages to emerge victorious. "So the brother in black offers to these United States the source of courage that endures, and laughter" (148). This remarkable story is filled with ironies and ambiguities, with the use of such words as "brother," "sister," "freedom," "kinfolks," and so on, in a time when segregation at home and in the military still existed and when lynchings still occurred. The story ultimately is one of laughter at the short-sightedness of white America—and of the heroism and courage of black America.

It would be a mistake to read Hurston's short stories only as a precursor to her novels, or even as glosses on them, interesting as that may be. The short stories stand on their own, revealing Hurston's insight into black life, its pain and its joy, and above all, its triumph.

4

Jonah's Gourd Vine
(1934)

Zora Neale Hurston wrote her first novel, *Jonah's Gourd Vine*, in a little more than two months, beginning on July 1 and finishing September 4, 1933. Although she later admitted that she'd had the story in mind since 1929, she nonetheless exhibits enormous skill and dedication to her craft of writing in this novel (Hemenway 189). While it is true that Hurston's *Jonah* is a novel based on her own life—more specifically on the lives of her parents, John and Lucy Potts Hurston—we should not confuse the characters and plot as exact replicas of her family or of her growing-up years. The family "history" that Hurston writes is a jumping-off place for the development of a remarkable work concerning African-American life after the Civil War in a South, and a country, undergoing rapid social and political change.

Reviews of *Jonah* at the time of its publication (May 1934) were generally positive, at least in the white press, which praised its language and story. At the same time, reviewers for such papers as *The Times Literary Supplement* and the *Boston Chronicle* totally misunderstood Hurston's attempt to portray the rich creativity of her culture (Hemenway 193–94). Perhaps *Opportunity* and the *Crisis* read *Jonah* without the racist bias of the white press, but Estelle Felton could muster only a tepid review (4–5), and Andrew Burris saw the novel as a failure (6–7). Today, such astute readers as Robert Hemenway, Eric Sundquist, Karla Holloway, and James Lowe recognize the daring and complexity of *Jonah's Gourd Vine*.

PLOT DEVELOPMENT

There are two main plots in *Jonah*: a family or a secular plot of love, loss, and regain and a spiritual plot of sin and redemption. The plots are intertwined to the point where they are nearly inextricable.

John Buddy Pearson of the Crittenden "ovah the river Niggers" lives in grinding poverty with his mother Amy and his stepfather Ned Crittenden. Set apart from his siblings by his light skin, John is abused, overworked, and humiliated by Ned, who refers to him as that "Yaller Bastard." The Crittenden family, riven with past hatreds, can barely sustain itself on its tenant farm; often there is little food and less money for bare necessities such as shoes. Education for any of the Crittenden children, John or his brothers Zeke and Zachariah, is out of the question. From this squalor and hopelessness, John leaves, swimming over the creek to the other side, to freedom from a postbellum slave mentality that threatens to keep John as ignorant and meanly vicious as his stepfather.

In Notasulga, Alabama, John goes to work on the plantation of Alf Pearson, who once owned Amy, and who in all likelihood is John's father. Pearson insists that John go to school to learn to read, write, and do simple arithmetic. His job on the Pearson plantation will be to check on the black tenant farmers to make sure that their financial accounts with Pearson are in order.

It is at school that John Buddy, himself only a teenager, meets Lucy Potts, the daughter of one of the elite black families in Notasulga. The Potts family owns their own land and home. They believe in education, and Lucy is "smart" as are all of the Potts family. John falls in love with Lucy, it seems at first sight, despite the objections of her parents, especially Lucy's mother Emmaline, who sees John Pearson as an ignorant, poor black man, without property and prospects.

But John does succeed: at school, in his work on the Pearson plantation, and in his courtship of Lucy. He marries her against her mother's wishes (Emmaline refuses to attend her daughter's wedding and disowns her own child) and takes her to live in a house provided by Pearson, who even provides them with a wedding bed. The good looks and charm that helped to win Lucy also work to captivate other women. John's relations with women persist after his marriage to Lucy, although he claims to—and indeed appears to—love only her.

Not only does John cheat on his wife, but he has a terrible habit of running away from any problems that confront them. When their child Isis (the fictional name that Hurston gives herself) becomes ill, John runs off to the comforting arms of another woman. At one point, when John has left Lucy alone during childbirth, her brother Bud demands and takes the very bed she lies in as payment for a debt her husband owes. When John learns of this, he beats Bud Potts badly and then steals a pig for food for his family. Both Bud and the man John steals from swear out warrants for John's arrest. Only because Lucy, still weak from childbirth, goes into town to beg mercy for her husband from the judge, who just happens to be Alf Pearson, is John released from jail into Pearson's custody. Pearson advises John to flee Notasulga, and he runs to Eatonville, Florida, where his family eventually rejoins him.

The early plot sequence of *Jonah*, then, concerns a man who moves from abject poverty as the hated stepson of a tenant farmer, who himself is next to being enslaved, to a family man with some education, a man who has the promise of making a good life for himself and his family. The main action in this plot is John's flight to freedom and his subsequent courtship of and marriage to Lucy Potts. Such a plot generally reveals the movement of a boy to manhood, but that movement is delayed here. John Pearson *could* be a man who moves ahead in life materially and who cares for his wife and children. Instead, he remains beholden to a white man, his unacknowledged father Alf Pearson. Moreover, John continues to neglect his family, running from his responsibilities as a husband and a father, to gratify his sexual desires. The attention from numerous women, their desire of him, seems to reassure John that he is in fact a man. When John beats Lucy's brother, however, the domestic plot threatens to turn into a tragedy as a consequence of his multiple betrayals of his wife and family.

When John moves to Eatonville, a town populated and administered by Blacks, he appears to have a second chance to redeem himself from his past neglect of his family. In Eatonville, John not only becomes a successful carpenter but a preacher, paving the way to become the moderator of the Baptist convention and the mayor of the town. It can and has been argued that John becomes a preacher only to gain power in the community, but he enters the church for at least two other reasons far more significant. First, he has a great gift for preaching. As Eric Sundquist states, John is like the African "griot," the "voice" of and for his community. He is a "blacksmith of the word," fashioning it, shaping it, as he calls and speaks to his community and to God (Sundquist 55). And second, Lucy encourages him and pushes him to be a great man, not only to his family and community, but also in his spirit.

And for a short while, John listens to Lucy and follows her advice. His advances in his careers as carpenter and preacher are mirrored in the well-being of his life with Lucy and their children. The life of family and church become as one, yet this unity lasts but a brief time. Soon John chases after other women, in particular Hattie Tyson. His betrayals of Lucy seem to kill her metaphorically as surely as the consumption that kills her literally.

As Lucy lies dying, John viciously turns against her, saying he does not need her any more; he needs no "guardzeen [guardian] atall" (128). When Lucy responds that she must tell the truth, that he is living "dirty," he hits her in the face. This horrific act seems to lead to Lucy's almost instant death and to John's subsequent marriage to Hattie Tyson. This marriage, doomed from the beginning by Hattie's desire for power over John and within the community, hastens John's downfall in the church.

Although Hattie contributes to John's leaving his church, ironically named Zion Hope, she does not cause his being ousted as the preacher. His own pride does that. Guilt-ridden over Lucy's death, John begins to despise Hattie and physically and verbally abuses her. He also neglects his children. Even John's gift of voice for preaching fails to save him, as the so-called good people of the church and Hattie conspire to remove him from Zion Hope. John's life itself becomes a waking sleep, where he seems to dream of the past so vividly, especially his courtship of Lucy and his life with her, that it overtakes the present and threatens to become his future (144–45). As his life remains mired in the past, the present for southern Blacks changes rapidly and radically. Blacks run from the South as if in a "stampede" for the North, leaving behind the ruins of an agrarian economy (151). John too leaves, though not the South, just Eatonville. Hattie divorces him and Zion Hope releases him as its preacher, driving John away from the community into self-imposed exile.

Paradoxically, when John is at his lowest point in life, he preaches one of his most intense and creative sermons on the wounds of Christ (174–81). At the end of the sermon, he pronounces that he cannot again participate in communion with his parishioners. In short, his life in the church, as well as his marriages, ended, John sees nothing but his trade of carpentering left for him. Yet even this is denied him, as the people in Eatonville turn against him in this craft as well.

Wandering, and without a home, John ends up in Plant City, looking for work and finding the widow Sally Lovelace. In a sense she restores him to his former self, and they marry. Sally, very much like Lucy, encourages him to go back to preaching, this time at Pilgrim's Rest Baptist Church. As was Lucy, Sally becomes an agent of redemption. With property and money, Sally buys John a Cadillac, suggesting that he return to Eatonville to see his best friend Hambo, as well as to let his former friends know how well he is doing without them, perhaps even despite them. His return, his pride in his well-being, and his separation from Sally prove to be his undoing. He cannot or will not dismiss the flirtations of the young Ora Patton (she calls him "daddy") who wants only to have a ride in his Cadillac, she says. He rebuffs her, thinking that now "God and Sally could trust him" (197), but he is too smug in his moral strength and too vain in his sensuality. He succumbs to the temptation. When he finds himself dressing in a "dingy back room" the next morning, John's anger vents itself on his own weakness by lashing out at Ora (199). His flight from her towards home to Sally ends in his death, as the train hits the car crossing the tracks. John Buddy Pearson never sees the train coming; for the first time in his life he is "looking inward," examining his self and his soul.

The funeral scene at Zion Hope Church reinforces the tight intertwining of familial and spiritual plots, of the secular and the sacred. The preacher speaks of the pale horse with its rider, Death, and of "Amen Avenue. Of Halleluyah Street" (201), all images from the Book of Revelation. These images are juxtaposed against a vision of the great drum O-go-doe, the ancient drum of Africa. The preacher says that in the end, as John was a man, only God knew him. And, as John was a man, the congregation feels his loss with the "drumming" of their feet. The mourning for John Buddy Pearson gathers together the secular and sacred plots: as Sally Lovelace mourns John personally, saying over and over that he was true to her, God delights in John's appearance in Heaven.

SETTING

There are three major settings in *Jonah's Gourd Vine*: the Crittenden side of the creek, and the Pearson side, both in Notasulga, Alabama, and the Sanford Zion Hope Church in Eatonville, Florida. In all three settings, family houses and the church prove the most important.

Ned and Amy Crittenden's household, a sharecropper's farm under a white man's control, is emblematic of the grinding poverty in which many tenant farmers and sharecroppers lived after the Civil War. The system of sharecropping was as close to slavery as one could get after Blacks received their freedom. Ned Crittenden, essentially as powerless as most slaves were to provide for their families, attempts to exercise some power by dominating his family. He and his wife Amy, and their three children, live in a shack not fit to be called a house, let alone a home. As Ned is used by the white owner, so he uses his children: like slaves, worse than animals. Ned works for the landowner, and in turn Ned's children work for him. The very existence of Ned's family revolves around their ability to produce enough to give to the landowner to his satisfaction; what is left over, no matter how little this may be, belongs to the worker and must maintain him and his family. Thus Ned treats his children the way he has been treated: with bullying, violence, and intimidation.

Ned warns his children that they should not look white folks in the face. Such action could get them lynched, especially John, who seems to show no fear of white folks—or of Ned, even when his stepfather threatens to take a "trace chain" to him or to "stomp" his guts out (2). Amy reminds her husband that to beat her children is to bear her wrath.

For Ned, his sharecropper's farm, with its shack for a house, is no different from slave shacks, and the farm no different from the white slaveowner's plantation that Blacks formerly worked. The only way any of the children can rise above this psychological as well as literal "enslavement" is to escape. This John does by swimming over the creek to the Pearson side.

Alf Pearson's plantation formerly housed slaves, Amy Crittenden being one of them. Now his land, too, is sharecropped, although he runs his farm in a benign way contrasted to the running of the farm on which Ned lives. Pearson's black workers tend the farm and work in his house; however, the separation between house and field Blacks continues as in slave times. For example, after John and Lucy marry, they move into a house-servant's living quarters "just back" of the "big" or plantation house (81).

On the Pearson plantation, black rituals and folk games, which can be traced not only to slavery but to Africa, continue (22–24). Children play the dozens (24), attempting one-upmanship in classic verbal "put-downs. Dances are held and the ancient "man skin" drums (clapping of hands and stamping of feet in rhythm) are played—not the fiddles of the white man. The rhythmic bodies of Africa provide the music of festivities held on the Pearson place; the Beasley place, where Ned and his family live, allows no time for any such festivities. On the Pearson plantation, the older generation of Blacks teach their children to get the clapping right, in time (31), as folk songs are sung (30–31). These activities are held out-of-doors, in nature, around fires on the tamped down earth. The setting may be in America's Southland, a place of humiliation, degradation, and death for many Blacks, but the sounds and soul of the setting are triumphantly African, played against and out of that which is American.

Although Pearson's plantation is in clear contrast to Beasley's land, Hurston clearly lets the reader know that vestiges of slaveholding remain in both settings. The major difference is the care that Pearson takes of his workers. Pearson would like to use John Buddy as a "house nigger." Ned Crittenden is right when he says the "yaller" slaves were always used as house servants, whereas black slaves worked in the fields. If Alf undoubtedly recognizes John as his son, his wife also probably recognizes the physical likeness between her husband and John Buddy. She will not have him in a position visible to the society in which she moves, and thus John becomes a sort of overseer, just as in the days of slavery, after he is sent to school to learn how to read, write, and do sums.

Juxtaposed against both the Crittenden and Pearson settings of sharecropping is the independent black farm of the Potts family. Richard and Emmaline Potts have worked hard to own their land and home. Richard has a horse and buggy, not merely the mule that was the staple in the South to plow the land. The house itself is a sort of marvel, with separate bedrooms, a kitchen, and a parlor. The parlor is decorated with art reproductions on easels; there are gold-trimmed mustache cups and saucers in their stands; and there are various religious sayings hanging on the wall. There is even a porch to this house. Yet for all its material comforts, the house is filled with Emmaline's stiff-necked pride and self-righteously harsh religion. This is a house which shows off the family's acquisitions and, at least, Emmaline's desire to hold on to them and to acquire more.

On the Pearson side of the creek, then, it is possible for a black family to rise in respectability and material possessions. There are also institutions on the Pearson side of the creek, as well. There is a school for black children, and there is also a church. And above all there is the law, ruling the town like a little fiefdom, and presided over by a white judge, Mr. (not Massa on this side of the creek) Alf Pearson himself.

It would be a mistake to minimize the natural setting of both sides of the creek. On the Crittenden side of the creek, nature spells danger, Amy thinks, for her son John. He takes too many risks, runs and jumps in dangerous places and ways. The creek itself has its strong current and could easily drag him under. Snakes abound on both sides of the creek. Lucy is afraid of them, and John kills at least one for her, leaving the other as a possible sign that this land is no paradise. As Lillie Howard points out in her book *Zora Neale Hurston*, snake images abound. The snake is the whip that Ned beats Amy with, in a scene that causes John to leave his mother's house. Howard notes that the snake images become more powerful as John gets ready to cross the creek; even the train that John sees for the first time on the other side of the creek is like a snake (85). Yet there are other wonderful images of nature: black workers in the woods celebrating their harvests; the birdsong that John notices; in fact, the very beauty of nature that John seems so attuned to. Both the beauty of nature and the references to the poisonous aspects of the cottonmouth moccasin are put to good use in John's great sermon on the "Wounds of Jesus," which he preaches at Zion Hope Church.

The third major setting, Eatonville, a town of black folks, managed and incorporated by Blacks, is the place that John determines to live in and eventually to be a "big man" there. The most important building, aside from the house John and Lucy live in, is the church where John becomes pastor, Zion Hope.

Like Richard and Emmaline Potts, John Pearson acquires "proppity," a house that is similar to Lucy's family home, but without the emphasis on material goods and acquisition. It is a house, however, filled with love of children and—astonishingly, considering John's philandering—of parents. There is never any doubt that Lucy and John Pearson love each other, even though guilt and bitterness seep into the house as a result of John's many sexual betrayals. Also in this house, John commits the sin of hitting his wife, and in this house Lucy dies. Lucy Potts Pearson leaves in her "little" coffin from this house on her final journey to Zion Hope Church. This same house falls into chaos and ruin under the carelessness of Hattie Tyson, who becomes John's second wife.

In addition to family households, Zion Hope Church is crucial to our understanding of Hurston's novel. She links the church to plot, character, theme, and meaning in *Jonah's Gourd Vine*. Zion Hope is not only the church that calls John to preach, it is the church that ends his career as a preacher and sends him into exile. Hurston does not so much describe Zion Hope—she tells us virtually nothing about its exterior or interior architecture—as she makes us *feel* it. Those readers familiar with the black church in the rural South know what it looks like: its austerity, its raised platform for the pulpit, the chairs for preacher and deacons, its communion table. The very name of Zion Hope reminds us of what the church looks like and represents: the spiritual community, theoretically a harmonious community, devoted to God and to doing God's work. Zion stands for Mt. Zion, the temple mount in Jerusalem. Zion imagery has to do with return from exile and the restoration of freedom for the Jewish people who were once enslaved just as Blacks were. And just as the Jews were set free, so too were Blacks.

Instead of description, Hurston gives us spiritual markers: Communion Sunday with the sermon on the "natchel" (natural) man (122), the "Dry Bones" sermon (158), Pastoral day, the Covenant Meeting, the "Wounds of Jesus" sermon (174–81), and the requiem service after John's death (201–2). These markers give us the spirit of black people, their celebration and pain, their aspirations and pragmatism. At the same time that the church represents the best of its people, their goodwill and charity, it also exposes their worst: the petty factions, the gossips, the mean-spirited, and the hypocrites. Hurston does not make it easy for readers to accept the self-righteous piety of many of those who worship at Zion Hope.

At the end of the novel, Zion Hope takes John Buddy to its heart. On the day of John Pearson's memorial service, mourning covers the village, but flowers fill Zion Hope: small bouquets of wood flowers alongside elaborate flower arrangements. The high-back chair of the preacher—John Pearson's old chair—is also adorned with flowers. Hurston marks the memorial occasion in the country church with the funeral preacher's images of Death and his icy hands. But Zion Hope is also marked with the gold streets of glory, of "Amen Avenue," and of "Halleluyah Street." Hurston's black readers then and now would instantly call to mind the physical setting of the church, crowded with congregants, the women fanning themselves, the cries of Amens, the children restless. Hurston keeps us riveted in our church seats, as we too hear the singers around God's throne. Under Hurston's craft, Zion Hope Church expands to include Christian images from the Bible's Book of Revelation, cosmic images of the weeping sun and moon, and resounding sounds of the African drum of death, O-go-doe, its beat an African-American rhythm, of "drumming . . . feet," a "mournful dance of . . . heads" (202).

CHARACTER DEVELOPMENT

John Buddy Pearson is undoubtedly the major character in *Jonah's Gourd Vine*. As Mary Helen Washington notes, Pearson is the "heroic center" of the novel; his voice and his presence dominate the text from beginning to end (*Invented Lives* 250). But one can hardly understand him without understanding the father figures in his life or the women surrounding him.

John Pearson is the illegitimate son of Amy Crittenden, a former slave, and her white plantation owner. John's stepfather Ned Crittenden, also a former slave turned sharecropping farmer in the post-slavery South, is both servile and self-serving. His ingrained slave mentality leaves him fearful of being abused by the white man and afraid to look at his white bosses. Ned remains caught in the grinding poverty of the sharecropper, all too frequently cheated by his white landowner. Crittenden's crippled foot seems to be a symbol of his impotence against the all-powerful white father figure for whom he works, Mr. Beasley. In a sense, psychologically like Oedipus (Lowe 116–17), Ned desires to kill the authoritative father in order to take his place. Yet Crittenden remains totally incapable of any action—except against those most vulnerable to him, his wife and his children, especially his half-white stepson, John. If Ned can not even look his white bosses in the face, let alone strike them, he can vent his rage on his wife Amy. Though he wants to strike John, he cannot because Amy protects the boy. As John grows older, he protects himself, becoming too strong for Ned to attack physically, and his stepfather's abuse becomes mostly verbal. But he also decides to indenture John to Mimms, a white landowner notorious for ill-treatment of black workers. Ned's decision, thwarted by John's running away, replicates the system of slavery to which Ned himself had been bound.

John had left his family once before, with Amy's blessing, swimming over the Songahatchee Creek to work on Alf Pearson's plantation. Though not much more than a boy, John exhibits raw physical courage: he not only stands up to his stepfather but swims a river full of dangerous currents. Hurston's description of John's flight to freedom is telling: he sings a "new song"; he stomps the beats of its rhythm in time to the roar of the creek. Indeed, he creates the words to go with the "drums" of nature. A man-child of nature, he will proclaim himself a natural man later in the novel in one of his most moving sermons. As John swims the creek, he thinks of the "many girls" on the "new and shiny side" of the creek and exults in his own physicality and sensuality (12). In this brief scene of John's crossing over the creek, Hurston reveals much of John's character that will not so much be developed as expanded upon as the novel progresses.

John makes two trips over the creek, both to escape his stepfather, and each time ends up working for Alf Pearson, his white father. Hurston ironically represents Alf Pearson as a former benign slave-owner, now the benign manager of sharecropping tenants on his plantation. As Alice Walker so clearly demonstrates in *The Third Life of Grange Copeland*, sharecropping was only another form of servitude. While it is true that Pearson treats his sharecroppers decently, he does so because it is in his best interest. Alf hires John Buddy because he looks like a "splendid specimen" (18), and because he knows "how to work 'em" (18). Although slavery has been abolished, the view of black workers as slaves has not. Blacks are looked over like farm animals; strong and healthy specimens are crucial for productivity.

Pearson also hires John Buddy because he remembers his mother Amy and because he was born on the plantation. There is little doubt that Pearson recognizes himself in the boy and initially plans to make a "house nigger" or at least a carriage driver out of John. Alf's wife puts a stop to this plan because she too likely recognizes the similarity between her husband and John.

Alf never acknowledges John as his son. He does, however, take a perverse pleasure in his son's sexual prowess, as though he vicariously relives his own sexual desires and promiscuity through John. Readers understand, even if John does not, Alf's ambivalence towards his son's sexuality. He calls John a "walking orgasm. A living exultation" (50). John asks what that means, and Alf responds by telling him to never mind but to "keep up with the pigs" (50). Alf seems to know everything John does with women, and his interest in John's sexual activities borders on the obsessive. He knows with whom John is sleeping and tells him to leave "Big 'Oman," one of the plantation tenants, alone, for example, as she may prove dangerous. Alf presents John and Lucy with their wedding bed. Alf's relationship with his son is both furtive and salacious. Although he seemingly disapproves of his son's sexual behavior, he seems oddly proud of it, urging John at one point to leave rather than face the consequences of his actions. History truly repeats itself here: like father, like son.

Both Ned and Alf, neither of whom takes responsibility as a father to John, are the only role models John has for manhood. One beats his wife and exploits his children; the other does not own up to his sexual activity and its consequence—a son—and winks at his son's sexual promiscuity. The lack of any positive male presence in John's young life appears to keep him emotionally in a state of perpetual adolescence, looking for solace and support from one woman after another. Since neither Ned nor Alf takes responsibility for John, he fails generally to take any responsibility for himself or his actions. Ned and Alf's neglect of their wives and children seems doomed to be repeated in John's neglect of Lucy and their children.

Children in slavery frequently did not know their parents, nor did they have stability in their home life. In many instances, slave-owners calculatedly and repeatedly broke up family units to discourage strong bonds that might prove disruptive to the slave system and, of course, to make a profit. The slaves' first and only allegiance belonged to their masters. What is so chilling in *Jonah* is that Hurston reminds us how little had changed in the postwar South. Amy tells Ned at one point that Blacks must *learn* to love their children and to care for them. It seems that Alf Pearson needs to learn these lessons as well.

John's lack of self-understanding reflects his lack of knowledge concerning his origins. Hurston takes a great risk in creating a central character who appears to be so unaware of who he is. But this seems to be one of her main points concerning the character of John Buddy, and perhaps of the African-American male all too frequently. Richard Wright deals with this topic in his novel, *Native Son*, in the character of Bigger Thomas, who comes to have a glimmer of self-awareness only after committing a violently horrendous murder. John Buddy's awakening to the kind of man he is comes slowly and painfully; he learns about himself through the loss of everything he cares about: the loss of Lucy, the only woman he truly loved, the loss of his children through his own neglect, and the loss of his church, Zion Hope, because of his pride. The loss of Zion Hope means not only the loss of communion but also the loss of community, as John Buddy goes into self-imposed exile.

John's failure to know himself may be seen in his relationships with women. Set adrift when not much more than a boy, John learns early on that women are attracted to him. M'haley and Phroney, as well as Big 'Oman and others, are eager to please him sexually. John is equally eager to accept their easy pleasure and comfort. All of these women, and certainly Hattie Tyson early in her relationship with John, provide sensual pleasure. Through his encounters with these women, John seduces himself into believing he is a man.

Lucy Potts clearly is different from these women, and there is little doubt that John falls deeply in love with her (one is tempted to say, forever). Lucy is innocent and lacks the sexual aggressiveness of the women who usually associate with John. Even as a young girl, however, Lucy is sensually alive to John, willing to risk the wrath of her mother by stealing a few moments with him. She writes John love notes when she is little more than a child. Smart, tough enough to stand up to her mother Emmaline's demands, and courageous enough to leave her home and even her hometown to be the wife of John Pearson, Lucy Potts is the most formidable and unforgettable woman in his life.

The love of John and Lucy suggests the possibility they could have a radically different marriage from the ones they had seen in their respective families. On their wedding night when John carries Lucy over the threshold into their house on the Pearson plantation, he tells her not to worry about losing her folks. Indeed, he promises to be both mother and father to her. She can depend upon him, as he says, "tuh prop [her] up on eve'y leanin' side" (79). Unfortunately, he never lives up to this promise. Yet, Lucy remains fiercely loyal to her husband. When John beats her brother Bud, Lucy goes to the sheriff's office almost immediately after giving birth in order to save her husband from being put into a chain gang. She remains loyal to John when he runs away from Notasulga to Eatonville, Florida, in order to avoid a trial, and later she follows him to Florida, uprooting herself from the town she has known all of her life.

Lucy also acts as guide and teacher for her husband. Even as a child she inspired and helped him to read and write. When John writes her name on the chimney of his birth-granny's house on the Pearson plantation, he does more than profess his love for her; he demonstrates that she has taught him how to use language.

Lucy also inspires and guides him into the church. Although others also recognize his oratorical skills, she encourages him and helps him to use them. Moreover, she gives him advice not only on how to get a congregation but on how to keep it. It is Lucy who forces John to better himself, and when John brags about himself at Joe Clarke's store, the men remind him that he owes his ambition and his rise in the world to the "l'l' handful uh woman" he has (109). For all of this John is both grateful and resentful. He is perhaps most resentful of the moral advice Lucy gives him from time to time.

John desires and needs Lucy's moral strength, her comforting presence, and her guidance, but these things also make him feel guilty and diminished as a man. Yet it is she who steers him onto the path of greatness as a preacher, and she who admonishes him for his womanizing. When Lucy dies, John is left, as Hurston puts it, writing about her father in *Dust Tracks*, with no steering mechanism: without a moral compass, without comfort, without a life companion. Although John attempts to replace her with numerous other women, in particular Hattie Tyson, he never forgets Lucy. He remembers especially her eyes, shining like a light (her name, Lucy, means light) into his soul.

Hattie Tyson, who so often had provided physical solace to John, works especially hard to be his new wife after Lucy's death. If Lucy represents intellect, loyalty, and spirituality, Hattie represents the opposite. Her body defines her character. She marries John three months after Lucy's death for what she thinks he can give her. Hambo, John's best friend, sees her as seeking only personal pleasure, a loose woman who goes from one sawmill camp to another. Her looks are as hard as she is. Hattie had gone to a conjure woman, Dangie Dewoe, to "fix" Lucy, that is, to get rid of her and get John for Hattie's use. The death of Lucy convinces Hattie that the conjuring indeed worked. Despite the conjuring—or maybe because of it—John reaches the point where he tells Hattie he does not know why he married her. It is as if he has been sleep-walking (143); by contrast, he was totally awake with Lucy and remembers everything about her—their courting, their marriage, their life together. Even in the same room with Hattie, he claims to remember nothing about his second wife. Perhaps Dangie Dewoe's conjuring spell goes too far with John.

John's unfavorable comparison of Hattie to Lucy brings only trouble. Hattie is, as John says, unlike his first wife. Hattie turns on him, threatens to expose him and his lust for other women, and dares him to beat her. Her challenge to John brings only disdain, as he tells her he doesn't beat women; his sudden vivid remembrance of striking Lucy as she lay on her deathbed, however, leads to the kind of guilt that turns vicious. He frequently beats Hattie, who, unlike Lucy, does not simply turn her face to the wall and die. Hattie strikes back underhandedly by conspiring with the church faction that wants to oust John from Zion Hope. In contrast to Lucy, Hattie's loyalty is only to herself.

Hattie's desire for John had nothing to do with love but only with the pleasures of the flesh. Her goals were simple: the house and marriage bed John had shared with Lucy, dresses and shoes to wear. In addition, she assumed she would gain instant respectability and social power by marrying a preacher of John's reputation and popularity. When she discovers little pleasure and less power, she channels the full force of her hatred into "fixing" John by getting rid of him as a husband and as a preacher. Dangie Dewoe, long dead by this time, could not have done a better conjure job.

The third significant woman in John's life, Sally Lovelace, seems to be an older version of Lucy. A widow with property, Sally remembers her late husband saying John was a great preacher. She hires him as a carpenter but tries to persuade him to preach the communion service at Pilgrim Rest Baptist Church. The word "communion" brings more awareness to John than he can stand, and he tells Sally everything of his past. As he puts his head in her lap, crying "like a boy of four" (189), Sally comforts him as a mother might. She runs her hands through his hair until he falls asleep "at her knee." One cannot escape the image of mother and child (perhaps even the Holy Mother with the Christ Child), an image reminiscent of Lucy, yet different.

Lucy, although also comforting, had some of her mother Emmaline's righteousness in her. Or perhaps Lucy had some of the loving, yet stern, preacher in her. Not allowed to preach to a congregation, she preached to her husband instead. Sally, in contrast, is all loving forgiveness, comforting and maternal. With Sally, John feels "lak Samson" (189), surely an unconsciously ironic comment, given his life with women; he regains his strength and his preaching voice. Sally, not shy with words herself—in this, she is like Lucy—not only tells him that Pilgrim Rest wants him to be its pastor but that they should get married immediately. John's answer is a quick thank you. The roles that Lucy and John filled are reversed with Sally and John. On their wedding night, Sally is matter-of-course in going to bed, but John is "shy as a girl—as Lucy had been" (190). When John prays that night, he asks God to keep him from the "snares" (of women), but he also prays that Lucy see how he would keep his vows to Sally.

Sally's generosity with herself and her possessions—she buys John a Cadillac—is a sign of her happiness with him. She also trusts John to be faithful on his own. Thus, his betrayal of Sally the first time they are separated seems particularly shocking. As he drives away from Oviedo after spending the night with Ora, the links between Sally and Lucy are made clear as John thinks of how Sally was God's answer to John's prayer for Lucy's return. Sally's generosity of spirit remains even after John's death, as she promises to give the $7,000 railroad money in recompense for the accident to his children. Sally obviously mourns him, wanting to be buried with him "off" by themselves. Moreover, she regrets nothing about their short life with each other, ironically saying—to readers, at least—that John was always true to her. In fact, she repeats this belief as if it is a heart-song (201).

In part, Hurston uses the three women to shed light on John's character: his dreams to be greater than he was, and his belief that he was chosen by God because of the gift of voice. They also help to reveal his sheer physical strength, his charm, and his great capacity for life, including his sensuality. If these women help to show his moral frailty, they also show his ability to feel guilt and remorse. Hurston lavishes the most care and attention on Lucy. She not only reflects John, she shines as a character in her own right. Tough, courageous, gifted, with a moral depth John lacks, Lucy demonstrates the great capacity for love possible to men and women. She lives up to her name, illuminating not only character, but theme and meaning in *Jonah*, and lighting the way for Janie in Hurston's novel to come, *Their Eyes Were Watching God*.

THEMATIC ISSUES

Jonah's Gourd Vine does not lack for themes. On the contrary: Hurston packs the novel with so many themes, so intertwined, that they are difficult to sort out. One of the most powerful themes, however, has to do with the impact on both black and white Americans of the slavery system. *Jonah*, set in the early years of the twentieth century, depicts the force of slavery in the post-slavery South. This force can be seen of course in the geography that Hurston maps for us. In Notasulga, on the Crittenden side of the creek, violence rules the family. As Ned was abused during slavery, so he abuses his wife Amy and his children. As he was bought and sold into slavery, so he binds his stepson to Mimms, himself a (white) throwback to slavery's cruelty. John Buddy escapes, as other slaves escaped, by putting distance between himself and the man who would bind him to another.

Slavery systematically worked against the formation and maintenance of black families. Indeed, it worked against any form of love between man and woman, parent and child. In John Buddy, we find the harvest of such a system. When John swims the creek to the Alf Pearson side, he discovers a more benign world. One of the first signs of this world are the voices of happy children as they exit school. On this side of the creek, children have a higher value than animals; they are educated, even loved. John himself will have some education, if only to make him more valuable in his work for Alf Pearson.

Hurston is quick to show us that even the benign remnants of slavery expose the rottenness of the institution. Alf Pearson not only rules his land, kindly to be sure, but he rules the whole community; he is the judge, literally, of all. If Ned never loves or treats John as his son, Alf never acknowledges he is John's white father. How can he in a society that demands, legally and socially, strict separation of the races? There is a certain poignancy in Alf's knowing his white son remains in Europe under the pretense of getting an education, but essentially doing nothing, and that his black son, who must always be no son, is bright, learns quickly, and works hard. The lack of a positive father—indeed of any father—in John's life permeates the novel from beginning to end, coloring John's relationship with women and his own children.

In addition to, and as a result of, slavery, gender is also of strong thematic concern in *Jonah*. The roles women play in the rural South during this time have a narrow range for the most part. Women exist to give men pleasure, as Amy did for Alf Pearson. Because she was black and in his employ, he felt free to do with her what he wished. Even Alf's white wife must live with the results of her husband's liaison with a black woman; the best Mrs. Pearson can do is to make sure that John Buddy is kept out of her sight. It surely is not coincidental that Alf's wife has no character, indeed, not even a name. Ned Crittenden shares Alf's attitudes towards women; Ned simply is more brutal. Women exist to serve him, to work for him, to produce children for him. But Ned does not want to hear Amy's voice and would deny her language altogether if he could.

As Debra Beilke demonstrates in her critical essay, " 'Yowin' and Jawin,' " John Pearson is little different from Ned. John stifles Lucy's voice as surely as Ned does Amy's (22). As a young girl, Lucy was the ablest performer at school in her use of language and in her speaking ability. In fact, Lucy's linguistic talent is one of the things that impresses John and causes him to fall in love with her. Once they are married, however, he pointedly tells her that he does not need to listen to her; he is a man who needs no guardian. As Beilke points out, John must "squelch Lucy's voice in order to maintain his own masculine identity" (22). It is Lucy, however, who guides John in his own use of language and who gives him advice on his sermons. In short, she gives him his effective use of voice. For all that John attempts to stop her voice, every man at Joe Clarke's store knows that Pearson is a "wife-made man" (113). Indeed, John's slapping

Lucy because she refuses to tell him anything but the truth (128) appears to be his most heinous crime.

Gender roles in *Jonah* appear on the surface to conform to strict rules. Men, like Ned, Alf, and John, rule women. They treat them as objects and feel threatened if women try to "take over." Women's mouths represent subversion of and opposition to masculinity and male power. John slaps Lucy and beats Hattie because of what they say. Women, according to Ned, Alf, and John, exist for pleasure and servitude. Yet both Lucy and Sally Lovelace are powerful women in their own right. Both reveal intelligence, loyalty, generosity, and love; both have voices which will be heard.

In addition to themes of family, gender, and race, there is also the theme of rapid change. The "monster" train that so surprises and fascinates John represents the industrialization coming to the rural, agrarian South. Moreover, the train signifies mobility for Blacks who left in droves from the South to the North to work in factories and to find a better life for themselves. (Toni Morrison would later write of this migration, in an unflattering way, in her first novel, *The Bluest Eye*.) In *Jonah*, the migration of Blacks from the South results in the end of a southern agrarian economy. There was no stopping the great migration of Blacks to what seemed the promised land of the North (151).

Perhaps the most powerful of themes in *Jonah's Gourd Vine*, however, is the theme of sin and redemption. John Buddy's failure to recognize his responsibility to his family, indeed his responsibility for himself and his own actions, stems from his arrogance, his own pride. Out of pride, John sins over and over again. Even his confession to Sally Lovelace is not enough to save him, for like the biblical Jonah, John Buddy needs to look inward and to understand his own pride. John Pearson has run from his capacity for betrayal all of his life. Only at the end does he accept responsibility for his promiscuity. For the first time he accuses himself of pride and hypocrisy. For the first time, John Buddy looks inside himself and reflects on his own soul. In this act lies his redemption.

It seems fitting that a train kills him at this moment of reflection. One of John's earlier and most memorable sermons on communion Sunday had been preceded by the hymn "Beloved, Beloved, now are we the sons of God" (174). In his sermon, he preached on the subject of betrayal and sin, and the powerful motif in that sermon was the train: not only the damnation train that pulls out of the Garden of Eden but also, through Christ's death, the train of mercy, the redemption train. When John Buddy dies, Hurston has the engineer of the train that kills him blindly say, "Damned, if I kin see how it happened" (200). If, as readers, we have been paying attention, we understand both how and why it happened, as well as its meaning.

Underlying all of the themes in Hurston's novel, however, is that of second chances. Just as the biblical Jonah is given a second chance, so too is John

Buddy Pearson. As Walter Brueggemann points out in his *Theology of the Old Testament*, the Book of Jonah is a story with a "predilection toward forgiveness, restoration, and rehabilitation" (525). Like Jonah, John Buddy attempts flight— physical, psychological, and existential—and in each case he is saved by compassion (Trible 473). The preacher at John's funeral tells us that only God knew him, but Hurston makes quite sure that we know him almost as well.

A READER-RESPONSE READING

Robert Hemenway writes that the "sum" of *Jonah's Gourd Vine* "may be less than the parts, [though] the parts are remarkable indeed" (201), and most scholars tend to agree. What then are we to make of the fact that one of the more crucial "parts," little more than halfway through the novel, is left out, omitted from the text altogether? John Pearson's famous "Dry Bones" sermon is his answer to the conspiracy of Zion Hope Church and Hattie Tyson to have another preacher, Rev. Felton Cozy, take John's place in the church and to send John into exile.

Hurston makes only a quick reference to the Dry Bones sermon, spending merely a brief paragraph pointing to it; the rest of Chapter 21 deals with Rev. Cozy's sermon. If Pearson's Dry Bones sermon is so famous, why does Hurston not include it? She includes two other sermons of Pearson's in the novel: his "Natchel Man" sermon (122–23) and his climactic "Wounds of Jesus" sermon (174–81). Surely Hurston could have included the Dry Bones sermon without its slowing down the plot. Indeed, the sermon would have effectively contrasted with Cozy's, revealing not only his character but also that of John. Moreover, the sermon would have directly reinforced the themes of the novel. Why this gap, then?

Reader-Response criticism may be useful in helping us to understand what seems to be a glaring, yet intentional, omission within the overall context of *Jonah*. Wolfgang Iser, in his *The Implied Reader*, explains reader response. For Iser, the meanings of any text require and depend upon the reader's participation, upon his or her response to the literary work. He points out that in looking at a literary work one must take into account not only the text created by the author but also the realization of the text by the reader. The reader brings to a text certain cultural experiences, emotions, and so on—"pre-intentions"— but also has "intentions" awakened by the reading process itself (Iser 274). According to Iser all literary works have "gaps" to be filled in by readers, though to be sure readers—and readings—may fill these gaps somewhat differently (280). For example, readers note obvious gaps in Laurence Sterne's novel, *Tristram Shandy*, where he deliberately leaves blank pages, spaces in the text to be filled in by the reader. Readers are invited to participate in the text, to fill in the gaps left open. Such gaps affect what readers anticipate to come in the narrative and how readers retrospectively interpret the text as a whole. Roman Ingarden refers to such gaps as "spots of indeterminacy," causing the reader to go beyond what is presented or projected by the text itself (Ingarden 252).

Hurston's omission of the Dry Bones sermon suggests several things. She knew that her black readers had in their cultural repertoire the Dry Bones text; she need not repeat it for them. She expects that white readers won't recognize the reference to Dry Bones and perhaps would not understand it if she did include the sermon. So the focus in the chapter seems to be her biting portrait of Rev. Cozy, a portrait that both white and black readers would understand as stinging. For observant readers, however, the reference to the Dry Bones sermon adds another and richer layer to both the chapter and the novel itself.

The Dry Bones sermon, based on Ezekiel 37, was a familiar and traditional sermon to black preachers and congregations alike; perhaps some white people would recognize its text through the spiritual, "Dem Bones, Dem Bones, Dem Dry Bones." The connections between the sermon and John Pearson, as well as Zion Hope congregation, are clear. Ezekiel was a prophet but also a preacher like John Pearson. Ezekiel, along with the best of Judah's leadership, had been carried into captivity in Babylon, where he began ministering to a group of exiled Jews living near him. No wonder African Americans have identified so closely with the text of the Dry Bones sermon, for they too knew what it was like to be carried off into exile and captivity. Pearson himself identifies with Ezekiel, for John knows that Zion Hope, with Hattie's help, intends exile for him. Ezekiel's complaints against his own people were that they were self-righteous and full of pride in their turning against God, who calls upon him to prophesy against them concerning dire consequences, including death. The people pay little heed to Ezekiel's voice until Jerusalem is destroyed, after which he, in turn, prophesies a new Israel.

The Book of Ezekiel is more than a story of exile, of despair, and of dry bones in the desert. It is also a story of transformation and of cleansing, a story of hope and resurrection. Like the Book of Jonah, it is a story about second chances. The Dry Bones sermon contains these motifs as well. Just as God calls Ezekiel to pastor the valley of Dry Bones, so God calls John Pearson to pastor the Dry Bones of Zion Hope. Both men believe themselves filled with the breath of God when they preach the Word of life. When Ezekiel begins to preach, he hears the rattling of bones as they are put back together, to rise and to live, by God's spirit within them. Like Ezekiel, John pastors to his people, the dry bones of Zion Hope, who are broken into squabbling and self-righteous factions. And both Ezekiel and John share in that brokenness. Just as the exiled Jews rise up to live in response to the breath of God through Ezekiel, so

Zion Hope congregation becomes "alive from the pulpit to the door" in response to John's preaching. Their "frenzy" calms down only when the Deacons move Pearson from the pulpit to his chair, fanning and wiping his face.

In *The Art of the American Folk Preacher*, Bruce A. Rosenberg discusses the Dry Bones sermon, remarking on its flexibility (one version of the sermon is reprinted in his book: 200–208) and its powerful meanings. Paradoxically, Hurston intensifies the meanings of the text by the ambiguity of its exclusion from the novel. Yet, the very allusion to the Dry Bones sermon, as well as the response to Pearson's preaching, serves to point out the contrast between John and the Rev. Cozy, brought into Zion Hope to unseat him. Whatever we may feel about John Pearson's moral character, God "called" or chose him to be a preacher; thus when John preaches, he is inspired with God's word speaking through him. As John says in his "Natchel Man" sermon, when he is not preaching, he is merely a clod of earth, a man like every other man. Rev. Cozy apparently has no such calling to be a preacher but has chosen to be a "race man," a "Race Leader," as Hurston would call him (see her essay, "Art and Such," reprinted in *Reading Black* 22). Cozy begins his sermon by asking what black folks are going to do about the race problem. Sister Boger represents many in the congregation when she says to Sister Pindar, "Ah ain't heard what de tex' wuz" (158). Although all sermons, including black sermons, retain a flexibility of form, they do, nonetheless follow a certain order, and the sermon proper follows the text.

As Bruce Rosenberg and Henry Mitchell both agree, black preaching concerns itself with "affirmations of faith" and "celebration" (Mitchell 59, 119). Although black preachers may use a variety of structures (folktales, folk games, rituals, family histories, biblical stories, and so on), they generally follow a pattern loosely referred to as a "text-and-context" form. "The preacher begins with a quotation from Scripture (the "text"), proceeds to explain it ("context"), raises a doctrine from the passage and then, in the section that most interests the preacher, applies that doctrine to every-day affairs" (Rosenberg 14). That Sister Boger does not know the "text" of Cozy's sermon is telling, not only about Cozy as a preacher, but also about Hurston's strategy here.

Hurston parodies the sort of preacher who is in the pulpit for personal gain. Cozy lacks all skill for preaching; indeed, he is so bad at it that he must ask the congregation at least four times to say "Amen," and to say it as if they mean it. The usual call and response between preacher and congregation, the very spontaneity and life of the worship service, nearly disappears here. Although Cozy attempts to shame them into response, the Amens are lackluster at best. At the end of the service, when Deacon Harris asks Sister Boger how she liked the service, she annihilates both Rev. Cozy and Harris' plan to get rid of Pearson: "[t]hat wan't no sermon. Dat wuz uh lecture" (159).

Hurston demonstrates her skills with parody and satire brilliantly in this little scene, using Felton Cozy (including his name) to show her utter disdain for those Blacks who capitalize on race issues for their own gain. But the chapter does more than show off Hurston's craft as a writer. The gap of the Dry Bones sermon is a call for our response; our reading of the gap, perhaps not fully at this point, but retrospectively by the end of the novel, is analogous to the call and response in the black church when we know the text and context.

Through the contrast between Cozy and Pearson, we come to understand more about John Pearson's character. His moral failings may be obvious to us, but we do not doubt that, like Ezekiel, he is inspired by God's Word . We also understand the viciousness of some of the "good" churchgoers; if John Pearson needs to turn away from sin, so too does the congregation. If John's body and soul need to be mended and restored, so do the dry bones of the churchgoers. And if Pearson needs a second chance, the congregation requires it as well, for if John seems unaware of his sinning, the church is equally blind to its own sinfulness.

The reference to the Dry Bones sermon resonates with the meanings and themes of the novel itself. The sermon looks backward to Pearson's earlier sermon on the Natural (and therefore sinning) man and forward to his climactic sermon on the Wounds of Jesus, who takes on the sins of humankind. If one sermon speaks of the propensity of humankind to break faith and to be broken, the other speaks of a second chance, a restoration of brokenness.

In addition, Hurston's reference to the Dry Bones sermon connects to the folk festival at the end of cotton picking on the Pearson plantation (28–32). This festival is in itself an African "sermon" on the order of Dry Bones. Kata-Kumba, the great African drum, speaks with a prophetic voice filled with the spirit of the African god. The drum also tells a story of exile and despair, of Cuffy (the African) brought in chains, through the horrendous middle passage, over the Atlantic to America. Cuffy carries Kata-Kumba hidden "in his skin under the skullbones"; he beats the drum with his own shinbones (29–30). African Americans understand the text and context of the Dry Bones sermon; they have lived it.

Moreover, the sermon Pearson preaches, in its poignant omission, prophetically looks to the death of John Buddy, smashed and broken by the train that hits him, with only his foot twitching to remind us of the vitality of the man. It looks to the requiem "poem" of the preacher at Pearson's funeral in Zion Hope church. Indeed, his sermon speaks of hope, of resurrection, of God's celebratory delight in John before his throne. The gathering-up of Christian themes fuses with those of African Traditional Religion (see Mitchell, who notes that "it is very close to that of the Old Testament" 13), fuses with the voice of death and tears sounding from the drum of O-go-doe (202). The last line of the novel binds the African tradition with the Christian even more tightly; the line ends in the rhythm of drumming feet and the dance of heads moving in mourning. The last words of the novel, "it was ended," echo the words of Christ on the cross, words that breathe the promise of a new beginning, of a second chance for all of those who, like John Buddy, are broken and would be whole.

Their Eyes Were
Watching God
(1937)

Most scholars consider *Their Eyes Were Watching God*, Hurston's second novel, to be her best. Many readers, who know little about Hurston or her work, know Janie Crawford and Tea Cake Woods. Any critic attempting today to write about *Their Eyes* must acknowledge the numerous authoritative voices of earlier critical views. For a number of years Robert Stepto's influential essay in *From Behind the Veil* (1979) marked other critiques of *Their Eyes* in one way or another. Stepto called for a fresh look at African-American works, including Hurston's.

In response to Stepto's call, it may be helpful to look at Hurston's autobiography, *Dust Tracks on a Road*, in which she writes that she tried to "embalm" in *Their Eyes* all of the passionate and tender feelings she felt for a man she loved and yet gave up for the sake of her career (211). Not only is *Their Eyes* a love story, but it is a story of a young girl growing up, a *Bildungsroman* or a coming-of-age story.

PLOT DEVELOPMENT

Hurston structures the plot of *Their Eyes Were Watching God* by using a brief prologue that leads into a framing device. Within the frame is the story proper, divided into three segments, marked by the marriages of the novel's protagonist, Janie Crawford. What appears simple in structure, however, turns out to be complex in development.

The third person narrator opens the novel by contrasting the dreams of men, mocked by time and death, with those of women, in whose dreams there is truth. More importantly, unlike men who merely wish passively for dreams, women act upon them: they "act and do," as the narrator tells us (9).

The narrator moves from viewing all women to focusing on one woman, Janie Crawford, as she returns home to Eatonville, Florida, after burying her third husband, Vergible "Tea Cake" Woods. The novel opens, then, at the end of the narrative, as Janie paradoxically prepares to begin the story of her life adventures, relating them to her "kissin'" or best friend, Pheoby. Janie begins her tale with a flashback to when she was a child, living with her grandmother, Nanny, a former slave, then a domestic servant for a white family, the Washburns. At sixteen, Janie awakens to her sexuality. As Janie watches the bees pollinate the pear blossoms, she sees the "dust bearing bee sink into" the blossoms, and she watches the "thousand sister-calyxes arch to meet the love embrace" of the bee (24). From this view, Janie envisions what marriage is, an organic and harmonic union that produces an "ecstatic shiver" in nature itself. As a result of her vision, Janie kisses a boy, transformed in her imagination from a boy in rags to a lean youth covered in golden pollen. When Nanny discovers her granddaughter kissing the ragged boy, she determines to marry Janie to the widowed Logan Killicks, a farmer. Despite the fact that Killicks is much older than Janie, he seems favored by his ownership of sixty acres, a mule, and a house with an organ in the parlor. To Nanny, Killicks is a good "catch."

It does not matter that Janie has no affection for Killicks and does not want to marry him. Nanny demands the marriage as protection for Janie, who has no parents to look after her. As Nanny approaches her death, she fears that her grandchild will be left vulnerable alone. Shortly after Janie's wedding, Nanny dies, and it does not take long for Janie and Killicks' marriage to sour. Essentially Logan perceives his wife as someone to serve him and to work on the farm. When Killicks buys a second mule with the clear intention to have Janie work with it in the fields, she desires only to leave him and the farm.

Joe Starks, who just happens to stop by the farm one day, enroute from Georgia to Eatonville, Florida, fulfills Janie's desire. Starks, who had worked and saved his money, has heard about Eatonville, a town lived in and run by black folks. An ambitious man, Starks aims to rise in the world, and he wants to take Janie with him as his "lady"-wife. Because Joe (or Jody, as Janie calls him) speaks for change, for movement, and for new horizons, Janie decides to leave Killicks and run off with Joe Starks.

In comparison to Killicks, Starks initially treats Janie like a queen. He buys her gifts of new clothes, apples, and candy. When they arrive in Eatonville, Janie, obviously younger than Starks, is mistaken for Jody's daughter, a mistake Starks immediately and defensively corrects. Before long, Starks not only owns the only store in the town but becomes its first mayor. As his material life prospers, however, his personal life suffers. Jody spends most of his time being important, "a Big Voice" who buys "big," and who spends very little time with his wife. Unlike Logan, Jody does not attempt to work Janie to death. In fact, Starks had been attracted to Janie because she seemed like a "doll-baby," someone to keep as an object for others to admire (49). Jody intends for Janie to dress up, to be an ornament for him and a model for other women. In short, Starks views Janie as his prize possession. As such, he keeps her at a polite distance from the rest of the townspeople, regulating not only her use of language but her movement in the town. Starks flatly states that Janie knows nothing about making speeches: "She's uh woman and her place is in de home" (69).

Again, Janie finds herself in a marriage that demands she serve her master, that is, her husband. In response to Killicks, Janie ran away; in response to Starks, she speaks out—publicly—and puts him in his "place." When Starks brutally calls Janie old in front of the townspeople, she retaliates by saying that when he pulls down his pants, he looks like the "change uh life" (123). Thus, she not only attacks his age but also his so-called "male-hood." Janie's assertion of self destroys what little remains of her marriage with Starks, and shortly thereafter he dies. As Joe Starks had attempted to make himself a big man in Eatonville, so his funeral is big, full of the show of pomp and circumstance. Even Janie shows herself as Starks would have liked: starched, ironed, and finely dressed.

Starks leaves Janie with property and money, and thus she is courted by men who hope to move up in class. Much to the chagrin of the townspeople, a laborer and a guitar-playing singer, Vergible "Tea Cake" Woods, wins Janie's heart. Tea Cake, younger than Janie, loves her for who she is; he does not try to remake her into a mule driver, as Logan Killicks had, nor a doll-baby, as Joe Starks had. Instead, Tea Cake treats Janie as an equal, teaching her games and sport, how to play checkers, how to fish, and how to shoot a gun, for example.

Janie and Tea Cake move from Eatonville to go on the "muck," to work together in the rich bean fields on reclaimed land from Lake Okeechobee in the Everglades. Here they share not only their work, but their play: song, feasting, festivity. Most importantly, they share their love and thus a life together.

The equality of their love and life make for a different relationship from Janie's two earlier marriages. The love between Janie and Tea Cake is both spontaneous and giving. Although Janie has enough money for them to live in one place, she willingly goes with Tea Cake to what might appear to be a demeaning job. Yet their marriage cannot survive a hurricane that sweeps everything away, including many people in the Everglades. In the scenes in which the hurricane ravages both people and landscape, we understand the meanings of the novel's title; truly, the eyes of the people are "watching God." Although Tea Cake and Janie escape death by hurricane, Tea Cake is bitten by a rabid dog. He contracts rabies and goes mad; in his derangement he attempts to shoot Janie. In order to save herself, Janie shoots him, ironically killing the person she loves most. At an inquest, a white jury acquits her of murder, finding that she acted in self-defense.

After the trial, Janie buries Tea Cake in a "royal" funeral; she buries him with a guitar she buys so that he will be able to play songs for her when she rejoins him after her life is over. When Janie buried Joe Starks, she attended his funeral in expensive clothes and a veil, with her face—and her emotions—starched and ironed. When she goes to Tea Cake's funeral, she goes in her overalls, too full of grief to wear grief's trappings.

The novel ends at its beginning, with Janie's return to Eatonville. She passes the cold eyes and spiteful tongues of the townspeople, as they sit on the front porch of Joe Starks' store and judge her without knowing anything of her or her life away from Eatonville. Only Pheoby, Janie's friend from earlier days, arrives at her door, generously bringing her supper. The novel ends with Janie finishing her story, and with Pheoby's response that she has grown "ten feet higher" just listening to Janie's story. If Janie's love for Tea Cake changed Janie, causing her to grow up, so too does Janie's story change her listener.

The end of Janie's narration to Pheoby, however, is really no ending. As Janie closes up her house, the narration is given over to the voice that opens the novel, the voice that told us about dreams and truth. When Janie climbs the stairs in her house with a light in her hand, her face reflects "sun-stuff," the beginning of life itself. Nothing is dead until she stops "feeling and thinking" (286), Janie knows. So, too, do we know this truth. Like Pheoby, we have grown ten feet higher.

SETTING AND SYMBOLISM

Hurston's sense of place looms large in *Their Eyes Were Watching God*. Janie grows up in the backyard of the Washburns, the white family for whom Nanny works. We learn little of the plain house Nanny and Janie share, but we do have a sense of how it compares with the slave quarters in which Nanny gave birth to her child (Janie's mother) Leafy. It is certainly a more benign location than the plantation slave quarters, with Mrs. Washburn a kinder and gentler mistress. Nor do we learn much more about Logan Killicks' house. To be sure, we know that it has an organ in the parlor, evidence of his being a successful farmer. There is, however, no music in his house that we know of. Still, the very materiality of the two houses is used metaphorically to delineate character; Nanny is a "cracked plate," nearing the end of her function as a guardian over Janie; Logan is alone, and lonely, a "stump" in the middle of the woods, just like his house. Killicks' house has no "flavor," like the man himself.

In Eatonville, Joe Starks' store figures importantly in the town, just as the man does. The store is not only the very center of the town, literally and figuratively, but it represents acquisitiveness. Joe Starks is a buyer and seller of consumer goods, all for profit; the canned goods piled on the floor even before the store's roof is complete demonstrate Joe's obsession with materialism. For Joe Starks, the store is one of his means of power. For Janie, the store simply means work. The store is also the cultural center of the town, where stories are told and embellished and where gossip, like the canned goods, is exchanged.

In addition to the store, Starks' house is the most magnificent structure in Eatonville; in comparison, the other town houses look like the servant's quarters clustered around the "big house" of the master (75). Starks' house is huge, with two stories, porches, and bannisters. Moreover, Starks had it painted white, inside and out. One can hardly miss Hurston's irony here; she makes clear Starks' emulation of white acquisitiveness at the expense of other Blacks, including his own wife. Once Starks nails down the important posts in the town—mayor, postmaster, landlord, and storekeeper—he acquires things: a desk with chair, just like the white entrepreneurs in nearby Maitland, and a "golded-up" spittoon, plus a lady's spittoon with little flowers printed on it (for Janie). As Killicks kept an organ in the parlor for his wife, Starks keeps a spittoon in his parlor for his. As Killicks owned sixty acres, Starks does considerably better, ending up with two hundred acres.

Yet Starks' house, for all its grandness, lacks "flavor" as much as Killicks' house ever did. Even after Starks dies, the house keeps the sound of loneliness; it creaks and cries. Starks' house also represents the high market value of Janie as suitors come to call on the widow. At the same time, the house means freedom for Janie; as a woman of property, she is not compelled to choose anyone to take Starks' place as her husband. Paradoxically, when Tea Cake arrives, the house for the first time gains flavor from the laughter that fills it. Yet Janie has no trouble leaving it to go with Tea Cake to the "muck" in the Everglades.

On the muck, the soil is rich, black, and fertile. Not only does sugarcane grow wild, so too do the people. Everything is alive on the muck; people work hard together, and they play hard. Whereas Starks' house stood outside of and above everyone else's, Tea Cake's house is the center of the community. People are drawn to Tea Cake's house like a magnet. Not only does Janie make huge vats of food to be shared with everyone, Tea Cake sits in his open doorway, playing his guitar. Unlike Starks' house, which was for show, Tea Cake's house overflows with hospitality, song, and laughter. The house on the muck, unlike the one in Eatonville, does not imprison Janie; she and Tea Cake share their house, just as they share their work on the muck during the day. Love flows out of the house in the morning to return in the evening. When Janie thinks of the past in her big white house and store, she can only laugh.

If the muck is a place wild with life, it also holds death. When the hurricane strikes, Lake Okeechobee awakens into a monster. The lightening and thunder come from "Big Massa," moving his "chair upstairs" (235). The world becomes one house that we all live in, a house threatened by destruction. No matter the houses humans acquire, great nature links us all, Hurston suggests.

At the beginning of the novel, Janie perceives herself as being part of nature itself, when she finds herself under a blossoming pear tree. To her, the pear tree signifies the mysteries of spring and the universe. "From barren brown stems" to the buds of leaves to "snowy virginity of bloom" (23), all life is contained. The mystery of life becomes clear to Janie in the pollen-laden bee as it lends itself to the innermost reaches of the pear bloom. In the flower's embrace of the bee comes the ecstatic, divine marriage at the core of life itself. Janie's view of the orgasmic shiver of the tree, a shiver that runs from root to branch to each blossom "frothing with delight," leads to Janie's own orgasmic response. As Robert Hemenway, Hurston's biographer, writes so eloquently in his book on Hurston, "The orgasm described here comes to represent the organic union Janie searches for throughout her life" (233). The image of the pear tree permeates the novel and comes to stand for the organic growth of Janie's "emotional life" (Hemenway 233).

Paradoxically, the huge storm in the Everglades is but one part of Janie's growth. As the pear tree signifies the sacred marriage and life of the universe, the storm represents the "monstropolous beast" that seemingly destroys life. The storm looses the chains of the beast that appears all too humanly alive, running to uproot dikes, rolling people and houses like dice. The sea walks "the earth with a heavy heel" (239).

In the beast of the storm, Janie comes to recognize a significant part of the diurnal round of nature, just as, when a young girl, she recognized the significance of the pear tree in that round. Thus the mad dog of the storm does not obliterate Tea Cake; instead great nature absorbs him unto itself. At the close of Janie's story, she begins again with life. If Tea Cake embodied the organic marriage of the universe, so too a packet of seeds Tea Cake left Janie will be a reminder of that marriage into the future. Janie plants the seeds not only for remembrance of the past but for the present and the future. In this planting, of course, we recollect the pear tree, in which not one aspect of birth, growth, and death is ever really lost.

CHARACTER DEVELOPMENT

Even though Nanny's role in *Their Eyes* may seem small—she dies, after all, early in the novel—she looms large in Janie's life. Nanny, born into slavery, has her own history which determines not only her actions but the decisions she makes for her granddaughter Janie. As a slave, Nanny was impregnated by her master and bore Janie's mother, Leafy. Nanny's mistress, who discovers the child is part white, with gray eyes and yellow hair, threatens to have Nanny whipped one hundred lashes and to sell her child when she is a month old. Instead, Nanny escapes with Leafy to a new and so-called free life, in which she sends her daughter to school, hoping she will be a teacher. However, Leafy's teacher abducts her and rapes her; the result is Janie. Leafy never recovers, takes to drink, and disappears, leaving Janie for Nanny to raise.

In a way, Nanny, too, never recovers from her own devastating experiences on a slave plantation or from her daughter's rape. As a result, Janie becomes her last hope to be a woman who is not a "spit cup" for men, white or black. Thus, when Nanny realizes that Janie is no longer a girl and finds her kissing one of the local boys, she acts quickly. The die has long been cast for Nanny to marry off her granddaughter to a man who will provide her security and protection.

For Nanny, Janie's marriage to Logan Killicks, older, settled, with property, means respectability just like that of white folks; moreover, such a marriage means that Nanny, old herself and worn out, can now die knowing Janie will be cared for. As far as Nanny is concerned, love does not enter into and has no place in what amounts to a transaction, a marriage contract signed and delivered in return for protection.

For Janie, Logan's sixty acres represent only her own lonesomeness. Nature seems as barren as Logan himself. Indeed, Logan appears to be as insensate as the stumps on his property, as unappealing as his own mule. Logan is even described as having a "skull-head" and mule feet. Unclean, nearly inarticulate, Logan sees Janie as a part of his property; he acquired her not only to chop wood and to do chores, but to help him acquire more property. She is Logan's capital investment, for he intends to buy a second mule with which Janie will be able to help plow more ground to increase Logan's property value. Nanny's value was that she and other black women were used as the work mules of the world for both black and white men. Blinded by Logan's ownership of sixty acres and a mule (most likely acquired, ironically, as slave reparations after the Civil War), Nanny marries Janie to Logan to prevent her from being turned into a mule. She could not or did not want to see the mulishness of the very man she selected for her granddaughter. Nor did Nanny know that Logan Killicks would come to perceive Janie as merely an extension of his mule, yoked to it to plow his sixty-acre world.

No wonder, then, that Janie has no qualms about leaving Logan for Joe Starks. Younger than Logan, but still older than Janie, Starks seems to be both affable and charming. Unlike Logan, Starks is not tied to a lonesome sixty acres in the woods. Starks promises to take Janie away from the drudgery of Killicks' life; in addition, Starks' gifts of elegant clothing to Janie seem like daybreak after relentless darkness. Yet the differences between Killicks and Starks are merely superficial; Starks is the same as Killicks: aggressive and acquisitive.

Joe Starks sets out to be a "big" man (50) by buying up property in Eatonville, which he then rents to the townspeople. Starks embodies the capitalistic marketplace. He owns the only store in town and thus controls all buying and selling in the community. Moreover, the store is in the center of the town, its porch containing and regulating social, moral, and even cultural behaviors. Although Starks allows Janie to work in the store, she does so under his direct supervision. His property, then, includes, as one person tells Starks, "yo' belov-ed wife, yo' store, yo' land—" (67). Because Janie is property, Starks insists that her place is in the home; he displays her, his lady, at his pleasure (50). Although she may witness much of what may be called porch behavior—its playacting, its social banter, and its storytelling—Janie is not allowed to participate in any of its vitality or the life of the community. If Starks owns town property and store goods, he believes he surely owns his wife.

Starks solidifies his status as a big man when he becomes Eatonville's mayor. He also becomes the postmaster, as well as the storekeeper, and thus controls the significant institutions of the town. He is also Eatonville's chief orator, speaking for everyone in the community. Literally, as well as metaphorically, Starks electrifies the town and demonstrates his power over the community when he throws the switch turning on the electricity.

For good reason, then, Joe Starks' tag line, his favorite exclamation, is "I God." Indeed, he thinks of himself as God, superior to everyone and all-powerful. Even his body suggests power; he is physically a big man, portly. However, despite Starks' size, his gift of oratory, and his apparent power in Eatonville, he remains a "small" man, one who bullies his wife and one who merely apes the white men he so admires. He hires a boy to work in the store, who in turn apes Starks, including not only his language and walk but his attitudes towards those around him. Even Starks' house, his desk where he keeps his accounts, and his spittoons are mere imitations of the trappings of white men's power. One might well argue that Starks' treatment of Janie imitates the propensity of white men to place their wives, along with their other goods, above all else, displaying them prominently for others to admire.

Starks demonstrates just how small he is when he publicly berates Janie, calling her an old woman. Her retort that Starks, when he pulls down his pants, looks like the change of life does more than shock her husband; it humiliates him and reduces him both in stature and power. Janie's words both wound and destroy Joe Starks.

Janie's ability to speak out in self-defense is a major step towards self-expression. Indeed, she had earlier told Logan Killicks that she had not married him to be his servant. The granddaughter of a former slave, Janie was brought up by

Nanny to know her "place." In fact, Nanny coerces her to marry Logan Killicks, a man of property, to ensure for Janie a respectable and secure place as his wife. Initially, Janie passively accepts Logan's demands for her to work on the farm. She accepts Nanny's vision of life, albeit reluctantly. Gradually, however, Janie begins to speak up to Killicks, as she recognizes that their marriage will never fulfill the promise of love she envisioned under the pear tree. Finally, Janie refuses to stay in her place. She physically leaves the place Nanny and Killicks assign to her. Although easily seduced by Starks with the promise of travel and gifts, Janie later steps out of her assigned place with him, shaming Starks with her well-chosen words.

After Starks dies, Janie, herself now with property, can choose who she wants to be her mate. She can, of course, choose not to have a mate, but this choice would be out of character for one who found in the natural flowering of a pear tree a vision of union, of marriage. After marriage with two men who believed a wife was merely one more acquisition of material goods, Janie finds someone quite different in Vergible "Tea Cake" Woods. His very name indicates how closely he is linked to nature: Vergible or veritable, the "true" woods, perhaps even verdant woods. Whereas Logan Killicks' land looked like a barren old stump, and Starks tore down nature to build up his town, Tea Cake follows the cycle of the seasons and the land itself in his migrant farm work.

As a well-off widow, Janie has what everyone tells her is a comfortable place, but she leaves it behind to go with Tea Cake. Nanny, Killicks, Starks, the townspeople who think she has many better suitors than Tea Cake, Mrs. Turner who tells Janie she could do better than Tea Cake—all attempt to define Janie's place for her. The struggle of Janie's life is to define her place for herself.

For Janie, whose vision of life itself comes from nature at work in the pear tree, is it any wonder that she chooses to follow Tea Cake, who himself follows nature? Both Killicks and Starks, older than Janie, viewed life as work leading to self-aggrandizement. Tea Cake, younger than Janie, views life as play. A man of music, Tea Cake plays his guitar and sings. A man of stories, he plays with words. And he teaches Janie to play: from checkers, to fishing, to her story-making. Work on the muck becomes simply a different kind of play. Of course, the most serious play is the "game" of love—as Tea Cake says, his feeling for Janie is not business; it is a love game (171)—a game played for a kingdom of life itself, to which Janie holds the "keys."

Although Tea Cake fulfills the vision Janie had under the pear tree—he is the "bee" man, associated with trees in bloom, with the gold of the sun, with the scent of the breeze—this does not mean that he is perfect. Just as Killicks threatened to hit Janie and as Starks actually slapped her, so does Woods beat her. Despite attempts by critics to acquit Tea Cake of any flaws, his beating is not in "play"; it is all too serious. He beats Janie after overhearing Mrs. Turner say that she could do better than to be married to Tea Cake; he beats her to re-assure himself that he has control over her. At the same time, Janie herself is not perfect; she beats Nunkie, a plump, younger girl who Janie believes is attempt-ing to seduce Tea Cake. In addition, she also beats Tea Cake because she fears he will leave her.

One of the problems for readers of *Their Eyes*, particularly in terms of the characters of Janie and Tea Cake, has to do with the fact that they are portrayed both mythically and realistically. That is to say that Tea Cake, on the one hand, is a product of his historical time, a black man with little power, working in a world dominated by the power of white men. The sense of powerlessness in ev-eryday life leads all of the black men in Hurston's novel to behave in aberrant ways; if white men brutalize black men, black men in turn brutalize the women in their lives. We find the pattern of this in the black schoolteacher's rape of Leafy. Even though the schoolteacher tries to make amends to her, white men track him like an animal and lynch him. Had it been a white man who raped Leafy, no action would have been taken.

Even women are not immune from the pattern of violence that spins out of racial hatreds. Just as Nanny's mistress threatens to whip her to death, so Nanny slaps her granddaughter into submitting to the marriage with Killicks.

Both Tea Cake and Janie exhibit all of the real frailities of human beings: jealousy, fear, and anxiety. Tea Cake succumbs to madness when bitten by a ra-bid dog and attempts to kill the one person he loves more than life. At the same time, Tea Cake is associated with the god Orpheus, the maker of music, and with the world of nature itself; Vergible seems to be the veritable god of living things: of the woods, of the earth—the fertile muck—of the sun. He arrives with the air into Janie's life. He literally and metaphorically carries with him the seeds of life itself in his serious game of love.

Similarly, Janie suffers hurt, jealousy, and remorse. Her desire to *be*—to be able to know and express herself—is the realistic goal of all of us. Her desire to share who she is with someone she loves is something we can all share. At the same time, her journey to reach her goal and desire are particular to a young black woman. Janie struggles to know who she is in the face of racism and sex-ism. Janie kills Tea Cake out of her deep-rooted will to survive, to live, and thus, ironically, she snuffs out the life of the only man she loved. Janie's charac-ter is also the stuff of myth, akin to the goddess Isis, who is associated with the flood waters. Janie, herself saved from the flood, casts forth her net at the end of her story, pulling in all of life in its meshes. The close of the novel paradoxically opens up Janie's story so that it seems to open out beyond real facts, just as she opens the window of her house and the four primal elements surround her: air, fire, water, and earth. The light in her hand becomes the fire of "sun stuff," and the breeze blows the "road dust" from her hair. She holds the seeds Tea Cake had given her, which, when planted, will bloom into new life.

In telling her life story to Pheoby, Janie demonstrates that she has found her own voice. Instead of others defining her role—her place—for her, she has made her life her own.

THEMATIC ISSUES

The intricate interlacing of the themes of racism, sexism, and class in *Their Eyes Were Watching God* accounts in large part for the novel's richness. Add to these themes those of love and spirituality, and the complexity of Hurston's best known novel becomes evident.

Some fifteen years ago, Barbara Christian, in *Black Feminist Criticism*, rightly noted that African-American women's fiction often mirrors "the intensity of the relationship between sexism and racism in this country" (172). Christian warns us that although we may understand this relationship "in terms of economics or social status," we neglect to understand its impact on individual self-expression. "To be able to use the range of one's voice, to attempt to express the totality of self," is a constant and "recurring struggle" in African-American women's writing from the nineteenth century to the present day (Christian 172). This struggle undergirds the plot, the character development, and the thematic issues of *Their Eyes*.

Nanny's "text" at the beginning of the novel instructs her granddaughter Janie in what it means to be black, female, and a slave to the white world. It is to be a "spit cup," for the white master to use for his sexual pleasure, as well as to be his mule of all work on the plantation. It is to be threatened with the whip by the white mistress for being sexually abused by the mistress's own husband. It is also to be threatened with the impending sale of the newborn, gray-eyed, "yaller" child, the product of master/slave abuse. Nanny's text also has to do with the resultant horror-filled flight from slave-owners in order for her to protect her child Leafy, who would become the mother of Janie. Janie herself, like her mother, was also born of a rape, this time by the black schoolteacher. Nanny's insistence that Janie marry Logan Killicks, a man of property, is an attempt to raise her granddaughter out of the mire of such abuse, to give her a life where she is both respectable and respected, where she will not have to be either a "spit cup" or a "mule" of the world.

Ironically, Nanny's statement becomes fulfilled by both Killicks and Starks, themselves products of the racism that was integral to slavery. Killicks, probably not much younger than Nanny, most likely owns his sixty acres and a mule as part of the reparation given to Blacks at the end of the Civil War. Like his former white masters, Killicks determines to acquire more property, and also like his former masters, Killicks also will use "slave" labor—his wife Janie—to improve his financial status. With another mule and Janie hitched to it, Killicks aims to increase his holdings and thus his power. Starks is no different from Killicks; Starks' plan is more ambitious and turns out to be more successful. Younger than Killicks, Starks has worked for white men and recognizes the power one gains through material wealth.

Starks sees Janie as an asset in his plan to become a big man. She represents his "trophy" wife: a good-looking, light-complected woman, a possession owned by Starks and put on display. She is the visual proof of his power; as Starks dominates her, so he dominates the town of Eatonville. Janie's headrag, which Starks demands that she wears, is the type worn by slave women as a visual sign of their status. Clearly Janie's headrag signifies Starks' presumed ownership of her. When Starks slaps Janie for not cooking his dinner properly (112), he does what countless slave owners had done to their black cooks on a bad day in the kitchen. Not only is Janie punished for her supposed inability to cook, she is also punished publicly for thinking. When Janie reminds Starks that God talks to women as well as to men, Starks tells her she is getting too "moufy" (117); as he prepares to play checkers with one of his cronies, he orders her to get the checkerboard "*and*" (Hurston's emphasis 117) the checkers, implying that Janie is too ignorant to understand both are needed in order to play the game.

Starks' constant reiteration that Janie is old demonstrates merely another attempt to degrade her at the same time that he shows his power over her. Inwardly filled with his own sense of inferiority in a world run by white men, Starks attempts to deny Janie's womanliness and her sexuality. Janie responds by turning his cutting remarks back on Starks. As she points out, she is a woman, and he knows it. His sexuality, his maleness, is highly questionable; when his pants are down, he looks like "de change uh life" (123). Although Starks strikes Janie a mighty blow, he never regains domination over her. Indeed, his inability to wield power over her—verbally or physically—leads to his death.

Racism, indelibly imprinted in the system of slavery, fueled and formed the basis of white male economic aggrandisement; slave-owners controlled not only black production but reproduction. Killicks and Starks represent the legacy of such white oppression even as they perpetuate it among black people. Vergible "Tea Cake" Woods for the most part seems to have somehow escaped such a legacy. But not entirely. He slaps Janie, just as Starks had, because Tea Cake fears he will lose her to someone lighter in color than he. Beating Janie alleviates his fear, reassuring him that he retains "possession" of her (218). Tea Cake overheard Mrs. Turner, herself light-complected, tell Janie that she could do better than be married to someone as black as Tea Cake. In short, he beats Janie to let Mrs. Turner know who is "boss" and who is in "control" (220). Generally, however, he treats Janie as an equal, in ways that Starks never did; Tea Cake takes her fishing and plays checkers with her. Although money and material goods seem of no consequence to either Tea Cake or Janie, yet paradoxically Starks' money and property make possible Janie's return to "*her*" (my emphasis) house in Eatonville after Tea Cake's death.

Nor does Hurston allow readers to overlook the connection between class and racism. Although Blacks were free of slavery, free to own property, and free to be mayor of a black town, in the white world Blacks counted for little. In *Their Eyes*, Blacks are not seen so much as a part of the lower class, as they are beneath class consideration. For example, after the monstrous hurricane sweeps through the Everglades killing many people, black and white, Blacks are immediately pressed into burial service. Even though the storm does not discriminate between class or race, white authority in Florida does: Blacks are buried separately from Whites. As Tea Cake sarcastically queries, do the guards think God knows about Jim Crow laws?

Not only Whites believe they are superior in both race and class; light-skinned Blacks are sure they are superior to those who are darker. On the muck, Mrs. Turner, who runs a restaurant, chastises Janie for marrying such a black, low-class man as Tea Cake. Mrs. Turner sarcastically comments that Tea Cake must have had a great deal of money (which, of course, she does not believe) for someone like Janie to marry him. As far as Mrs. Turner is concerned, there are "too many" black people; the black race needs to become lighter to advance in the world. Not only are black people ugly, according to Mrs. Turner, they are also stupid. Thus, Mrs. Turner goes to white doctors when she is ill. Moreover, Mrs. Turner attempts to disrupt Janie's marriage to Tea Cake, urging her to meet her brother, who has "dead straight hair" (211).

Janie rejects Mrs. Turner, along with her self-hatred and sense of class. After all, Janie knows what it means to be "classed" off, as she was when married to Joe Starks (169). As Janie realizes, Mrs. Turner demonstrates cruelty to those she sees as inferior, at the same time that she grovels before those who have power over her. However, even Janie is not totally immune to the idea that the world is separated into classes along the lines of race and economics; she calls upon a white doctor to help Tea Cake when he suffers rabies. And at the trial held after Tea Cake's death, Janie clearly knows she must select her words carefully for the white legal institution controls life and death, particularly over those de-classed by race.

For all the thematic power of such issues as racism, sexism, and class, the driving force in *Their Eyes Were Watching God* remains love, along with its concomitant spiritual expression. When Janie as a young girl lies under the pear tree, she has a vision of love in what she perceives is its natural form: the perfect, harmonious marriage between bee and blossom. It takes Janie quite a while for her to find her "bee" man in Vergible Woods, and, although not perfect, he is as close to bringing her into harmony with the world as one can find outside of Paradise. There is no denying that Tea Cake is flawed; subject to jealousy and feelings of inferiority, he wants things his way and strikes Janie. So too is Janie flawed; she also suffers jealousy and beats Tea Cake. Their relationship is not founded on business, as were Janie's first two marriages. As Janie puts it, she and Tea Cake are not running after "property and titles" (171). Their relationship remains throughout the novel a "love game" (171). Tea Cake is a "glance from God," just as she holds the "keys" to the kingdom.

Yet if Tea Cake is God's glance, God can, apparently, take that glance away. The hurricane is as much a part of nature as the procreating pear tree. Although Tea Cake is bitten by a rabid dog in the wake of the hurricane, Janie is saved. Thus, even though the hurricane kills many people, it also gives life to many believed to be dead (236).

When Tea Cake is dying from rabies, Janie questions God: Was God paying attention to what was happening on earth? Did God "mean" for the rabid dog to bite Tea Cake? Perhaps the hurricane and the mad dog were part of some sort of cosmic joke, Janie thinks. Just as the people on the muck during the hurricane turned their eyes on God, watching for some sort of sign, so Janie watches for a sign. There are no answers to her questions, nor is there any sign from God. She finally believes that God "would do less than He had in His heart" (264).

The hurricane and Tea Cake's subsequent death cause Janie to reflect upon the meaning of her life with him and to evaluate the worth of their love. God may have taken back the glance that was Tea Cake, but through him, God had snatched Janie from a living death imposed upon her by others (267). It is as if Tea Cake had been on loan from God to give Janie the "chance for loving service" (273).

Janie and Tea Cake's love brought them to the dawn of a new day, a beginning, in which they had to shape new thoughts and new words and bring them into play. From their love springs new life, encompassing the world, which is always new, always changing (284). Their love allowed for individual growth, transforming not only Janie but touching others as well (284). When Janie tells her love story, Pheoby becomes dissatisfied with her old self and vows to change by going there, that is to love itself (284–285). To be fully alive, spiritually and physically, according to Janie, is to know love, to go to God (285). God and love, in Janie's text/sermon, are one and the same. Janie's telling of her story revivifies her love and makes everything taste "fresh again," as she remembers Tea

Cake. When Janie pulls in the net of memory, it contains the whole world, a world made vibrant with the breath—the very soul—of life.

A FEMINIST READING

In her dedication to Hurston in *I Love Myself When I Am Laughing*, Alice Walker explains her admiration of *Their Eyes Were Watching God*: "there is enough self-love in that one book—love of community, culture, traditions—to restore a world. Or create a new one" (2). Hurston indeed seeks to overturn an "old" world, bound by its history of racism and sexism, and to explore a new world, free and open to possibilities. In doing so, Hurston has written a novel that is both subversive and feminist.

To read Hurston's novel using feminist theory is to examine power relations in the text (and concomitantly in life) in order to break them down. Feminist critics view reading as a political act; in fact, contemporary feminist literary criticism sprang from the women's rights movement of the 1960s. Feminist critics examine representations of women in literature and question such images in relation to women's experiences. Images of women in literature are seen as important in terms of socialization, providing role models for good or ill. At the same time, feminist critics revalue women's experiences. More often than not such criticism is polemical; it seeks not only to explore female relationships and values but to bring about political and social change for women. Because of its broad goals, feminist criticism draws from a variety of critical positions, including psychological, historical, cultural, and the like. For example, the French philosopher/critic Julia Kristeva uses a number of critical theories, including linguistics, psychoanalysis, and cultural studies, in her exploration not only of literature but of feminist politics and social relations as a whole.

Some feminist critics like Kristeva reject the male order of power in the name of sexual difference, arguing that there can be no real opposition between masculine and feminine because there is no fixed identity based on the biological sex of a person (Kristeva 33–34). In her work, Kristeva looks particularly at power structures, focusing on marginal peoples, those who are kept in their "places" on the fringes of society because of race, poverty, and/or sex. Her study of language, especially in literature, looks at various "ruptures, blank spaces, and holes [in] language" which indicate revolutionary potential. Such ruptures or spaces are viewed as disruptive, or even defining, moments in a literary text, moments that force readers to examine their own expections or definitions of gender, for example, or of social order (Kristeva 13–35).

The very opening of *Their Eyes* may be read as a disruptive or defining moment. It raises immediate questions in the minds of readers as it indicates space between the lives of men and women. Men seem passively to watch ships on the horizon, filled with their dreams and hopes, and wait for them to arrive. The women also have dreams, but they "act and do" because of those dreams (9). The men resign themselves to their lives and eventually have their dreams "mocked to death." Hurston does not link women's dreams with death, but with truth. As she moves from all women to one woman, Hurston offers a paradox: the "beginning" for this particular woman comes after she is done "burying the dead" (9). Whereas death closes off the lives of men, it opens the life of a woman—Janie Crawford.

In exposing the space or rupture between men and women's time, Hurston forces readers to overturn certain expectations we may have: men as active participants in the world around them, women as passive. Nowhere in the passage are men and women linked irrevocably to biology, to some essential maleness or femaleness. In addition, readers are forced to rethink the accepted order of things: life ended by death; beginnings brought to endings; dreams stifled by resignation; hope beaten by hopelessness.

Even the order of how novels begin is brought into question. Hurston's novel begins outside of the narrative proper to move into its ending, only to go backwards to its beginning! The turning upside down or inside out of reader expectations continues throughout the novel. Janie Crawford's story calls us to reconsider Nanny's position on life and, like Pheoby, to begin to think new thoughts and entertain radical possibilities. However fascinating the men may be in this novel (including Tea Cake), Hurston focuses readers' attention on three women: Nanny, Pheoby, and especially Janie. Circulating around and through them are the "defining" moments of the novel.

Nanny's story reflects her experience of life, all of it based on a hierarchy sustained by white male power. In Nanny's world of slavery and post-slavery time, white men ruled from the top of this hierarchy—ruling even their wives—moving down the ladder to black men, black women, black children, and mules. Whether animals were lower than Blacks was questionable, since they were often lumped together, and when they died, buried together in the fields (Robinson 211–16). This powerful order, based primarily on a materialistic economy, as well as on pretensions of class and racial superiority, had the authority of law behind it as set out in the contract of sale specifying the trade of black men, women, and children between white buyers and sellers. The narrative behind Nanny's text was clearly structured and codified: as slaves, Blacks were property in the same way that animals were. Even though Lincoln's emancipation of slaves theoretically nullified the master/slave relationship, the legal narrative of the sale of slaves continues to haunt Nanny's story that she relates to her granddaughter. Moreover, the legal nullification of slavery did little to change the socioeconomic order of things. As far as Nanny can tell, black free men may have moved to the bottom rung of the social ladder, but black women, along with mules, lack even that foothold.

According to Nanny's way of thinking, the only way for a black woman to secure a place in the world is to marry someone who can provide it for her. Nanny's desire to protect Janie and to secure her a place where she will not be lumped together with a mule is understandable, but her choice of Logan Killicks as Janie's husband turns out to be disastrous. In fact, the marriage merely perpetuates the same hierarchical, patriarchal system. There appears to be little difference between the contract of sale that validated Nanny as property and the contract of marriage to which Nanny binds her granddaughter—sealed with a resounding slap to Janie's face.

Hurston makes clear the linkages between the marriage contract and the sale contract of slaves. Killicks' sixty acres and his mule stand as surety for Killicks in return for Janie. As Nanny did not possess any rights to remove herself from the slave trade, so she leaves Janie little choice about the marriage to Killicks.

Janie is "bought" for her youthful potential to work; as Logan Killicks admits, he married her anyway, despite her background. Logan expects her to chop wood, clean the house, and cook, since his deceased wife had done so without complaint. Moreover, Killicks intends to work her in ways most plantations did not: as a "house nigger" and as a "field nigger," hitched to a mule to plow his land. When Janie refuses to help Logan shovel manure, she tells him (from the doorway of his house) that he does not need her help; he is in his place, she in hers. Logan responds: "You ain't got no particular place. It's wherever Ah need yuh" (52). In addition, he threatens to beat her and even to take an ax to her. When Janie escapes from Killicks by running away, she repeats the same action as her grandmother, who ran from her mistress because she threatened to beat Nanny a hundred lashes with a whip. Nanny ran to save her daughter Leafy; Janie runs away with Starks to save herself.

The space between Janie's marriage to Joe Starks and that to Logan Killicks seems at first to be enormous. Where Killicks sees her literally connected to his mule, Starks sees her as his "queen," a "doll-baby" that he buys with gifts of new clothes, food delicacies, and promises of far horizons (50). Starks is physically different from Killicks, with his skull-like head and mule feet. Although seal-brown in color, Starks seems, in his attitudes and actions, to be more like the white Mr. Washburn than like Killicks. Janie, seduced by Starks' charm (in contrast to Killicks' mulishness)—and by her own desires to be loved and to see distant places—voluntarily chooses to enter into a marriage contract with Starks. He is a bad choice. In the end, Starks' marriage contract turns out to be little different from Killicks'. Alice Walker goes to the heart of the matter in her poem, "Janie Crawford," when she writes about loving the way Janie left her husbands: one husband who attempted to turn Janie into a mule, and one who attempted to turn her into a queen (*Good Night Willie Lee* 18).

To both Starks and Killicks, Janie is a possession, property. As property, Janie, like a slave, is bound to her "master's" orders. Starks drives this point home by requiring her to wear a headrag to bind her hair, both de-sexing her at the same time that he forces identification of her as merely a black woman. In Nanny's days on the plantation, slave women were required to wear the headrag as a sign of their "place" in the social order. Nanny alludes to the danger of black women's hair being unbound when she relates her history to Janie: Master Robert, before leaving to fight Yankees, went to her cabin and made her let down her hair. He wrapped his hand in it "lak he always done" (33). The enjoyment of the black woman's hair and her body was reserved for the master at his will.

Not only does Starks' insistence upon the headrag link him to slavery, but just as Killicks has his mule, so does Starks. He "frees" Matt Bonner's mule after much mule-baiting on the part of the townspeople. Janie, who empathizes with the dumbly passive mule, tells Starks that freeing the mule makes him a big man, like Lincoln, a man of enormous power, like a king (92). Although Starks welcomes the adulation and beams "all around," he misses the irony here. He may have freed Bonner's mule, but for all his power, he does not "free" his wife—from work in his store, from her headrag, or from his wife abuse.

When Bonner's mule dies, the linkage between it and Starks becomes both more humorous and serious. Starks foreshadows his own death when he uses the dead mule's distended belly as a pulpit from which to deliver a funeral oration. Later Janie accuses Starks of being nothing more than a big-belly that brags (123). As Sharon Davie points out in her essay, "Free Mules, Talking Buzzards, and Cracked Plates," the mule story itself is filled with ruptures that overturn social order. Sam Watson, one of the porch-talkers—and husband to Pheoby—preaches a sermon that turns the world upside down: mules go to mule heaven and become mule-angels riding on people (448–50).

Following hard on the mule story, Janie, in a brief scene, demonstrates the same radical rupture of order. When Starks attacks Janie by calling her not only stupid but old (121), she retaliates by admitting she may be nearly forty, but he is already fifty: "Talkin' bout *me* lookin' old! When you pull down yo' britches, you look lak de change uh life" (123). In one swift verbal moment, Janie de-sexes Starks, not only calling his male identity into question, but transposing him into a menopausal woman, by using the same contemptuous words men hurl at women. Sexual identity, supposedly fixed, unitary, and stable, suddenly becomes open to question. This imagery recalls the mule, a sterile hybrid, the cross between a male ass and a female horse. The mule is also a symbol of the stubbornness of both Killicks and Starks. Janie's words mortally wound

Starks, who, like Bonner's mule, becomes ever more helpless, the butt of town jokes. When Joe Starks lies on his deathbed, he, like the mule, is mere skin and bones, with his own distended belly protruding from him.

These ruptures—spaces with seemingly no alternatives to fill them—eventually become filled with Tea Cake's presence. Unlike her relationships with Killicks and Starks, Janie freely chooses Tea Cake as her partner. He has nothing to offer her but himself. Without property or money—and therefore without social power—he is also younger than Janie and blacker. Tea Cake himself seems a disruption of the natural order of things. The townspeople, including Pheoby, believe Tea Cake means trouble; he must be after Janie's money and will soon leave her for a younger woman.

Tea Cake and Janie's relationship proves as disturbing to us as it would to Nanny if she were alive, for they demonstrate that gender roles, as well as color and economics, are not necessarily part of an immutable order. Tea Cake, who is a field laborer, living moment to moment, speaks and sings like a poet. He teaches Janie to play checkers instead of merely fetching them. Neither seems to care about material wealth. They work, play, make love, and care for each other. Janie and Tea Cake seem disinterested in the market and sexual exploitation that enslaved Nanny and continues to color and poison the lives of Blacks like Killicks and Starks.

Significantly, Tea Cake and Janie defy gender roles. Unlike Killicks and Starks, Tea Cake freely expresses his emotions to Janie, thus freeing her to express herself and the passionate feelings she had at sixteen under the pear tree. Tea Cake nurtures Janie, and she in turn nurtures him. He also teaches her to fish and shoot like a man. In the end, she must shoot the madness in him to save herself. As bell hooks points out, Janie defies "traditional notions of romantic love, which encourage female masochism; she is not willing to die for love" (hooks 185).

However, Tea Cake, like Starks and Killicks before him, beats Janie because he needs to reassure himself "in possession" when he overhears Mrs. Turner tell Janie she should never have married such a black man; rather, Janie, light-skinned, should meet her brother for a better "match." And Janie beats Tea Cake when she fears he will leave her for a younger woman. Their verbal and physical assaults, mutually inflicted, reveal the difficulties of both Janie and Tea Cake to imagine a relationship outside of or beyond accepted sexist and racist roles. In their life-and-death struggle at the end of the novel when Tea Cake madly attacks her with a gun, Janie courageously shoots him.

But the shooting of Tea Cake is not the end of the story; it is merely a beginning. Janie Crawford returns to Eatonville, demonstrating to the community that place—social class and gender—is not fixed. She returns with her hair swinging down her back like a much younger woman, yet dressed like a man in a faded shirt and muddy overalls. The townswomen are aghast at her hair and her clothes and see them as a sign of her unwomanliness; they are also sure Tea Cake has taken her money and left her for someone younger. The men reduce her to female parts: "firm buttocks" and "pugnacious breasts" (11). Unlike Janie, the black community, it seems, remains caught in the oppressive categories of sexual and class roles. Only Pheoby Watson feels called to hear Janie's as yet untold story.

Pheoby's openness to her friend's story evinces an openness to change itself. If Janie's story is one of transformation, where she changes from being someone's property, and where her place is located according to a contract of sale/marriage, it is also a story of regeneration. Just as the pear tree renews itself each spring, so Janie and Tea Cake's love brings renewal to her. The seeds Tea Cake hoped to plant are now seeds for Janie to plant. The seeds are her story—for Pheoby and for us.

In the beginning of Hurston's novel, Nanny tells Janie that she wanted to preach "a great sermon about colored women sittin' on high" (32), but she had no pulpit. Hurston gives Janie a pulpit. Pheoby, who hears her friend's testimony, responds with her own regeneration: she grows "ten feet" merely listening to Janie's story. Pheoby is no longer satisfied with herself (her place), and she aims to "make Sam take [her] fishin' wid him after this" (284). She plans to help Sam grow as well. In addition, Pheoby will not allow "nobody" to criticize Janie in her hearing (284), suggesting she may transform others within the community. As "listeners," along with Pheoby, to Janie's story, readers may also be transformed.

If the task of feminism has to do with the breaking down of arbitrarily defined social roles according to race, class, and gender, Hurston's novel not only was radical for its time but remains radical today. Perhaps what makes *Their Eyes Were Watching God* so subversive is its reliance on love, both sexual and spiritual. After all, Janie defines her own individual place through eros, in her passionate and sensual love for Tea Cake. When he dies, she cradles his head to her breast, weeping, in an image evoking the pieta. At the same time, she thanks him, wordlessly, for "giving her the chance for loving service" (273). This remarkable—and significant—prayer of Janie's echoes one of the Apostle Paul's letters to the Galatians, a letter that takes as its text the whole notion of liberty and freedom from the yoke of bondage. We are called to liberty, writes Paul, not to use one another, but "by love [to] serve one another" (5:13). Out of such service, suggests Hurston, we can create a new and radically different world.

6

Moses, Man
of the Mountain
(1939)

Hurston wrote *Moses, Man of the Mountain* between 1937 (when *Their Eyes Were Watching God* was published) and 1939. She had already written about Moses in a short story, "The Fire and Cloud," in which Moses fakes his death and, sitting on his grave, describes to a lizard his deliverance of the Hebrews from bondage (*Challenge* 1). The figure of Moses had long played (and continues to play) a significant role in African-American culture, from sermons of black preachers, including Hurston's father, to the poem, *Moses, A Story of the Nile* (by Frances Harper, 1869), to black spirituals such as "Tell Ole Pharaoh to Let My People Go," to *Go Tell It on the Mountain* (by James Baldwin, 1952), and to Martin Luther King, Jr.'s allusion to Moses in his famous speech "I See the Promised Land."

Hurston's *Moses* has received, at best, mixed reviews over the years. Critic Robert Hemenway finds the novel limited because Hurston is "unable to find a consistent tone" in her treatment of Moses (260); Lillie P. Howard writes that "the book falls short of its mark" (132). Among critics, John Lowe, Timothy Caron, and Deborah McDowell seem to be most aware of the power inherent in Hurston's fanciful retelling of the biblical story of Moses.

Hurston "reconfigures 'bone by bone' " the black folk hero of Moses, the great cultural figure who delivers southern Blacks from bondage into the promised land of freedom (Caron 47). She does this by reinterpreting the biblical Moses, transforming him into a great conjurer/hoodoo man. Conjurers tell stories that attempt to explain the riddles of life; such storytellers often deal with origins and spiritual mysteries. Hoodoo (or voodoo as it is known in the United States) also deals with the spirit world and engages in magic, the art of transformation. Although the terms conjurer (or conjure) and hoodoo are often used interchangeably, hoodoo makes use of conjure to work its "miracles" or magic. Hurston viewed hoodoo as a "folk religion" (Pryse 15). Hurston saw Moses not only as a conjurer/hoodoo man, but as a liberator of African Americans from the violence of white racism. In order to do this, Hurston translates the King James Bible back into a black folk story (Hemenway 212).

PLOT DEVELOPMENT

Hurston uses the basic biblical story of Moses as a framework for her elaborations and improvisations. In the Bible, Moses is born to a Hebrew couple and saved from certain death when Pharaoh's daughter rescues him. The Hebrews, enslaved by Pharaoh, eventually are led by Moses from Egypt to the Promised Land. The story is replete, on the one hand, with numerous adventures, ugly plagues, narrow escapes, grumbling and complaints during the exodus, and blazing interventions on the part of God. The biblical narrative is a salvation story as well as a history of the shaping of a nation, the community of a people. The great story of Exodus 3:1–4:17 is also a "call and response" narrative: God hears the cries of the Hebrews and calls Moses to deliver a divine ultimatum to Pharaoh. Moses responds to God, and in turn, calls the Hebrews to follow him into the wilderness and finally to the Promised Land.

Hurston loosely follows this narrative, using as its backbone the call and response not only of Moses, but of the enslaved Hebrews. But she also elaborates on the biblical story of Moses and changes a number of details. For example, in the Bible, when Pharaoh's daughter discovers the baby Moses, she asks for a wetnurse to be hired for the baby. The woman who is hired is Moses' biological mother. In Hurston's adaptation, Pharaoh's daughter declares that she needs no wetnurse and sends the mother away. By changing the biblical story, Hurston deliberately obscures Moses' origin: is he the adopted or biological son of Pharaoh's daughter? Such ambiguity, of course, leaves open the question of Moses' color. In addition, Hurston makes changes in the characterizations of Miriam and Aaron. There is also no biblical basis for Moses' killing of his brother Aaron. Perhaps the clearest change from the Bible that Hurston makes is to shift the focus in large part from God to Moses. By doing so, she makes it possible to infuse the biblical tale with the language and culture of African Americans.

In many ways, the plot of *Moses* is familial. Moses, the son of Hebrew slaves Amram and Jochebed, must be hidden, since Pharaoh, the Egyptian ruler, has decreed that all newborn Hebrew male babies will be killed. Jochebed saves her son, or so she believes, by placing her son in a reed casket (an ark) and sending it down the Nile. Moses is no ordinary baby, just as perhaps no mother's child seems ordinary. Jochebed frequently remarks how beautiful Moses is, how bright and alert.

Moses' birth proves traumatic to the entire family, as most likely every birth to African-American slaves must have been. Typically, the slave child would not have been killed but was often taken from the mother to be sold. In a real sense, such a baby was "dead" to the family. Moses' brother Aaron and sister Miriam are witnesses to their mother's birth pains as well as to her husband's attempt to stifle her cries for fear that the secret police will discover the birth and kill the child—and perhaps even the parents. Aaron, still a child himself, must stand watch to alert the parents if the police come near; Aaron's fear is palpable in this scene.

Because Jochebed fears for her baby's life, she decides to place the child in a basket and place it in the river. In doing so, she hopes that someone will find the boy, rescue him, and keep him safe. Hoping for the best, Jochebed commands Miriam to stand watch in order to see that the baby is safe. Miriam's attention not only wanders, she falls asleep and awakens to find the child gone, "that was all." She invents a story to tell her parents that Pharaoh's daughter found the baby and took him to the palace to bring up as her own child. Jochebed, who wants to believe her son has been saved—and by the princess, no less—spreads the story of his rescue. The Hebrew slaves, in turn, want to believe that one of their own is now "kinfolks" to the Pharaoh; indeed a Hebrew baby is now Pharaoh's own grandson. A mighty trick has been played on the very man who decreed the killing of Hebrew male babies; one of these babies is now "passing" for royalty. Jochebed even goes to the palace to offer to nurse the baby; the palace informs her that her services are not required, for there is no new baby in the palace. However, the legend of Moses, the Hebrew in the palace, never dies.

In Hurston's novel, Moses is brought up by Pharaoh's daughter as a young prince of the court. He is educated by tutors, the high priests of Egypt, and taught the arts of warfare under the tutelage of Mentu, the stableman. Mentu (a pun on Mentor) teaches the boy about nature and, in particular, he teaches Moses animal language. He instructs Moses through the use of African folktales, similar to the folktales of Charles Chesnutt's Uncle Julius stories. In addition, Moses studies magic with the Egyptian priests at the palace. From Mentu, as well, Moses learns how to be a great military leader, strategist, and warrior. Indeed, Moses' military abilities lead to his command of Egyptian armies and the conquest of lands and peoples; he even gains a "trophy" wife to cement political alliances.

Moses' rapid advancement and his brilliance as a leader create jealousy on the part of Pharaoh's son, Ta-Phar, who perceives Moses as a threat to his position. Thus Ta-Phar delights in hearing Moses' wife's accusations that her husband is nothing more than the son of Hebrew slaves. The accusations arise from a rumor started by Miriam who comes to the palace seeking her brother Moses. Although Moses vehemently denies any Hebrew ancestry, he is unable to avert imminent disaster. When Moses, out of a sense of justice, kills a brutal Egyptian overseer who is beating a Hebrew slave in a work camp, he realizes that he must flee Egypt.

Moses escapes to Midian by crossing the Red Sea: "Moses had crossed over . . . now he was not an Egyptian" (78). This crossing over, reminiscent of John Buddy's crossing the river in *Jonah's Gourd Vine*, makes possible not only Moses' freedom from Egyptian power but also the possibility of discovering or even creating his identity. In Midian, Moses, free of his trophy wife, falls in love with and marries Zipporah, daughter of Jethro, chief of the Midianites. Jethro, however, is more than Moses' father-in-law: he becomes Moses' teacher, friend, and surrogate father. Jethro also seems to be an intermediary of God and teaches Moses how to talk to God, as well as how to save the Jewish people. In addition, Jethro gives Moses language; that is, he teaches Moses how to talk in idiomatic dialect instead of the exalted language of the palace. Like John Buddy in *Jonah*, Moses becomes a "man of words," expert in the use of folk language, the key to folk culture itself. If God speaks to Moses, Moses comes to speak *for* God, translating Almighty power and humanizing it. The importance of language in *Moses* cannot be underestimated. Critic John Lowe recognizes this power when he notes how Hurston "brilliantly refigures" the biblical story of Moses in which he relies on Aaron to be his "spokesman to the Hebrew people instead of [Moses] communicating with them directly" (223). In order to lead the people, Moses believes he must be able to speak their language. The resultant language taps into the power of repetitions, of exaggeration and humor, and perhaps especially of slang (Lowe 224).

Moses lives with the Midianites for twenty-five years, with time for a trip to Koptos, to read the Book of Thoth, whereby he further prepares for his mission of leading the Hebrews to freedom. He crosses the Red Sea again, this time returning to Egypt to win the release of Hebrew slaves. Moses' confrontation with Ta-Phar, who is now the Pharaoh, and the court emphasizes what Hemenway refers to as the mentality of a people who assume superiority over others and who justify slavery as a benign, even kind, system (267). In spite of a series of plagues (frogs, lice, locusts, and so on), Ta-Phar and the court nobles refuse to free the slaves.

At the same time, Moses' task of uniting the slaves appears to be no less of a challenge than convincing Ta-Phar to let them go. In Goshen, the slave ghetto,

Hebrews seem afraid to acquire freedom. Their long period as an enslaved people has created a dependency on their masters. While slaves know the masters and what they are capable of, Moses is an unknown. As slaves, they have become grateful for the crumbs thrown to them because they believe that is all they are worth. In addition, Moses comes to the slaves talking of one god, a god they don't know. Asked to fight for freedom, the slaves respond that they had not bargained on joining an army.

The only people clearly on Moses' side, it seems, are Joshua, a young slave boy, who freely offers his service to Moses, and Aaron and Miriam, who have their own personal agendas. Only Moses' charismatic leadership, coupled with God's divine intervention, sets these people on the move from Egypt. Again Moses, this time with a fledgling, anxiety-ridden nation following him, crosses the Red Sea, destroying Ta-Phar and his troops in their wake.

Right from the beginning, grumbling and dissatisfaction mark the Hebrews' journey with Moses. Aaron and Miriam, out of envy of Moses, who they believe to be their brother, and a desire for power, help to foment trouble and rebellions. Moses himself despairs over whether these people will ever form a nation; only Moses' talks with God keep this reluctant leader focused and on track, requiring of him hard choices and decisions. Miriam, who for years tried to wrest power from Moses for herself and her brother, attacks Zipporah, calling her worthless because of her blackness. In punishment, Miriam contracts leprosy and must remain outside of the community until well. Although Miriam is cured of her disease, she never really becomes healed in her mind and soul. She becomes silent until near the end of her life; her voice remains still until she begs Moses to allow her to die.

Whereas Miriam attacked Moses by slandering his wife, Aaron encourages the former slaves to worship a golden calf in order to forget the hardships of their journey. Moses orders the killing of many Hebrews who turned away from God in their worship of the golden calf and forces a whole generation to wander in the wilderness for forty years in order for a new generation of men and women to be born: "The third generation will feel free and noble" (260). Only after those forty years can there be a free people ready to make their way to the promised land of Canaan, the promised land of freedom. Like his sister, Aaron cannot be part of this group. Aaron, like Miriam, jealous and petty, spent a lifetime trying to attain the power of Moses. Finally, Moses takes Aaron to the mountaintop to speak with God and there kills his brother in the cause of nationhood. Aaron's son, Eleazar, becomes the high priest, replacing his father, just as the younger generation of the early Hebrew slaves will be the ones to cross the River Jordan into Canaan.

Moses declines to make this last journey with the Hebrews, instead sending the younger Joshua, who will lead them. At the end of the novel, Moses climbs

Mount Nebo, to sit on the peak of Pisgah. In front of him, he sees Israel spread before him, a free people about to become a nation. At the same time, Moses looks inside himself, at his own desire for freedom. On Mount Nebo, he builds himself a tomb and talks with a wise lizard before turning to descend the other side of the mountain. Hurston's novel, then, comes full circle, in which we have no ending, but a new beginning of a nation of free people.

SETTING

The setting of *Moses* includes the Old Testament geography of Egypt, the Red Sea, and the wilderness between Egypt and the Promised Land of Canaan. In addition, there are stopovers in Midian and in Koptos. Because space is always linked to time, Hurston suggests that the place in which the characters live and interact could just as easily be the space in which we all live throughout time up to the present day. In our own time, for example, we continue to grapple with issues of freedom and power.

In *Moses*, although place is important, Hurston uses it far differently than in *Jonah* or *Their Eyes Were Watching God*, where she lavishes attention on the details of nature and on physical buildings. In *Moses*, there are few details; setting, for the most part, is nonspecific—and appropriately so. For *Moses* is the story of a people on the move, on a journey toward becoming a free nation. Their march toward freedom is marked by the miraculous and the mysterious, and as such, Hurston's lack of realistic detail seems fitting.

At the same time, the markers Hurston does use enhance theme and reinforce character. Goshen, the slave ghetto, and the supposed place of Moses' birth, reminds us of all ghettos, of space set apart for marginal peoples everywhere, space marked by poverty, darkness, isolation, and fear. The novel opens with the sounds of birth pains and fearful whispers. Moses has not yet been born, but other mothers give birth in caves, behind rocks. Birthing places in Goshen, because of Pharaoh's infanticide law, remain dark and secret, under the shadow of Pharaoh's secret police. Wombs and birthing beds, the most private spaces, now belong to the state. Space allotted to slaves exists "between the basement of heaven and the roof of hell" (1).

Fathers must suffer silently and try to muffle the birth cries of their wives, just as men and women must suffer silently each day as they work to build a new city as a monument to Pharaoh. Moses' father, Amram, along with other slaves, lives each day in space controlled by overseers who lash them bloody at the slightest provocation. The work place of Goshen is comprised of heavy building stones to be lifted on stooped and often whipped backs. Skies are cloudless, the sun hot and brilliant, leading to the mix of sweat and blood.

Later in the novel when Moses returns as God's emissary to set the Hebrews free, Goshen becomes "a land of moving feet. Feet, torchlights and whispers" (146).

In contrast, the palace world with its power-hungry men contains both seductive beauty and cold force. When Miriam, supposedly watching to see what happens to the baby Moses, sees Pharaoh's daughter at the Nile river, she discovers a world of beautiful garments, of ornate fans, of baskets filled with toiletries and oils, of the flute and strings, and of a sunshade held by black eunuchs, similar to the house slaves in America who looked after the masters and mistresses of the southern plantations.

The world of the court is quite different for males. Here we find a world of military planning and strategy, of horses and chariots, of conquests and alliances mapped out at home but carried out afield. Some strategies are enforced closer to home, for example the ethnic cleansing of newborn male Hebrew babies. The court of the Pharaoh, and later of his son Ta-Phar, prides itself on its hardness. In this court, Moses, growing to manhood, becomes a "perfect fighting machine" (83) in a world of death.

Midian, the place of Moses' self-imposed exile, remains the fulcrum on which Moses' destiny turns. But even before reaching Midian, Moses must cross over the Red Sea, vast waters which act as a threshold for him, separating him from what he was, the royal prince of Egypt, and what he becomes, the leader of a people. In the Bible, God parts the waters for Moses, but Hurston complicates matters: is it God who parts the Red Sea, or is it a natural phenomenon that Moses makes use of? Whichever interpretation is considered, Hurston uses the Red Sea as threshold territory. Once Moses crosses these waters, his life changes forever, just as the second crossing Moses makes with the Hebrew slaves changes them forever.

Midian seems to be a middle ground, a place that provides a waiting period. A land peopled by families, tribal by affiliation, Midian offers Moses the opportunity for his own family, with Jethro as his father/teacher and with Zipporah, whom he loves and marries. In addition, in Midian, Moses learns more of nature and especially of magic. Most importantly, in Midian, Moses sees his first mountain. In "[it] was all things to his inner consciousness" (84). The mountain directly contrasts with the pyramids built by and for such men as Pharaoh; the pyramids represent only hollowness. The mountain appears to Moses as "sublime," the "living place of a god," a place of both "peace and fury"; it is "rocky territory," where clouds hover around its brow and thunder and lightning play over it. The mountain and Moses seem almost to fuse; both have hardness, both exude calmness. Mystery surrounds the mountain, and from its top, God calls to Moses and enters into covenant with him, expressing His almighty and divine power through Moses' right hand. The mountain from which God speaks to Moses is called Horeb on one side, on the other Sinai, and represents all time. If this mountain marks the beginning of Moses' life as a leader of the Hebrews, a mountain will mark another beginning for him at the end of the novel.

From Midian, Moses returns to lead the Hebrew slaves to freedom. The wilderness through which they make their journey is named the Wilderness of Sin, and the Hebrews find it a harsh place, a barren wasteland, lacking food and good water. The former slaves respond to this landscape with whining, grumbling, and revolts. The epic of the Exodus plays out with all the dynamics of "call and response," not only between God and Moses, but between Moses and the Hebrew people. Betrayal occurs in the wilderness when Aaron creates the golden calf and disrupts the covenant between God and the Israelites. At this point, the drama of Exodus threatens to dissolve. Yet, also in the wilderness, God saves the people in spite of themselves, and the movement toward freedom continues. The wilderness, both in the Bible and in Hurston's novel, seems to represent the wilderness in all of us, that harsh and barren terrain that we must traverse within in order to gain self-knowledge and its concomitant freedom.

The sight of Canaan for Moses is a vision of a great free state. Israel at the Jordan can only be as strong and as free as the "well-blended mash" (278) of people waiting to cross over the river to the Promised Land. At the end of the novel, we are left at a pivotal moment; beautiful as it is, filled with hope, we somehow feel like the medieval King Arthur viewing Camelot, that this one brief, shining moment must constantly be fought for. Moses sees from the Peak of Pisgah the tents of Israel spread before him, glittering and shining. In the foreground is the Tabernacle, the Tent of Testimony, sheltering the Ark of the Covenant. Everything inside reflects gold and silver, glittering vessels and vestments of worship. And outside the Tent is the cloud of God, the mysterious Guiding Presence. We get this view from afar, as if through a wide-angle lens; even when the camera-eye zooms inside the Tabernacle or close to the cloudy pillar, narrowing the focus, we are left with Hurston's brilliant spectacle of mystery, made somehow both real and ephemeral, momentary and eternal.

CHARACTER DEVELOPMENT

Although Moses is clearly the major character in *Moses, Man of the Mountain*, other characters are extremely important to the unfolding of Moses' character. Even Amram and Jochebed, his parents, who disappear early in the novel, significantly contribute to some of the ambiguities surrounding Moses' origins; are they truly his parents? We are as uncertain as Moses whether he is an Egyptian prince or a Hebrew-born leader. Jochebed, however, is certain that Moses is her son; like all mothers, she perceives her child as beautiful and intelligent, a survivor. Why wouldn't an Egyptian princess rescue him from the Nile and adopt him? Amram, however, remains as uncertain as the readers about Moses' birthright. To Moses, the ambiguities surrounding his birth, his abandonment, and his subsequent rescue are not worth much thought. But Aaron and Miriam have no doubt that Moses is their brother, for to them he is a link to the royal house of Egypt, the country's center of power. When Moses returns to Egypt as a self-declared leader of the Hebrews, both Aaron and Miriam eagerly recognize him as their sibling in their desire to share power with him.

For Aaron, "a short, squatty" man, power means "clothes," "ornaments," and "titles" (131). In order to get such things, Aaron knows it is important that Moses recognize him as a brother. To be known—and feared—as a leader motivates Aaron's every action. At the same time, he shuns responsibility for those actions. Secretive and duplicitous, Aaron betrays Moses at every turn, complaining to his brother that he and Miriam do not have enough power. He incites the Hebrews against Moses, whining that they are worse off free in the wilderness than they ever were as slaves in Egypt. As Moses becomes more fluent in idiomatic Hebrew, Aaron speaks more "high-toned Egyptian," that is, when he doesn't forget (204). Even the Hebrew people note Aaron's hypocrisy.

Aaron's greatest betrayal of his brother occurs when he makes the golden calf for the despondent Hebrews to worship. Aaron, in order to ingratiate himself with the Hebrews—even as he tells them he would do nothing behind Moses' back (230)—not only willingly betrays Moses, but God. In so doing, of course, Aaron ruptures God's covenant with the Hebrew people.

When Moses comes down the mountain carrying God's sorrowful wrath, Aaron tries to hide behind the altar. The best he can do before Moses is to fawningly dissemble: "Lord, Moses, you're my bossman" (237), as Aaron lays the blame squarely on the people he led in false worship. Although Moses saves the people from total destruction, many are killed, including Aaron's two sons, Nadab and Abihu. From this point on, Aaron plots in secret, waiting for a chance to overcome Moses: "It's your time now, be mine after awhile" becomes Aaron's mantra (239).

Aaron's ceaseless self-promotion, his desire to go up the mountain with Moses to talk with God, leads him readily to his death. On that last walk, Aaron keeps Moses waiting because Aaron must first have his "beard boy" take care of his whiskers. Vain and self-absorbed, Aaron doesn't have time to look after his own beard, which he sees as a sign of God's favor, so he has a boy look after the whiskers. Indeed, Aaron's signature gesture throughout the novel tells us much about the man: he strokes his beard with a gesture "smug and flourishing." His self-satisfaction resembles the snake resting underneath the footstool of God

(272). On the mountain, Moses disrobes Aaron, who cries out for his clothes, "They're mine!" (273). Without the rich priestly garments, Aaron shrinks into the pathetic man he had always been, a man who used others as rungs on a ladder for his own paltry ambitions.

Aaron's sister, Miriam, also believes that she was never treated well by Moses. A prophet, with some power at least in the slave quarters in Egypt, Miriam finds herself with virtually no power compared to that of Moses—or even to that of Aaron. Thus, she joins Aaron in conspiring against Moses at every opportunity. Yet, we feel more sympathy for Miriam than Aaron, primarily because she moves in a world totally ruled by men. In comparison to male power, her prophetic voice is nothing. Indeed, her voice becomes ever more still as the novel progresses. In the wilderness, and powerless, Miriam blames Moses. She attacks Moses through the person he loves most, Zipporah. By using class and color, Miriam attempts to roil the Hebrew people against Zipporah, who, Miriam claims, "lords" it over the Hebrews. According to Miriam, Zipporah's blackness clearly indicates she should not dictate to anyone. Indeed, Miriam's hostility is ugly: "It's her color. . . . She's too dark to be around here" (244). Miriam not only hates Zipporah for her color; she hates her for her position. When she gazes on Zipporah, Miriam sees a woman in royal linens as contrasted with Miriam's work clothes and rough skin. In short, Miriam is made aware of class. When Moses responds to Miriam's attack by stating that he will protect his wife against such malicious attacks, Miriam does not back down. As she tells him, she won't be quiet, that the Lord speaks through her (and Aaron) as much as through Moses.

Miriam's punishment is leprosy. Ironically, she who complained of Zipporah's blackness has now turned white from her disease. For seven days, Miriam remains a leper and outside of the community until she heals. But in effect, she never returns to the community and thus remains tragically isolated. As Miriam tells Moses, she knows that she hurt Zipporah, and that as Moses loves his wife well, he also punishes well. Miriam knows that her power is nothing against his.

Because Moses recognizes Miriam as a tragic figure, the reader also see her in that role. He notes that she, too, has served and that it has cost her dearly. A woman and a prophet, Miriam tries to lead in a man's world, in which women are punished well. Both Miriam and Aaron are petty, small, and mean in their jealousy of power. It is too simple to say that she and Aaron get what they deserve. With Miriam, especially, her punishment seems too harsh, too severe, for her crimes. Even Moses recognizes how Miriam has served both himself and a fledgling nation. Had she not claimed him as her brother, Moses would never have met Jethro or Zipporah, nor would Moses have gone to the mountain.

In addition to these siblings, Mentu, Jethro, and Joshua also help the reader to understand the character of Moses. Mentu, a cunning stableman of the royal Egyptian household, is Moses' first mentor, who teaches the boy about the natural world. From Mentu, Moses learns how to talk with animals. In addition, Mentu teaches the boy how to ride, as well as the intricacies of military strategy. Mentu's instructions go far in making Moses a great Egyptian military leader, attributes later necessary to the founding of a new nation. At the same time, Mentu acts as a surrogate father to Moses, who has no father. Clearly Moses and Mentu care for and about each other.

Jethro, a clan chief in Midian, follows Mentu as Moses' second mentor and second father-figure. Jethro and Mentu share similar traits: both have inner strength as well as self-confidence, even though one is a clan chief, the other a stableman and slave; both teach the natural world; both have folk wisdom; both love Moses and help to develop his extraordinariness. Jethro, however, has a "gift"; he can read others' minds. Moreover, Jethro knows the mountain and its God, and he sees in Moses the man the mountain has waited for. Thus Jethro helps to awaken Moses to his destiny. Where Mentu taught Moses about Koptos and the Book of Thoth (the great book of nature, including all heaven and earth), Jethro teaches Moses the ways of hoodoo. Perhaps most significantly, Jethro teaches Moses language. To talk the dialect of the people is to understand their culture as well as to be understood by the people. Moses' facility with the language of the people as well as that of the court helps him to lead the Hebrews out of Egypt.

Not only Jethro is important to Moses, of course, so too is Zipporah, the black, beautiful daughter of Jethro. Moses falls passionately in love with her and she with him. Zipporah, in many ways, remains a mystery to Moses, although he is wise enough to recognize he can never know her completely. Throughout Moses' life, she remains for him an oasis even though he leaves her behind a great deal of the time. Zipporah remains steadfastly in love with Moses. A woman proud of her heritage as a chief's daughter, Zipporah is like Miriam in her ambition and vanity. Zipporah, too, wishes to get ahead in a man's world, or at least see her sons elevated to princes. Zipporah glories, vicariously, in the fact that her husband is Egyptian royalty; she would like to see Moses made king. But she is unlike Miriam insofar as Zipporah lacks Miriam's petty jealousy and her mean-spirited tongue.

Moreover, Zipporah acknowledges and accepts Moses' lack of desire to be king. She also accepts his absences from her and their children; she realizes that Moses, as leader of the Jews, is on a mission that she cannot compete with. She even accepts the time Moses spends with Jethro instead of her. For all of her many disappointments in her life with Moses, she never turns away from him. If Moses is a man of the mountain, Zipporah is a woman of adamantine love.

Whatever Moses' relationship with his biological sons, there is no mistaking his love for his "adopted" son Joshua. When Joshua, as a boy, pledges to serve Moses without desire of personal gain, Moses embraces him as his own. Joshua works for Moses simply because he likes this imposing leader. As Moses says, Joshua is the first to offer his services with no thought of personal gain. In Joshua, Moses finds a "real man" (149). Thus, as Mentu and Jethro taught him, Moses teaches Joshua, particularly in military matters.

Joshua, the man of action, a great warrior, turns out to be Moses' left hand, not quite as strong and not as divine as Moses' right hand, yet still powerful. In his own way, Joshua proves to be as loyal to Moses as Zipporah and Jethro. Joshua remains Moses' friend and confidant, devoted not only to Moses but to his vision of a free people. Moses says of Joshua that he is respected for his virtues and understood for his vices (249). Thus Joshua tends to be the link between the superhuman Moses and the all too human men and women he leads.

Joshua might also be seen as the antithesis of Moses' uncle Ta-Phar. Where Joshua offers his service, Ta-Phar merely is self-serving. A king and a politician, Ta-Phar lacks any sense of integrity. He lies to his people and to Moses. Ta-Phar's idea of power resides in the inculcation of fear in his people through the exercise of brute force over them. Power means conquest and acquisition, as well as the maintenance of vast armies, upon which Ta-Phar depends. He has no sense of loyalty or of love. Women to him (as indeed they had once been to Moses) are simply war booty, good perhaps for forging treaties and cementing alliances. For all his power, Ta-Phar lives in fear of what the nobles of his class might say if he were to think of freeing the slaves. Rigid, unyielding, even in the face of his firstborn son's death, Ta-Phar resembles Aaron, who sheds tears when his sons die, but who vows to get even. Ta-Phar cannot admit any greater power than his own, and thus he marches to his ultimate death in the Red Sea.

All of the above characters, of course, can be read only in their relation to Moses, who looms larger than any of them. Moses' most striking characteristic is his intellect, always seeking knowledge about the world around him and even beyond. Nature is as a book, meant to be explored, read, and understood. Moses' mind acts as a sponge, soaking up information, whether from the high priests of Egypt or from the lowly, but wily, stableman Mentu. The information becomes filed in his mind to be retrieved and used when necessary. Moses takes a year to study and absorb the great Book of Thoth before returning it to its secret place. The knowledge Moses acquires seems to be arranged in systems or blocks of information, as in a computer, under such diverse categories as nature, politics, magic, military strategies, philosophy, and the like. At the same time, Moses does not view these as discrete, informational blocks; he recognizes where they overlap and, as a result, plays with them, mixing them, moving among them creatively.

"Knowing," then, proves not to be enough for Moses. "Thinking" is what finally proves to be significant to human beings, according to Moses. Knowing something may lead people down the wrong path to a dead end. A single thought, however, can set people on the road to knowing all sorts of things, as Moses tells Joshua. Of all the characters, except for God, Moses seems to be the only character who both thinks and knows.

Thus Moses finds meaning where others do not. He understands power as both the brute force of a Pharaoh and as the cunning duplicity of an Aaron. Moses sees power as ego-driven at the expense of others. Moses also understands slavery, not simply as fact but as a costly idea, branching out in subtle social and psychological directions, destroying not only the basic social unit of the family but whole nations as well.

In addition to his powerful mind, Moses has great physical strength. His right hand powerfully winnows out the weak and forges a nation of the remaining people. Yet, his physical strength has limits, as is shown in the battle scene with the Amalekites. The combination of mental and physical strength provides Moses with the ability to focus on his mission to lead a nation comprised of disparate and desperate people. The combination also lends itself to Moses' practice of hoodoo or magic in the many "miracles" he performs with frogs, lice, flies, and so on. Moses becomes known as the great hoodoo man, one who can transform water to blood, or turn light into darkness. No wonder the Hebrews follow him across the Red Sea and into the wilderness.

Hurston is careful, however, not to turn Moses into a god. For all of his extraordinary powers, Moses remains a man. He does not seek the mission required of him by God; indeed, like Job, he asks "why me?" Moses remains uncertain of whether he is up to the task demanded of him. Moreover, he suffers betrayal, feeling that suffering as much as Christ on the cross (238). In addition, Moses' friendship with others—Mentu, Jethro, and Joshua, for examples—presents him as human and touching. His love for the only woman he has known as a mother, the Egyptian Princess, is poignant; after her death, Moses returns to her gravesite in Egypt to honor her. Moses' love for Zipporah never wavers. His youthful passion for her, his warm humor with her, attest to his all too human love for the woman he marries. We sense the loss he feels when Moses responds to God's call.

Still, whatever Moses' capacity for warm and substantial human relations, he is also the man of the mountain. Indeed, the mountain *is* Moses: hard and unyielding. Nowhere is this clearer than after the Hebrews worship the golden calf, betraying both Moses and God. In this instance, man and mountain blend; Hurston describes the mountain from its shoulder to hips to ankles, and it seems to move as Moses does (235). When Moses first sees the mountain, not only is he awed, he is changed forever. He discovers in the mountain himself and God.

But also on a mountain—Mt. Horeb—Moses kills his brother Aaron. This killing is not integral to the plot, nor does it enhance it: Aaron could just as easily have died of natural causes. In this serious departure from the biblical text, Hurston includes Aaron's murder to show just how dangerous race leaders, even a Moses, can be. If Aaron resembles the Rev. Felton Cozy in *Jonah's Gourd Vine*, a man totally self-serving and ready to capitalize on the victimization of his people, Moses is a man who would use any means to attain the ends of his mission—including the murder of his brother. As Moses looks at the body of Aaron and asks, "Is this my brother?" (275), we are hard pressed not to remember the first murder in the Bible when Cain kills his brother Abel.

However, Hurston is not quite willing to associate Moses with Cain. Moses, to his credit, recognizes the real possibility of himself, his own dark capabilities, in Aaron. Moses realizes he may have created a nation, but he is also aware of the cost. By having Moses examine his own conscience and judge himself for killing his brother, Hurston takes some, but not all, of the onus off readers to do so. Still Hurston's hero troubles us—intentionally so. Moses, who sees Aaron as an obstacle to the establishment of a free nation, simply eliminates him. No matter the ends, the scene is a chilling moment that presents Moses as a deeply flawed hero.

It would be a mistake to see Moses as supplanting God in this novel. Moses comes down the mountain "like" God, but not as God. God remains a significant presence in the novel, if not a fully realized character. Hurston represents God as a burning "mystery," the burning bush, the cloud, the pillar of fire, a disembodied "Voice" on the mountain. The mystery is encapsulated in "I am who I am" (Exod. 3:4). God strikes a covenant with Moses and with a people in a single creative moment, which runs on God's time. If God is Being (Gilson 51), both Moses and the nation are in a process of "becoming." Hurston recreates the saga of the Exodus as a drama, and thus God is not simply a figure realized in stone; as in all drama, conflict and controversy arise. God, too, feels betrayed by the Hebrews. God feels incensed and desires to kill those who have turned from Him to the false idol of a calf. God is "*tempted*" (my emphasis) to kill all of the Hebrews as a result (235), although finally only some of the Hebrews are killed. In many ways, God and Moses seem similar. God, like Moses, has human qualities—he feels sorrow over betrayal but often responds with wrath, for example. Both God and Moses can be hard, like the mountain. Although Moses cannot look at God directly, face to face, yet Moses' face reflects the light of God, a sign of the strong bond between the Almighty and the man of the mountain.

THEMATIC ISSUES

Hurston packs *Moses, Man of the Mountain* with a number of themes related to power, racism, including slavery itself, and men's dominance over women. Infusing all of these themes is the idea of liberation or freedom.

In many ways, *Moses* can be read as an allegory containing both the biblical story of the Hebrews' march to freedom from Egyptian enslavement and the story of African-Americans' quest for freedom from enslavement in the United States. Hurston's use of call and response as a structural device in her narrative, as well as her use of folklore and dialect, makes it possible for readers to perceive every Hebrew in Goshen as a black American and every Egyptian as a white—almost. As John Lowe points out, Moses' uncle Ta-Phar uses the "hip language" of urban Blacks (226). Thus we discover that, knowingly or not, Ta-Phar himself has been "passing" as white. Ta-Phar and Moses' confrontations are marked by verbal duels that smack of "playing the dozens," as the two men strive to gain the upper hand. Moses and Ta-Phar's use of language contrasts not only in their dialect, of course. Ta-Phar's language has to do with the arrogance of power, Moses' with the power of freedom.

The novel opens with Jochebed giving birth to an as yet unnamed boy that can be taken from her and killed. She—and her husband Amram—can say nothing in response to Pharaoh's decree to kill all newborn Hebrew boys. The voiceless Hebrews depict the plight of voiceless black American slaves who often had their babies and children taken from them to be sold. The Hebrews also depict the near-voiceless Blacks of the 1930s who had their loved ones, their sons, lynched for no reason other than a display of white power.

Jochebed and Amram fight over whether their newborn child should live at all. Jochebed insists they secretly keep the child, whereas Amram wants to kill the baby rather than have him grow up a slave. The couple's life-and-death discussion captures the agony of slavery and reveals the fear instilled in them through the slave system. Similarly, black slaves were also powerless to keep their families together. Hurston's scene of despair between Jochebed and Amram finds its way, some fifty years later, into Toni Morrison's novel *Beloved*, when the mother Sethe decides to kill her own children so that they will never have to grow up as slaves. In *Moses*, the mother Jochebed prevents the father from killing his own child.

Considering this opening scene in the novel, one might think the Hebrews would be ecstatic to be delivered into freedom from Egypt. Yet, this is not the case. The Hebrews complain about the hardships of freedom; they resent being thrown on their own resources; they shuck off individual responsibility; and they prefer to return to Egypt (and its slave system), where at least everything in life—and death—was a known quantity. The Hebrews distrust Moses and remain in open conflict with him. As Moses notes, the condition of slavery has both external and internal consequences lingering long after slavery may have ended. Free people often continue to behave like slaves; as slaves they are not given responsibility and as free people they do not seem capable to practice it.

After Moses leads the Hebrews to Canaan, he questions ideas of slavery, freedom, and leadership. He discovers no one can *make* another person free. The best that can be done is to provide an "opportunity for freedom," but individuals have to liberate themselves (282). The whole journey to Canaan is fraught with conflict between Moses who attempts to emancipate a people who, in turn, seem determined to return to a life of slavery. These people fail to take responsibility for themselves over and over. The only thing that prevents the Hebrews from killing Moses is the fear of his awesome, God-given power.

Moses' power may be compared and contrasted with the power of racism itself. Racism carries with it the idea of "racial purity," with its own implicit power structure: those of the most "desirable" color should have "naturally" the most power. The notion of racial purity does not belong to a single group, as Hurston, an anthropologist, surely knew. As critic Deborah McDowell writes, Hurston is linked with other Harlem Renaissance writers who thematized racial passing: light-skinned Blacks passing as Whites. In this way Hurston, as well as others, "explored race as a cultural construct rather than a biological fact" (McDowell 235). Hurston's novel, published in 1939, undoubtedly also reflects her awareness of Nazism. McDowell notes that Hurston's *Moses* can be read as an attempt to intervene in discussions about race throughout the 1920s and 1930s. These discussions, both written and oral, tended to justify the low social and economic status of most Blacks in the United States. The arguments used in such discussions were the same ones used to call for the complete extermination of the Jews in Nazi Germany (McDowell 235).

The idea of racial purity is used by one group after another in *Moses* to gain superiority over peoples of mixed parentage or of some stigmatized race. Early in the novel, Hebrews question whether Pharaoh has Hebrew blood. Some of the older Hebrews believe that Pharaoh's grandmother was Hebrew. The Hebrews also believe that many of the Egyptian aristocracy have Hebrew blood as well; the aristocracy's desire to kill Hebrew slaves attests to their desire to keep their "dirty" little secret from leaking out. Indeed, in the story of Moses, it appears that no one is racially pure. The concept remains an unattainable "ideal" established by the dominant class to maintain power and superiority and then mimicked in various forms by the subjugated classes. One can say that the establishment of a "pecking" order allows all but the lowest members of such classes to feel in some sense "superior" to others around them. According to Hebrews, Pharaoh, a half-breed, merely "passes" as Egyptian. Moses, believed by many slaves to be a full-blooded Hebrew, also has "passed" as Egyptian. In

America, light-skinned Blacks passed as White in order to gain clear advantages within the socially constructed power structure.

The thematic complexities and permutations of racial purity may be seen in Miriam's attempt to stir up racial trouble because she is envious of Zipporah and her "high ways." Miriam questions Zipporah's so-called aristocratic manner because she is dark-skinned, suggesting that Moses' wife is no Midianite but rather Ethiopian. And because Zipporah has black skin, she needs to leave, to get "off the place." Miriam claims to be concerned that Zipporah will mix up the blood of the Hebrews and even though black, will assume a dominant position. The Hebrews will thus lose *their* place and become servants of people like Zipporah (243). Miriam's accusations concerning Zipporah's blackness remind us of the pejorative comments about Tea Cake's blackness in Hurston's *Their Eyes Were Watching God*; in particular, Mrs. Turner tells Janie she does not understand why a light-skinned woman would be interested in such a black man.

Hurston suggests that no one is immune to racism. The Hebrews, stigmatized by the Egyptians, turn around and do the same thing to the Ethiopians. Later in the novel, the Hebrews look down upon and crush other tribes in search of a perfect homeland, for the Hebrews perceive themselves the Chosen People, whom God singled out to give preferential treatment. Notions of race and nation seem inexorably linked in this novel.

The linking of class with race is another subtheme in the novel. Class certainly figures prominently in Egypt which bases its entire economy on slavery. The ruling class believes it cannot exist without slaves and sees nothing but ruin in social change. Who will do the work to build an empire? Paying people, the use of freed labor, will undermine not only the ruling class's economy but its power. In turn, Pharaoh cannot unilaterally free the slaves because his base of power rests on the aristocratic ruling class. The parallels to the plantation slave economy in America or even to the tenant farm structure that simply perpetuated a form of slavery in the 1930s are obvious. In Europe, the claim to Nazi superiority, with its subsequent rise to power, was being made on the backs of Jewish workers as Hurston wrote her novel. The Nazi slogan, *Arbeit Macht Frei* (Work Makes One Free), had ultimate consequences Hurston presciently seemed to realize in 1939.

Equally as powerful as the themes of race and class in *Moses* is the theme of women's subordination to men. Women in Hurston's novel exist in a world totally ruled by men. Jochebed and other women cannot call their bodies their own. Pharaoh owns all reproductive rights. To act contrary to Pharaoh's decree, women must enter into complicity with their husbands and be silent. In Pharaoh's court, women operate on the fringe of power; their only recourse is to withhold sex to get what they want. Moses' wife is a trophy wife, booty won in battle, and soon to be transferred to Ta-Phar. Moses, who has had many women, simply takes and dispenses with females as he wishes, until he meets and falls in love with Zipporah.

Even though Moses clearly loves Zipporah, he leaves her behind to fulfill his mission of making a nation. His father-in-law Jethro derides his own wife's physical structure and age, as well as his daughter's "female" silliness, her love of clothes, and so on. Jethro takes Moses to task over his passion for Zipporah and reminds him that his divine task is more important than love and marriage. To be fair, Moses at least laments his loss of family life and the sacrifice it has cost *him*; but what about the cost to Zipporah?

Aaron and Miriam may be seen as equally petty and mean-spirited, yet Moses has greater disdain for Miriam. In Egypt, Aaron, a high priest, can be of use to Moses; Miriam, a prophet, is allowed to speak only to the women. Arguably, Moses punishes Miriam disproportionately; he attributes her pettiness to the fact that she never married. Even though Moses grudgingly acknowledges that she "served" a purpose, he builds a tomb more for the Hebrews to have a patriot to admire than for Miriam herself.

We can be sure that God is He in this novel and that He envisions a male world in which women are merely subsidiary. God's vision and the man called upon to fulfill that vision have little or no time for women. Their lives, even their deaths, are turned into histories and legends fabricated by men. Still, in this story, a woman named Zora Neale Hurston has the last word.

A POST-STRUCTURALIST READING

Although a number of critics (Alain Locke, Ralph Ellison, and Robert Hemenway, for example) have given *Moses, Man of the Mountain* somewhat mixed reviews, others like Deborah E. McDowell and Timothy P. Caron seem to recognize the artistry of Hurston's novel as well as its radical import. Yet McDowell, who correctly notes Hurston's satiric view of male-dominated society and her disgust of eugenically-inspired racism, also sees the novel as "badly flawed" (231). Both McDowell and Caron recognize that for all the brilliance of Hurston's novel, it remains uneven; "problems" associated with ideas of freedom appear to remain "left over," unresolved for readers of *Moses*.

Using post-structuralist analysis may help readers to understand how Hurston exposes the problems and risks of emancipation projects. Post-structuralist critics attempt to "deconstruct" the text by reading against the very text itself. Such critics find within the text various repetitions and narrative patterns that seem to be designed to form a uniform or "model" text, one that coherently holds together. At the same time, post-structuralist critics take note of various gaps, or ruptures, in the text which run counter to and question the apparent overall coherence of the work. These gaps and inconsistencies provide the reader with a different story from that which flows in a well-organized pattern. Jacques Derrida called reading the inconsistencies or gaps in a text a deconstructive reading, an attempt "to make the not-seen accessible to sight" (158, 163). More precisely, a deconstructive reading tries to show that what may look like unity is in fact full of contradictions and conflicts which the text cannot stabilize or totally support.

On one level of narrative, Hurston's *Moses* contains the straightforward story of the exodus of the Hebrews from Egypt. As such the narrative chronicles the journey of the Hebrews from Egypt to freedom and the founding of a new nation in the Promised Land. In retelling this story, Hurston takes the Bible, along with black sermons on Moses, as the authoritative text. Indeed, she uses many of the same narrative techniques used in the bible story. At the same time, however, Hurston's retelling contains numerous contradictions and conflicts. By examining such conflicts, readers come to see the relationships—as well as the important disjunctions—between various parts of the novel.

In *Moses*, Hurston uses repetition upon repetition, techniques to be found in the biblical and black sermon narratives of Moses' life. Such use of repetitions reinforces the oral and folkloric origins from which Hurston's retelling draws. At the same time, the repetitions provide differing explanations of the same facts: the emancipation of the Hebrews from Egyptian slave-owners and the migration of the Hebrews to the Promised Land. One might expect that the constant repetitions would form some sort of harmonic coherence in the text, but this turns out not to be the case. Even the underlying repetitive structure of call and response fails to impose unity in the novel and instead points to disruptions and delays. The various calls and responses seem to work against each other. For example, God calls Moses, who initially resists a positive response. Later, Moses issues similar calls to the Hebrews and to Ta-Phar and also meets resistance. But the explanations of resistance vary according to individual motives and situations. The repetitive, yet subtly different, responses to the same call provide moral and psychological commentary on the novel's themes. At the same time, the repetitions point to ambivalences and fissures, or gaps, in the text.

In addition to repetitive narrative structures and situations, Hurston repeats certain key words within them, such as "power," "passes," and "crosses over," among others. Key words in the larger narrative segments of *Moses* make instructive connections between seemingly disparate episodes and simultaneously question the connections themselves. For example, the words "crossing over" (using variants of the verb "to cross") recur at significant junctures and pushes readers to reconsider meanings acquired in earlier contexts and question how they apply in present and future contexts.

When Moses leaves Egypt because he has killed an Egyptian, he crosses over the Red Sea into a new and unknown geography to him, where even the sun is "different." Hurston repeats the words "crossed over" thirteen times in the brief, final paragraph of Chapter 10 (78). In the context of its use here, the phrase indicates a freedom from the past, the liberation of a man from what he had been into someone new. Moses "felt as empty as a post hole"; "he was none of the things" he had been (78). He has been, in effect, emptied out of that earlier powerful, royal Egyptian self. He is no longer the military machine, no longer a part of a social, judicial, and political hierarchy.

We soon discover, however, that Moses' former life does carry over fairly intact into his new life. He maintains his military prowess, using it now in support of Jethro. Jethro fills the role of Mentu as Moses' mentor, as Moses acquires even more knowledge of nature and magic, the very subjects studied in Egypt. Zipporah displaces Moses' former war bride. And in a sense, God displaces Ta-Phar.

When the Hebrews leave Egypt, they repeat Moses' journey; they feel empty, as the new displaces the old. At the same time, however, they are quick to follow Miriam and Aaron, who represent the inability to transform the self simply by relocating to new geography. Although Moses places a great deal of blame on his sister and brother for the failure of the Hebrews to adapt to and adopt individual responsibility for freedom, Miriam and Aaron are simply more extreme cases of the desire to maintain the status quo and to emulate modes of behavior similar to their lives in Egypt. Even though Miriam and Aaron's behavior seeks to maintain hierarchical structures, which means someone has to be at the bottom of the ladder, the Hebrews have no trouble listening to Aaron, who in his rich robes must remind them of the powerful Egyptian priests and nobles they had left behind. The racist, class, and gender bias of Egypt carries over directly into the wilderness, just as the bacchanalian worship of the golden calf does.

Why then does Moses feel so betrayed? Why the dismay that the Hebrews feel no gratitude or loyalty to Moses for leading them out of bondage? As the "new" man Moses supposedly became after he crossed over, he too paradoxically displays many of the qualities he exhibited in Egypt. What made Moses so powerful in Egypt was his ability to focus single-mindedly on the task before him. He based his military prowess on his skill of envisioning not only enemy strength but upon the subtleties of the situation: the psychological nuances of his troops and the necessity of battle. For these reasons, Moses tells Joshua the folkloric tale of the rabbits and their victories over the frogs (208).

Hurston's inclusion of this folktale just before the great battle between the Hebrews and the Amalekites is unsettling in more ways than one. The story Moses relates has to do with a rabbit convention at which they decide to kill themselves because nothing respects them or feels afraid of them. They hop down to the river to drown themselves but have to "cross" over a marsh to get to the river. As they cross over it, they hop over some frogs who cry out for them to stop. At last the rabbits find something afraid of them and they return home, happy and victorious. The lesson of the folktale for the Hebrews is clear and simple: kill the Amalekites and thus be free of feeling inferior. The tale sends a message that the only way a disenfranchised group can deter suicidal impulses and gain empowerment is to exercise power over others. Only by feeling superior can a group live. The tale reminds us of the psychiatrist, Frantz Fanon's argument in his *The Wretched of the Earth*, in which he finds such oppositional antagonisms between groups of people doomed to be repeated. The design described in the folktale which Moses relates to Joshua as a model for the upcoming battle between the Hebrews and the Amalekites can lead only to further war and conflict.

Although Moses tells the story, he refuses to pick up the sword in the coming battle because he is "*the* [my emphasis] man of God" (208). Still, Moses does fight, using God's mighty power as it flows through Moses' arms. Joshua, who has been trained by Moses to be his fighting machine replacement, leads the Hebrews into battle and victory. Hurston emphasizes Moses' technical splitting of hairs when he tells Joshua that the powers of God will help to whip the enemy. Moses, who tires during the battle, requires Aaron and Hur, a companion of Moses, to prop him up. As Moses declares, they are "holding up the world." The Amalekite enemies are beaten at the cost of much blood; the battleground runs with it, and Joshua's shoes are filled with blood.

Both the folktale and the subsequent beating of the Amalekites make clear that the value of nationhood can cost a great deal in terms of blood. Ensuring superiority does not come cheaply. Since Hurston wrote *Moses* at a time when Hitler had already begun his own "crossing over" of borders, one suspects that she intended at least to raise serious questions as to how one arrives at notions of self-worth and empowerment.

The constant reiteration of how crossing over from one location to another changes people is constantly at war with how little change takes place. Even though the geography may be different, people remain locked into their view that one group must always prove themselves superior to another; for there to be rabbits, there need to be frogs. The new order of business with the Hebrews appears little different from the old: war and booty make for riches; one tribe (the Levites) is elevated above others; hierarchies remain; Zipporah and Moses' son becomes a prince. Where, Hurston seems to ask, is the vision of making a world beyond warring identities?

For all of Moses' leadership, for all his hoodoo, along with God's awesome power, the only hope to turn former slaves into free people rests in time. The

Hebrews wander in the wilderness for forty years until a new generation arises. During this period, warring factions continue to disrupt and delay the growth of a nation of free people. Also during this wilderness period, Moses kills his brother Aaron. Clearly, for Moses, the ends justify any means, no matter how horrific. The unspoken question and real tension of Hurston's novel show up in the textual fissures that are "crossed over," the space between the ends and the means. What kinds of corruption exist in that distance, and what sorts of corruption get carried over in the final crossing of Jordan into Canaan, into the Promised Land? When Hurston crossed over the Mason-Dixon line into the Promised Land of the North in the United States, she found not only white but black racism, sexism, and cutthroat competition.

Moses, Man of the Mountain is a dangerous book and the most radical one that Hurston wrote. Like the biblical story on which much of the novel is based, the narrative of an enslaved people freed from bondage threatens constantly to deconstruct, to implode from its oppositions and contradictions. Hurston's *Moses* calculatedly sputters with repeated beginnings and numerous falterings and failures. Events and situations spiral into near-dissolution at every turn. Racism, sexism, and bloody death are covered over by tombs, and phony legends arise out of funeral markers to misguided patriotism, whether ordered by Pharaoh or by Moses.

Moses, finally, is not about redemption and perhaps not even about getting to the Promised Land, but about *not* quite getting there. For if freedom represents the "ends," Hurston warns us, we had better be aware of the "means" and their meanings from one generation to another. There seems to be no real closure to Hurston's narrative; Moses crosses over the mountain to move back into the long reach of the past, while a new generation stands poised at the Jordan, ready to cross over into the future. Freedom, Hurston suggests at the end of her novel, is always beginning, as well as *a* beginning.

7

Dust Tracks on a Road
(1942)

Although Hurston would go on to publish her final novel, *Seraph on the Suwanee* (1948), and live another twelve years, dying on January 28, 1960, her autobiography details the poignant and sometimes bitter ironies of her life as well as its victories. Despite the fact that Hurston had published five books by 1940 and remained steadfast in her career as a writer, she also remained dependent on white patronage. She rarely had much money, working at temporary and never very satisfactory jobs. Her conversations with her publisher (Bertram Lippincott) about a new book brought his proposal that she write her autobiography, which he thought would sell to a wide audience (meaning, of course, a white audience).

Although Hurston seemed reluctant to work on this project, she agreed—most likely for the money and to keep her work alive in the publishing world—and traveled to California in 1941, moving in with a wealthy friend, Katharine Mershon (Hemenway 275). *Dust Tracks* was published in November 1942, and was a commercial success. As Hemenway notes: "It did not offend whites, it sold well, most critics liked it, and it won the *Saturday Review*'s $1000 Anisfield-Wolf Award for its contribution to 'the field of race relations' " (Hemenway 288). The irony of the Award, however, rests in the fact that the autobiography had to conform to what Lippincott believed to be white readers' expectations; portions of the book critical of racial policies within the United States and abroad were deleted—with Hurston's permission—because of Japan's attack on Pearl Harbor. Deleted passages of the text were restored in 1995 by the Library of America and included in the Harper Perrenial edition (1996). As Lillie P. Howard notes, Hurston had said what the dominant white society wanted to hear. Although she was praised by the white world, she was "suspiciously regarded and often lampooned by the black" (Howard 41).

Probably no other of Hurston's books, with the exception of *Seraph on the Suwanee*, has caused as much controversy as *Dust Tracks*. Her black contemporaries despised the work. Arna Bontemps wrote that she dealt with Negro life in America by ignoring it (*Herald Tribune*, n.p.); Harold Preece saw the book as "the tragedy of a gifted . . . mind, eaten up by an egocentrism fed on the patronizing admiration of the dominant white world" (*Tomorrow* n.p.). Roy Wilkins of the NAACP felt she spoke only to publicize herself (*New York Amsterdam News*, n.p.). More recently, Maya Angelou's Foreword to the Harper Perennial restored text (1996) suggests an ambivalence that admires her as "obstinate, intelligent and pugnacious," at the same time reading in Hurston's life story "enough confusions, contusions and contradictions to confound the most sympathetic researcher" (ix). For Angelou, Hurston's autobiography remains "puzzling" as a work that mentions no "unpleasant racial incident" (x). She finds Hurston pandering to Whites from the time she is a child and ends her Foreword with the awkward comment that "all creativity is imperious and Zora Neale Hurston was certainly creative."

In the Afterword to the Harper edition, Henry Louis Gates, Jr., offers a less jaundiced view of Hurston's autobiography by generally distancing himself from it. By focusing on Hurston's "two speech communities," those "masters" of the Western tradition and those of the "ordinary members" of the black community, Gates rightly praises her "*divided* voice, a double voice unreconciled," as "her great achievement" (294). Gates does not deal with the questions Angelou raises in her Foreword. The curious bookends that contain this edition of Hurston's autobiography exemplify the uneasiness with which we confront Hurston's view of herself, the discomfort many of us may still feel in reading *Dust Tracks*.

Dust Tracks confuses and disappoints if we intend to discover the "truth" of "facts" and the historical chronology of a life. As John Eakin points out, fiction is a "central constituent of the truth of any life as it is lived and of any art devoted to the presentation of that life" (Eakin 5). All of us "negotiate" our memories to fit present consciousness. Hurston not only mediated between the black and white worlds in which she lived but between dependence and independence, between inner and outer selves. The tensions inherent in Hurston's negotiations are found everywhere in her text, most notably in its gaps and disjunctions. In a way, her autobiography is an elaborate artistic device, similar to a detective story in which one discovers various clues and fragments of information. As readers we are drawn into a game of discovery, only to find out at the end that the story is incomplete. In a typical detective story, we arrive at the moment in the story where the controlling voice of the detective explains the meanings of clues and exposes character. In *Dust Tracks*, however, we discover only that there is more to discover. The nebulous meanings implicit in the very title of Hurston's autobiography underscore not only the somewhat elusive shape of her text but the mysterious textuality of her self.

PLOT DEVELOPMENT

Although it may seem strange to think of plot in autobiography, *Dust Tracks* is not simply an objective reconstruction of past events. Like most autobiographies, it is a life *story* of the self "engaged in an autonomous adventure" (Gusdorf, quoted in Eakin 199). In Hurston's text, the shape of that adventure follows union and separation, departure and return. Her autobiography repeats these rhythms as part of the narrative patterns which go into the formation of her identity. Indeed, the ending of *Dust Tracks* reaches into the future, projecting the same narrative form.

Dust Tracks proceeds in achronological fashion at times, looping from the present into the past, only to return to the present. At the same time, the reader can discern a loosely chronological time line, moving from Hurston's birth in Eatonville (although the location is not itself accurate; she was born in Alabama), to her childhood with family and community friends, to her initial haphazard education and multiple jobs, to serious education at Howard University and finally to Barnard, where she becomes an anthropologist, studying under the renowned Franz Boas. In New York, she is part of the "Niggerati" of the Harlem Renaissance, and begins to be a writer as well as a scientist. Following the "facts" of her adult life, the reader is carried along by the sheer energy and movement of Hurston as she maps out the terrain of her education, the collection of folktales and songs in the South and in Haiti, and the publication of numerous books and the production of theater pieces. Underneath this movement is a much darker geography of domineering white patronage, of alienation from and betrayal by family and friends, of utter poverty and illness.

We begin to see the narrative pattern of union, separation, and reunion emerge in the opening pages of Hurston's autobiography, beginning with her birth. Not only is Hurston's father missing from this crucial event, she tells us, but her birth is not attended, as would usually be the case, by a black midwife or "granny." Instead, a white man, nameless, assists Zora into the world and cuts the umbilical cord to her black mother. As Zora grows into childhood, this same white man takes her fishing and gives her advice on how to live in the world. Hurston's story, to a certain extent, reminds one of William Faulkner's story "The Bear" in which an older man, the half-Chickasaw, half-Negro Sam Fathers, initiates a white boy, Ike McCaslin, into the wilderness. Faulkner's story was part of his episodic novel, *Go Down, Moses*, published in the same year as Hurston's autobiography. Like Hurston's work, *Go Down, Moses* is achronological and its sequences are frequently difficult to follow. Both Faulkner and Hurston explore race relations in America. If "The Bear" gives us a white boy taught by a black man how to be a "man," Hurston's *Dust Tracks* gives us a black girl taught by a white man how *not* to be a "nigger," as he puts it.

In short, the beginning of Hurston's life, as she represents it, clearly demonstrates her union and separation from her black family. We need go back only one generation to discover the original plot she would use over and over in her writing. Her father was born the son of a black woman and a white man and grew up in a poor cabin on a white "plantation"; his marriage to the very black Lucy Potts had the effect of alienating them from their parents.

Hurston's childhood with her family and friends in Eatonville seems marred only by her visions, occurring when she was about seven, visions that emphasized the same pattern of her birth-plot: she would be orphaned and homeless (42). She describes the visions as being without continuity, indeed revealing disconnection, with only "blank spaces" in between scenes (41). These visions, Hurston recounts, mark the end of her childhood; her mother's death fulfills Hurston's first vision.

Lucy Potts dies when Zora is nine years old, and her death is poignantly described by her daughter. The death of Lucy is introduced by the mysterious death of her favorite nephew, Jimmie. He had literally been separated from her—he was beheaded, probably by a white man. Inserted into Jimmie's story is the pain of Lucy's separation from her mother who disowned her for marrying that "yaller rascal," John Hurston (63). Lucy instructs her daughter not to allow the community women to remove the pillow from under her head until after death, nor to cover the clock and looking glass, as was the folk custom of the time. The instructions are thwarted by the townswomen, with the complicity of Zora's father. John Hurston holds his daughter "tight," as he allows the women to carry out their folk preparations for Lucy's death. Zora's father and the women compound the sense of separation the daughter suffers here, repeating Lucy's suffering in being separated from her mother. As Zora notes, her father comes down on the side of community mores, betraying both wife and daughter. Later when John Hurston remarries, Zora feels alienated from and betrayed by him once again: he failed to be present for her birth, he failed her at her mother's death, and he failed to care for his daughter (indeed, any of his children) during her life.

John Hurston basically abandons his daughter when he sends her to Jacksonville after Lucy's death. He installs Zora in a school/orphanage, urging the school to "adopt" her. In Jacksonville, separated from home and family, Zora *becomes* colored; that is, she becomes aware that she is black. In Eatonville, where everyone is some shade of black, Zora is no different from anyone else. The white people she meets in Eatonville differ from her only insofar as they do not live there. As Barbara Johnson points out, the Zora of Eatonville disappears in Jacksonville and becomes a colored girl. "The acquisition of color is a *loss* of identity," Johnson writes. Moreover, color seems not to be "fixed" but a "function of motion" from Eatonville to Jacksonville (Johnson 320). Although Johnson is writing primarily about *How It Feels to Be Colored Me*, published in 1928, her comments are equally valid for *Dust Tracks*, since Hurston reuses, revising only slightly, many of the same passages from her earlier work. Hurston's sense of separation from her warm and safe familial life and her subsequent departure from Eatonville to Jacksonville begin a lifetime of wandering from and returning to her roots.

Although Zora returns to Eatonville after her father's second marriage, she is never able to return to her mother's home; it has become simply a house. Zora's knock-down, drag-out fight with her stepmother, whom she never forgives for usurping her mother's place, emphasizes Hurston's displacement from her home and family. In one sense, however, her alienation precipitates her journey from Eatonville to Washington, D.C., and later to New York City to gain education and a better life. This journey echoes that of many Negroes who moved from the black belt of the South to the North. Hurston's journey repeats in a way the migration by slaves to gain life and freedom, followed by subsequent migrations made by Blacks to find work in northern factories and to improve life for themselves and their children. The plot development of Hurston's autobiography, then, owes much to a black tradition, going back to slave narratives and to early black autobiographies (William L. Andrews *passim*).

Although Hurston's story is one of separation or displacement, it is also one of return or reunion. Her major work brings her South time and again, as she collects folktales and folk songs, and studies voodoo as well. For all the displacement and alienation that is plotted in *Dust Tracks*, the interpolated stories emphasize reunion. Stories of the jook joints, the sawmills, of tough, hard-talking men and women, the fragments of folktales, the descriptions of the natural world of the South—its wild lushness, its color, its birdsong, its waterways— all depict Zora Hurston's reunion with her home.

And finally, *Dust Tracks* is meant, as the early slave narratives and black autobiographies were, to be an exemplary tale in which the action is a model for others. Its plot is that of a pilgrim's progress, of a poor, black, orphaned girl who becomes a respected scientist, a well-known author, the winner of Guggenheims and other awards; if all of this is possible for her, then it is possible for other marginalized people. Hurston's plot, as was her life, is a black story. It is also a very American story, though one that she manipulates to serve her own uses. She takes the Horatio Alger story: of the young poor, always white, boy, who, by trickery, gumption, and a willingness to learn, becomes successful (that is, he acquires wealth, with the help of—always—a rich white man who becomes his mentor). Hurston takes that plot and turns it inside out, indeed, explodes it. The Alger plots were all the same: simple, one dimensional, racist, and most assuredly sexist. Hurston's plot overflows with its subtleties, its richness, its ambiguities, and its poignancy. In short, her plot overflows with life itself.

SETTING

In *Dust Tracks*, Hurston maps a geography that is important to a number of events in her life and to her work as a writer. She is, first of all, a writer of nature. As a child, nature calls to her and talks to her. Many of the folktales she hears are those in which animals talk. As Hurston points out, life becomes larger by including the mysteries of nature. The wind and trees speak to her; one tree is so "friendly" that she names it "the loving pine" (52). Nature provides the impetus and framework for the stories the child Zora tells her mother, such as her walking on the lake or climbing upon a bird to chat with it. Nature encourages full range to the imaginative play of her mind. Nature also contains the possibilities of transformation, as in the alligator man story (58–59), as well as the terror of the unknown.

When Zora's father sends her to Jacksonville after her mother's death, she suffers the loss of the "loving pine, the lakes, the wild violets in the woods and the animals" she had known. As a result, she can feel only despair. Nature is analogous to her feelings and experiences. Losing the natural environment in which she had been a child coincides with the end of her childhood; the loss of her mother coincides with the loss of the natural landscape surrounding her home. Away from home and family, away from her loving pine, Hurston enters the twilight world of school in Jacksonville.

When Hurston returns home from Jacksonville, she describes the thrill of seeing the water life, the lushness of foliage and flowers. Nature demonstrates to her its extraordinary variety of detail, its complexity, not revealed all at one time, but absorbed, read, understood over long periods of time, and felt even retrospectively. Hurston would imaginatively recreate her feelings toward nature in her novel, *Their Eyes Were Watching God*, in the character of Janie Killicks-Starks-Woods.

Set against this natural background—carved out of it—is Eatonville, a "pure Negro town" (1), though started by three white ex-Union officers.

Eatonville was a frontier town, forged like America, out of generally unsettled country, in this case South Florida. It was a town, like many, created out of the blood of Spanish, French, English, and Indian people (2). Eatonville grew out of Maitland and was chartered as a Negro town in 1886, the first of its kind in America. As Hurston points out, in a raw frontier town, the experiment of Negro self-government began. Her father, John Hurston, and her mother, Lucy Ann Potts, put down roots there. He was mayor of Eatonville for three terms and helped to write its laws. As Hurston tells us at the beginning of her autobiography, to understand her one needs to understand the *place* she comes from.

Eatonville provided Zora Hurston with her own sense of roots. It was a place of community, one that lived side by side with white Maitland and without enmity. It was a place where her spirit could grow and not be "squinch[ed]." Out of such a place it was possible for Hurston to take with her the belief that she had "no race prejudice of any kind" (231). However, she follows this comment with the rather ambiguous statement that she could love both kinfolks and skinfolks. By kinfolks she most likely refers to her relatives; but who are her *skinfolks?* Only blacks, or is she including white folks as well?

Within Eatonville was the home Hurston's parents built on land they planted. The home was filled with eight children and surrounded by the lush harvest of nature: flowers and fruits, fish and game. Hurston's yard was a place for folk games—hide and whoop, chick-mah-chick—and of folk songs and tales. She lavishes detail on the house itself, down to her mother's rocking chair, the towels used, even the kinds of toilet paper.

The Hurston home is analogous to her hometown of Eatonville. In both home and town, she discovers the uses of language, its source and its power. It is not such a long walk from her parents' home to Joe Clarke's store and its porch, the "heart and spring" of Eatonville. Here could be heard the specifying and signifying, the lying sessions, as men sat around "pass[ing] this world and the next one through their mouths" (45). Joe Clarke's porch, however, is a male world. Women are peripheral, objects to be talked about along with the folktales of God, Devil, Brer Rabbit, Brer Fox, and so on. Joe Clarke's porch is reconstructed in *Their Eyes Were Watching God* as Jody Starks' porch. In her novel, Hurston makes a point of giving Janie Starks a voice on that porch.

In addition to her home and Joe Clarke's store, Hurston "tumbled" into the Missionary Baptist Church at her birth. Her father was a preacher there, and Hurston grew up learning the stories of God's ways and hearing Negro spirituals. She experienced Love Feasts and speaking in tongues, and she attended revival meetings and heard testimony. She grew up listening to the cadences of the black preacher: the sonority and musical speech, with its dignity and its sophistication. In black preaching, Hurston heard not only the great stories of the Bible, but the meanings they had for black people. When the preacher told the story of Moses and chanted for Pharaoh to let my people go, he was preaching a story of self-liberation. The call and response of black preaching, which Hurston demonstrates in *Dust Tracks* (219), demands the congregation's participation, just as Hurston herself invites reader participation. From the black preaching of her father and others, Hurston would have learned the musical rhythms of speech, role playing, elaborate character development, dialogue, and rhetorical flair (Henry Mitchell 88, 97, 101).

While the community of Eatonville has much to offer Hurston about her culture, its absoluteness and certainty also threaten to stifle her. Indeed, the young Zora's sitting on the gatepost in front of her family home represents Hurston's unwillingness to accept community authority on the porch, in the church, or in her father's house. From this gatepost, quite obviously a threshold position, she looks to the horizon and offers to go with white passersby to show them her town and beyond. As much as she may romanticize her home and her hometown, as much as they comfort her, Hurston recognizes there is a wider world and that she must wander in it. Although Hurston would always claim Eatonville as her home, it was the place she was *from*, not the place she remained. As Annette Trefzer notes, Eatonville provided Hurston with a "communal affiliation," out of which she "not only (re)invents her hometown, but she creates a positive sense of her self" (Trefzer 71).

When Hurston leaves Eatonville as the result of her mother's death and her abandonment by her father, she begins a life of wandering from house to house, in temporary living spaces occasioned by various jobs, by her education in Washington, D.C., and later in New York City, and by her work as an anthropologist and writer. In *Dust Tracks*, she never lavishes attention and detail on any setting other than Eatonville, including New York—not even when she returns to Florida. In fact, she comes to see New York as cold, filled with enmity, betrayal, and outright viciousness. Hurston's nostalgic reinvention of Eatonville suggests that she sees it as a kind of "Paradise Lost," a standard against which all other places are compared to and fall short.

CHARACTER DEVELOPMENT

In *Dust Tracks*, Hurston's construction of the character Zora follows the mythic pattern of the monolithic hero described by Joseph Campbell in *The Hero with a Thousand Faces*. Such a character does not reveal psychological nuances but is expressed more through action and situation or event. Although other characters exist in Hurston's life-story, they remain character *sketches*: Zora's parents; her benefactor, Mrs. R.W. Osgood; Fannie Hurst; and Ethel Waters, to name a few. Hurston comes closest to developing the characters of

Big Sweet and Miss M—(the actress Zora served in an early job), but both remain no more than vivid portraits. All figures other than Zora merely provide the backdrop for her performance.

At the beginning of *Dust Tracks*, the scene of Hurston's birth alerts us to how special Zora is. As in the hero's birth, a certain mystery surrounds Zora's birth: the absence of her father and her untraditional birthing by the unnamed white man. Zora seems to take credit for her own birth—it's a "trick" she "play[s]" on her father—as if she were self-created. Perhaps Hurston is letting her readers in on the joke of this autobiography, a self-creating genre in itself. Even the naming of this hero is special, an act of her mother's friend, Mrs. Neale. The first name, Zora, "perhaps" came from something Mrs. Neale read or from a pack of Turkish cigarettes. Hurston continues to maintain a humorous distance from Zora, the character, throughout the text, except when she interrupts her life-story with comments on race and politics, for example.

As with all heroes, the events surrounding Zora's birth and naming serve to set her apart as extraordinary. Her first steps, humorously recounted as a folk-tale itself, are taken to get away from a sow attempting to get the child's food. The animal perforce teaches Zora to walk, and she never stops; she takes to wandering as her "fate." Her mother believes an enemy had "sprinkled 'travel dust' around the doorstep" at Zora's birth (22–23). Clearly in this text, event and situation shape character.

Even though Zora feels a part of her hometown Eatonville, she also has a sense of being set apart. If she is an insider, she is simultaneously an observer and outsider. The center of her world may be the family home, and by extension her hometown, but that world is too small. Zora would climb to the top of the chinaberry tree to look over a wider world and to the horizon, yearning to discover the "end of things" (41). Her discovery comes through mysterious visions, experienced at the age of seven; these visions foretell what will happen to Zora up to the end of her life (41).

Hurston strategically places these visions immediately after Zora's being given a number of books by two white women who had marveled over her reading in school. Among the books were fairytales, Greek and Roman myths, and Norse tales, which she liked the best. In addition, she read the Bible, especially the Old Testament. These books contain stories of heroes who often spring mysteriously from humble beginnings, are set apart from their people in special ways, who are visionaries. The heroes of these texts participate in adventurous journeys, seek their way in the world, to return to save their people. It is hardly coincidental that Hurston links these texts of heroic figures with her character Zora.

Zora never tells anyone of her visions: "They would laugh me off as a story teller" (43). She recognizes her "difference" from others and her "vanished communion with [her] kind" (43). The hero's sense of difference, of being marked in a special way, never leaves Zora; she views herself as a wanderer in the world, a pilgrim journeying on a "strange road" (43).

When Zora sets out from her hometown of Eatonville, she, like all heroes, is tested and must overcome various obstacles. Along the way, she receives the boon or gift of education and is helped by different "guides" and benefactors. The cluster of words Hurston uses surrounding Zora—"way," "calling," "god-mother," "adventure," "road," "strange," "questing," "seeking"—are words found very often in tales of heroes, who are also, by the nature of their roles, pilgrims. None of the above is to suggest that Hurston creates a character totally dissociated from herself. The hero-pilgrim Zora is a metaphor of the self (James Olney, *passim*). In her desire to express the feelings of her self becoming, Hurston uses myths and images well-known and recognized by the dominant white culture. It is perhaps too facile to say that she does this merely to fuel her own ego and/or to appeal to her white publisher and predominantly white readers. Hurston most likely was familiar with a whole tradition of the hero-pilgrim trope used in black autobiography, beginning at least in the nineteenth century; William L. Andrews ably documents the complexity and subtlety of such usage in *To Tell a Free Story* (11–12; 143–144). Moreover, Hurston manipulates the character of the hero-pilgrim for her own purposes.

In the role of pilgrim, Zora becomes an example for her people—a poor black girl, orphaned, who becomes successful in the face of great adversity. At the same time, as a hero, she is "marked" as a visionary, who has a "true" calling; the stories she tells are intended to remind her people of the richness and artistry of their many voices. In her stories and collected folklore, Zora keeps these voices—and thus her people—alive.

Zora is not the only "character," of course, in her autobiography. She includes, for example, two remarkable portraits, one of Fanny Hurst and one of Ethel Waters, both of whom were close to Hurston. Chapter 13, "Two Women in Particular" (193–202), presents, side by side, character sketches of Hurst who was white, and of Waters who was black. Both women were important to Hurston, she claims, for friendship and for the inner experience they provide her (193). Fanny Hurst, white and successful, a very wealthy novelist and playwright, employed Zora as her secretary. Hurst is depicted as childlike and most likely childish, a woman still playing with dolls and subject to erratic mood swings. Hurston refers kindly to her as a lonely little girl in a huge house.

Hurst was born to wealth and all of the self-indulgences money could buy. She was fond of games, including those she played on Zora at her expense. Although Zora may have been hired as a secretary, she ends up a servant, often sent on fool's errands. For example, Hurst leaves the house one snowy day and decides to play a trick on Hurston. She calls Zora to bring her galoshes to a street corner where she will pick them up. Zora is left standing in snow and slush, waiting for Hurst to arrive and collect them. When Hurst fails to show up, Zora returns to the house only to find her employer stretched out on the sofa, beautifully dressed in an "American Beauty rose" robe (195).

Throughout Hurston's portrait of Hurst, she repeats such words as child, little girl, games, tricks. Zora is not only Hurst's secretary and maidservant but also her black chauffeur. The endless trips Hurst takes with Zora as her driver have no point or meaning to them; they are taken to satisfy the whims of a woman, who, when she is not writing, has too much time on her hands. Zora seems, in fact, to exist to indulge Hurst, to drive her around, and to walk her dog, Lummox (named after one of Hurst's most successful novels). Hurston refers to Fanny as a "runaway" who is irresponsible (197). It is the closest she comes to overt criticism of Hurst.

The subversion of Hurston's portrait of Fanny becomes clear at its end. Fanny Hurst was her most level-headed when it came to dressing, notes Hurston. Fanny's vanity, her desire to create an effect and to flaunt her looks, becomes all too apparent. Hurston's last line on Hurst is that she "will never be jailed for uglying up a town" (197). Of course not. Hurst's money, class, and skin color ensured that she would not be jailed. Spoiled, given to tantrums, vain, and at times mean-spirited, Hurst's physical beauty belies her real flaws.

Running alongside Hurst's portrait is one of Ethel Waters, "This Ethel Waters," as Hurston phrases it, immediately marking Waters as someone extraordinary. Ethel Waters, the great black blues and spiritual singer, also was successful, but not born to wealth as Hurst was. Waters was formally uneducated and came from the slums of Philadelphia. She too has moods, but they stem from the difficulty of expressing herself. When Hurston meets Waters, she has an opportunity to help her. Waters was advised not to sing spirituals at Carnegie Hall because she would be unfavorably compared with Marian Anderson, Roland Hayes, and Paul Robeson, who had all sung there recently. Hurston points out to Waters that her spirituals would be different—and better—because she would not concertize them; she would sing the spirituals as her mother had sung them to her.

Through Waters, Hurston educates blacks and whites as well to the enormously inventive creativity of black folk. Hurston's biggest fear is that the world will not know of Ethel Waters, just as it will not know of the wonderful artistry of many of her people. For Hurston, Waters is not simply an artist— she grants Hurst her talent—but a person with soul. Waters not only brings her artistry to the audience, she brings her whole person. In short, Hurston views Waters as a national treasure who should not be kept within national boundaries.

Even with the inclusion of these remarkable character sketches of Hurst and Waters, the focus of the text remains unalterably on Zora. At the same time,

Hurston's personal story remains elliptical, at times withheld, at times presented as hearsay. For example, chapter 14, "Love" delivers little in the way of Hurston's personal feelings on the subject. Her relationship with a shadowy figure of a man, who is unnamed, remains abstract. Zora attempts to interpret the private experience of love in a public fashion, but she gives up. She informs us she will tell us little. At the same time she promotes her novel, *Their Eyes Were Watching God*, promising that she expresses all of her personal passion there. Finally she admits the impossibility of love for her: she must "follow" the "charge laid" upon her (210). The chapter ends, not with a comment of Zora's, but with a folk saying:

> Love is a funny thing; Love is a blossom;
> If you want your finger bit, poke it at a possum. (214)

Chapter 14, which seems to promise to reveal the "real" Zora, reinforces her characterization as a hero-pilgrim who must fulfill her fate. The chapter on love cannot be personal because the characterization of Zora is ultimately not personal but transpersonal; Zora's life is meant to be an instructive model for both black and white readers. The ending of *Dust Tracks* projects Zora's instruction into the future in a wonderfully performative way: with an epilogue, similar to those used by Shakespeare. The ending is inclusive, gathering up (she hopes) a diverse audience and the numerous paths of the pilgrimage, even the dust, ready to carry all into the future. Zora speaks to all of us, irrespective of race, out of generosity and hopes for our applause. She also reminds us, rather ironically but nonetheless seriously, of our own journey together in the world, pilgrims all, who may be able to breed a more "noble world in a few hundred generations or so" (232).

THEMATIC ISSUES

There are numerous thematic issues in *Dust Tracks*, many of which occur in other works: family relations and tensions, violence and poverty, nature, love, and religion, to name only a few. Contrary to critical views that Hurston failed to deal with race or gender in *Dust Tracks*, both are thematically powerful in this work.

Hurston begins her text by describing her birthplace as a "pure Negro" town and goes on to explain how Negro slaves came to be in that area. She recreates the history of Eatonville, with its black leaders and lawgivers and disclaims any "enmity" between whites and blacks who lived next to each other in the twin towns of Eatonville and Maitland.

At the same time that she disavows any racial disharmony, her recreation of her family history, and specifically her own childhood, emphasizes racial tensions. Her father, John Hurston, was a "mulatto," whose own father, a white man, never claimed him as a son. John courts and marries the very black Lucy Potts, whose family disowns her for marrying "dat yaller bastard." Lucy herself thinks of John as a "stud-looking buck," a phrase connoting a great deal of money during the slave trade. Lucy and John begin their married life in a cabin on the plantation of the white man who probably is John's father. They leave that cabin, making their way to Eatonville, to pull themselves out of post-slavery tenantship, with John becoming mayor for three terms, writing laws, carpentering, and preaching, all rather successfully.

The fact that Hurston begins her autobiography with an emphasis on race, foregrounding the remnants of slavery and degrees of blackness, demonstrates her insistence on bringing racial issues in America to our attention. Though Zora claims that she was unaware of race until she went to Jacksonville, Hurston makes clear that racial conflict intruded in her own family, right down to her parents' view of how to bring up children in this country. Lucy encouraged all of her children, but especially the precocious and independent Zora, to "jump at de sun" (13). John wanted his children to be more passive to survive. He believed white people would not stand for Zora's feistiness and that she would be hanged before she grew up. In short, Lucy encouraged freedom for her children; John encouraged meekness.

Hurston's education, the center of her life as of her text, reiterates the significance of racial structures in this country. When Zora attends Howard University in Washington, D.C., she feels as if she has reached heaven. Howard represents the great institution of learning for Blacks; it bespeaks wealth, beauty, and power. Zora claims singing the Alma Mater to her was like singing the Star Spangled Banner. At Howard, Zora is her most humble before the greatness of learning and the most grateful to her black teachers and mentors.

If Howard deepens Zora's sense of pride in her people, her job as a manicurist in a Washington barber shop teaches her that self-interest can be far more powerful than racial solidarity. The barbershop, run and staffed by Blacks, caters to white legislators. When a black man tries to integrate the shop and demands to have his hair cut, one of the barbers tells him that he does not know how to cut his kind of hair. When the would-be integrationist tells his fellow Blacks not to be Uncle Toms, they throw him out on the street. Zora remarks how she too approves, since her own livelihood is threatened. Yet she knows she has just sanctioned the rule of Jim Crow, and she recognizes the hard truth that self-interest, her own included, often overrides racial, as well as national, religious, and class concerns. This seeming digression, sandwiched between Zora's educational progress at Howard and Barnard, is telling.

Zora's experience at Barnard is meant to be compared and contrasted with her earlier situation at Howard. Hurston's story "Spunk," published in Charles

S. Johnson's *Opportunity* magazine, brought her to New York City and to Barnard, as well as into the Harlem Renaissance. Although Zora notes that she has no awful stories of race discrimination at Barnard, she also notes that the socially prominent crowd at Barnard makes of her blackness a "sacred" cow. At Barnard she studies under Ruth Benedict and Franz Boas, the two most eminent anthropologists in the country, and this study would give her the opportunity to write about her race.

If race is an important theme in Hurston's autobiography, so too is gender. Nowhere is this more apparent than in her commentary on her mother. Lucy Potts encouraged her children to get off the ground, to move forward, to love themselves. Lucy, when she is dying, desires her daughter to speak for her when she cannot, and perhaps Zora's sense of failing to be her mother's voice pushes her to speak for many of the rural poor women, black and white, who lack their own voices. Hurston does this, of course, not only in her novels but in the folklore she collected.

In *Dust Tracks*, the women at Joe Clarke's store do not speak. The men who sit on the porch pass "worlds" through their mouths—and women. Women to them are sexual objects to be desired and feared. They are to be taken by men if and when they want them and to be beaten if they refuse. The men on Joe Clarke's porch do the talking; women are silent. We recall Janie in *Their Eyes Were Watching God* when she defies the rule of silence and speaks up to her husband, Jody Starks. Both lives are changed forever. When Janie meets and falls in love with Tea Cake, they are equals; her voice is never silenced again.

Hurston's collection of folklore included the stories and lives of poor black women of the South, exactly those women who lacked voice in the larger world. In some cases, these women were filled with rage that exploded in violence against men and against each other—one need only think of Big Sweet of Polk County (152–56)—and at times against Hurston herself, who was lighter in color, different in education and in class. Hurston makes no judgment of them but presents them in their own voices as they are.

In America, it was considered bad enough to be born black, and worse to be born black and female, as John Hurston reminded his daughter from the day she was born. Male children contributed work to the family; females wore out shoes. The costs of being black and female were unlikely to have ever been forgotten by Zora Hurston; they are part of the folklore she collected and recur as themes in her fiction and in her autobiography.

A DIALOGIC READING

Zora Neale Hurston's *Dust Tracks on a Road* has proven mystifying and maddening to readers ever since its publication. A text that purports to be an autobiography, it disdains chronology and often facts for discontinuity and disjunction. At the same time, *Dust Tracks* conjoins portraiture, philosophy, literature, and social science methodologies as it seeks to establish an identity that is paradoxically and fluidly always in a state of evolving. Hurston uses a multiplicity of texts in radical and subversive ways, attempting not merely to engage her readers but to transform them.

To understand Hurston's autobiography is to understand how she uses different approaches to comment on the texts and to revise them. Obviously, Hurston writes her own narrative text, her story, but she writes her story against and out of similar narratives that she may have read or heard. Throughout *Dust Tracks*, Hurston carries on what might be called a dialogue between these numerous texts. The process of reading and interpreting such a dialogue in a literary work is called *dialogics*. Mikhail Bakhtin, the Russian scholar, notes that there is always dialogue going on, not merely in oral but in written communication, both within and among texts. Certain literature presents readers with an interplay of different texts, or voices, which negotiate with each other, just as voices do in our day-to-day understanding of dialogue. Without the negotiation of different voices, dialogue would cease. In Hurston's autobiography, dialogue is diffuse, permeating the text as a whole. This dialogue contains memories, echoes, and transformations of Hurston's earlier works and those written by others. In the critic Henry Louis Gates' terminology, Hurston's text may be seen as "speaking to" or "signifying" on other texts, including her own (*The Signifying Monkey* 64–124).

Discovering the internal dialogue in *Dust Tracks* helps readers to understand the meanings of Hurston's multitext project. At times her texts seem to compete with one another and to challenge the values and expectations of the readers (as, for example, in the portraits of Hurst and Waters). Through Hurston's manipulation of texts, she forces readers to rethink their positions in the world around them.

From the beginning of *Dust Tracks*, Hurston deliberately includes narratives that by their shape and content inform other texts which in turn form her own. The story of John Hurston's birth follows the slave narrative of the absent white father; this narrative informs the shape of her own birth story, a story that radically subverts the master (a word I choose calculatedly) text. In Zora's birth story, her "yaller" father is absent, and the white (metaphorical) "father" who births her is present. This white father, however, fulfills the role of the traditional black, female midwife (often called "granny") who usually attends the births of black babies. In describing her birth, Hurston pushes readers to examine black familial relationships insofar as both her biological father and the traditional black midwife are absent. Readers also see firsthand the intrusion of white male power in the figure who usurps the black male's place.

Furthermore, Zora's text reiterates the whole question of identity for African Americans. During slavery, black families were given, or, rather, *denied* shape by white masters who consistently broke up family relationships. White fathers were conspicuously absent in any familial role and usually denied biracial offspring their names. The unnamed white "father" who births Zora does not give her a name, but neither does her black father, just as he would not have done so under slavery. Instead, she is named—creatively—by her mother's woman friend, thus establishing a strong linkage among women.

However, the white "father" renames Zora, calling her Snidlets. This same white man initiates her, as a father might his son, by taking her fishing, introducing her to the natural world, and warning her not to be a "nigger," which he considers the opposite of a truth-telling, upright person (30). Hurston's note (she repeats it within the text two pages later) explains that the word does not mean race but a person who is "weak" or "contemptible" (30, 32). The very fact that she feels compelled to include such a note forces our attention to the implications of the word and perhaps to her own contradictory feelings. Hurston's white "father" is a self-made man who accumulates property and teaches her his philosophy: one must be strong in the face of fear and one must learn to recognize power. Yet Hurston clearly undermines her portrayal of this white father figure. On the one hand, he is kind (to her), successful, seemingly wise, a powerful frontiersman; on the other, at her birth he is feminized by the role he plays as a black midwife.

The inclusion of this lengthy narrative of the unnamed white man, a surrogate father/teacher to Zora, both speaks to and revises not only a master narrative all too familiar to black families but perhaps also addresses William Faulkner's story, "The Bear," in *Go Down, Moses and Other Stories*. ("The Bear" was published about the same time as Hurston's autobiography; there is no way of knowing if she was familiar with this particular work of Faulkner's, but she was surely familiar with the initiation narrative.) "The Bear," similar to Hurston's autobiography, relates personal, familial history and contains complex narratives of memory. Both are not simply narratives of past events but contain things left unfinished, incomplete, vague. Both reveal a vision of the future. And both Hurston and Faulkner see slavery as an evil that has corrupted the new world of America (it is not coincidental that Hurston describes Florida in frontier terms) and has tainted any sense of social justice. Yet both perceive possibilities of transformation and thus of freedom for blacks and whites. Faulkner's hero is a boy, Ike McCaslin, who is taught by a half-Indian, half-Negro, Sam Fathers; Hurston's hero is a girl, Zora, taught by her white surrogate father, unnamed.

Hurston's revision of Faulkner's story, as well as her revision of the black family narrative, mastered in both cases by a powerful white "father," is tantalizing in the tensions raised and left unresolved. Zora's father-midwife initiates her into a world run by white money and power; he refers to liars (like God, he apparently sees who they are and judges them) as *niggers*, implying that the model liar comes from this "race." At the same time, he gives money to *Negro* schools. He represents the highest "virtues": he is a hard-drinking, cussing, riding, shooting man, who has amassed wealth (32). He promises Zora that she will get along well if she does exactly what he (the white master) tells her (31). Zora points out that this is a man the community (that is, Maitland) approves of; he is the kind of (white) man who conquered the frontier.

Faulkner's Sam Fathers is the dark mother-midwife who initiates the boy McCaslin into the fear and power of killing and marks the white boy forever with the blood of the doomed animal he kills. Faulkner romanticizes Fathers, the son of a slave and an Indian, making him one with nature and the slain beast. Neither Hurston nor Faulkner's story is a pretty one, in terms of racial perceptions, in terms of what is taught. Hurston gives us a narrative of a white father figure who embodies the frontier spirit that supposedly made America great. Simultaneously, she questions the narrative and forces attentive readers to do the same.

Hurston's dialogue with and revision of earlier slave narratives, of frontier narratives, and perhaps of Faulkner's initiation narrative represents her dialogue with America and with herself. Within her multitext project, Hurston raises the question of what it means to be born black and female in the presence of white male power, where the words liar and coward are synonymous with "nigger." Her work looks forward to the radical drama of Lorraine Hansberry's *A Raisin in the Sun* (1959). Hansberry also asks a similar question: how does one forge a black identity in the face of such abusive white power?

Zora Neale Hurston's *Dust Tracks on a Road* is a coda to her life and work. Like Walt Whitman before her, she praises America for its visionary promise and at the same time takes her country to task for its social injustices. In those sections excised from her original text, she especially castigates this country's political goals and its racial policies here and abroad. Yet Hurston, also like Whitman, believed in America, its very potential of inclusiveness, and it is that song she sings most clearly. She reminds us that we share common human bonds, that we all walk in the dust together.

8

Seraph on the Suwanee (1948)

Zora Neale Hurston's last published novel, *Seraph on the Suwanee*, appeared in 1948. It has proven to be her most puzzling and controversial. Most likely because the novel deals predominantly with white southern characters, Robert Bone criticizes the novel as assimilationist, that is, of pandering to white readers (169). Critics such as Robert Hemenway finds *Seraph* to be less exciting than her previous works (314), and Lillie Howard, in her book *Zora Neale Hurston*, does not understand what Hurston's view of sexual relations is in the novel (146). Recent critics such as Ann Rayson, Hazel Carby, and Mary Helen Washington are also puzzled or outright dismissive of *Seraph*.

John Lowe is one of the few Hurston scholars to give the novel not only a sympathetic but a thorough and provocative reading, noting Hurston's complex combination of psychology and religion in the love story that drives *Seraph* (259–340).

PLOT DEVELOPMENT

The plot of *Seraph*, as Lowe notes, operates on at least two levels: it follows the psychological development of Arvay Henson, who withdraws into an unhappy private world, and the successful rise of Jim Meserve, her husband, as he makes his way through one industry after another in Florida. The plot is also a journey-narrative, one that tells the story of Arvay Henson's growing up (arguably to what her husband expects and wants her to be). Most of all, the plot maps out the romance of Arvay and Jim, encompassing a period of twenty-plus years, beginning in the first decade of the twentieth century. We come to understand the narrative primarily through the consciousness of Arvay.

The novel opens in Sawley, a backwoods town on the banks of the Suwanee in west Florida. The white folks heading to church go not out of religious desire, but out of personal desire to witness Arvay Henson being escorted to church by Jim Meserve, the handsome, dark Irishman, recently moved to Sawley to work at its main industry—turpentine. His courting of Arvay is unusual because five years earlier, at the age of sixteen, she had renounced the world, intending eventually to become a missionary in India or some other distant part of the world. We discover that her religious vow, made publicly in church, resulted from her anguish over her sister Larraine's marriage to the Rev. Carl Middleton, who Arvay thought had loved her. In fact, Arvay somehow believes that he still loves her just as she continues to love him; as far as Arvay is concerned, Carl just made a mistake in marrying Larraine.

Arvay's singular, slender beauty in a town of especially robust women marks her as a target of male desire. A number of young men, believing her religious fervor to be merely a passing phase, attempt to court Arvay. She responds by falling into fits and scaring them away. Thus she becomes thought of as queer, peculiar, and strange. Her father Brock and mother Maria talk about her—and at her—as being a girl of no sense. Both parents want her to quit being the "tom fool," find a husband, and not be a burden (that is, an expense) to the family (13). When Jim Meserve shows up, ambitious, aggressive, and hardworking, he is thought to be a "good catch." Moreover, Jim's ancestors had been Alabama plantation owners, aristocrats who owned slaves. Although the family lost all of their wealth during the Civil War, Jim remains quality folk, especially in contrast to Brock and Maria, who are "crackers," that is, poor, white, uneducated people.

Although Arvay is attracted to Jim, she cannot believe that he might be interested in her, with her cracker family. Meserve is too handsome, always joking, and, to her, higher in class. Brought up to believe that Larraine was both brighter and better-looking, Arvay thinks that Jim intends merely to make her look foolish. She also feels unworthy of his attention because of her guilt over her lustful feelings for her brother-in-law Carl and because of her hatred for her sister Larraine. Arvay believes that she commits adultery in her mind and heart when she dreams and fantasizes about Carl. She often dreams that her sister dies and Carl turns to her for love. As a result of Arvay's sense of inferiority and her fears of rejection and ridicule, she attempts to dissuade Jim from courting her. At the same time, she secretly thrills at his attention to her. Jim refuses to be discouraged and courts her despite her objections. Even her throwing a fit does not scare him; Jim "cures" her with an oral dosing of turpentine, which he "accidentally" spills into her eye. Arvay recovers from the fits and never has another one.

When Jim asks Arvay to marry him, she replies that she needs some time to make up her mind. Jim's response sums up his perception of women and the relationship he expects to have with his wife: "Women folks don't have no mind to make up nohow" (25).

For all of Jim Meserve's brash and boastful talk, he is nearly as insecure around Arvay as she is around him. When Jim brags about being too tough for Arvay to get rid of, she asks him if he is all that tough, as she believes she feels his arm tremble (26). The very insecurity Jim feels around Arvay goads him to assert his claim over her: he rapes her. In a startling scene in its use of violence, pain, and guilt, Arvay takes Jim to her secret place under the mulberry tree in the Henson backyard. Under this tree she has spent much time pretending a life different from her own and thinking about heaven. As she tells Jim, from under the mulberry tree, heaven seemed a long way off: "I never could see a thing" (45). As Arvay swings on a low branch, Jim suddenly grabs her and rips off her underpants. Although Arvay tries to scream, Jim prevents her by his kisses. The rape ends in Arvay's knowing a "pain remorseless sweet" (47). Her first thought after Jim's sexual assault is not that she has been raped but that she has been made a fool. When Jim tells her of his love, however, an "unknown power" makes her hold tightly to him, kissing him over and over. Arvay and Jim become bound together for life, it seems. Afraid that he will leave her, she clings to him, eliciting another sexual embrace; still she is "not satisfied" (47).

This nearly unbelievable, soap-opera-like rape scene leads to its aftermath in which Arvay accuses Jim of raping her. She believes the rape was mainly to make fun of her! Because she feels inferior to Jim and because of her guilt over her lustful feelings for her brother-in-law, Arvay closes herself off from Jim, shutting him out of what she feels and thinks. Jim, cocky in his male assertion of power over her, tries to joke with Arvay, not realizing that she could not possibly find this a joking matter. Thus neither communicates to the other the depths of their feelings or the intensity of their emotions. This lack of communication dogs the couple's subsequent marriage with near tragic results.

Immediately after the rape, Jim elopes with Arvay to the courthouse where they are married. After their marriage, Arvay and Jim live in a turpentine camp outside of Sawley, but he does not plan to stay there very long. Arvay enjoys the time in the camp and even becomes fond of Dessie and Joe Kelsey, a black couple Jim hires on, Joe to work in the turpentine industry, Dessie to help Arvay. Joe becomes Jim's "pet Negro," so-called because he is always honest and loyal to his white boss (61). The only troublesome aspect of Arvay's life are Carl and Larraine's visits several times a week. Often Larraine alone visits her sister.

Arvay despises Larraine for her bossiness, and although Arvay does not want Carl around because of her guilty feelings for him, she fears her sister much more. Larraine, Arvay thinks, may tell Jim that his wife once loved Carl.

Arvay and Jim's first child, Earl David, is born in the turpentine camp. Unfortunately, Earl is deformed, physically—with a misshapen head and hands with fingers like strings—as well as mentally and emotionally. As Arvay looks at her baby, she recognizes that he looks like her Uncle Chester, her mother's brother, whom no one speaks of. Arvay fears Jim will leave her because of this child, who (in her mind) has been born as a punishment for her lustful thoughts of Carl. As a result, she sees Earl as a part of herself, a burden with her always.

Shortly after Earl's birth, the Meserve family, taking the Kelseys with them, moves from the turpentine camp to the town of Citrabelle, south of Polk County in Florida. Here Jim becomes foreman of a crew of fruit-pickers. Arvay sees the town as "too easy," a place where people do not have to work as hard as the people of Sawley. In part, Arvay's unease in Citrabelle has to do with her puritan religious fervor; it cannot be good for one, in a spiritual sense, if everything around seems too much like an imagined heaven. She remains, however, completely unaware of Jim's great struggle, not only to care for his family, but to thrive and get ahead in the world. Nor does he share this struggle, but thrive he does. He manages to buy five acres of fertile land next to what is known as the Big Swamp, a place that terrifies Arvay. She fears that there are snakes in the swamp and that Earl may wander into it and be lost. Jim promises that one day he will buy it for Arvay, who, of course, wants no part of it.

As Jim had done in the turpentine camp, he manages to manipulate and cajole his workers to help him clear his land and plant a citrus grove on it. They also help to build a house for the Meserves. Arvay never asks Jim how he does these things, nor does he volunteer any information; she accepts, however, what he does for her. Since she is again pregnant, her main worry is whether the child will be healthy and unlike Earl. Angeline Meserve is both beautiful and healthy, a baby who is her father's shining treasure, just as his second son, Kenneth, will be when he appears a few years later. To Arvay, Jim spoils these two children at the expense of poor, deformed Earl.

For all that Arvay enjoys the fruits of Jim's hard work, she never questions how they are able to acquire material wealth. Had she inquired, she would have discovered that a good portion of his money had been made through moonshining—running an illegal whiskey still—with Joe Kelsey. But Arvay eventually finds out the source of the Meserve's additional income, and because of her religious objections to liquor, Jim gives up moonshining. Arvay blames Joe for leading Jim astray and backhandedly drives the Kelseys off the Meserve land and into Citrabelle. Here, because of the money he has made, Joe becomes "people," that is, a big man who throws his money around importantly and works little, even leaving his new house unfinished. One is reminded of Hurston's essay, "My People, My People," in her autobiography *Dust Tracks*.

Jim replaces the Kelseys with a Portuguese family, the Corregios, who never seem quite "white" to Arvay. The Corregios speak funny-sounding English to her, despite the fact that Mrs. Corregio was born in Georgia. In spite of having hurried the Kelseys off Meserve land after the liquor episode, Arvay wishes they were back. She resents the Corregios and looks down upon them as inferior. She is jealous of not only Mrs. Corregio, but also of her beautiful daughters.

In some way, Arvay senses that the Corregio girls pose a threat to Earl, who has turned into a clearly disturbed, mentally deficient adolescent. Yet Arvay denies Earl's troubling behavior and sees Jim's desire to institutionalize Earl as a sign of his rejection of Earl and of her cracker origins as well. That the family is moving towards a tragic event becomes clear in the happy and healthy growth of Kenny and Angie in contrast to their brother Earl.

The novel builds to a climax when Earl attempts to rape Lucy Ann Corregio. He runs back to Arvay's house and hides under the dining table, springing from beneath it to attack his mother with an axe. Only Arvay's superior strength in her hands saves her from certain death by Earl. In a final attempt to save her firstborn child, she tells him to run and hide, and just as Arvay had always feared, he goes into the swamp. Alfredo Corregio, Lucy Ann's father, rounds up a posse who, along with Jim, go into the swamp after Earl. Unknown to them, Earl has a gun and ammunition he has stolen from his father. When Earl shoots and wounds his father, the posse shoots and kills the boy. The scene Hurston presents of the posse, with bloodhounds, tracking Earl into the swamp unmistakably follows those of real lynch mobs who tracked Blacks accused of rape. Quite certainly Hurston wants her readers, perhaps especially her white readers, to understand just what lynching means. In the horrific scene Hurston writes, the hunted represents all black sons.

The horror of Earl's attempted killing of his parents fractures the Meserve family irreparably through subsequent years. To be sure Angeline grows up, as beautiful as Arvay, but without her fears and sense of inferiority. Angie falls in love with Hatton Howland, a Yankee, who works in a gas station. Hatton is like Jim Meserve in many ways, especially in his aggressiveness and ambitions. In fact, Angie and Hatton play out a courtship scene that echoes Jim's rape of Arvay under the mulberry tree. Arvay overhears Hatton say to her daughter that if Angie continues to be so seductive, he will rape her (179). Angie's response is quite unlike her mother's, though: "So, rape me, and I'll help you" (179). Arvay is so shocked that she rises to get Jim's Winchester repeating rifle, a gun carrying immediate and painful memories of Earl. Arvay does not touch the rifle, instead grabbing a revolver and loading it. She fully intends to kill

Hatton but is prevented by Jim's sudden entrance. When she explains what Hatton has said about rape, Jim laughs that most likely Angie is the one doing the raping. Hatton and Angie shortly will elope, following in the footsteps of Arvay and Jim.

By careful use of repetitions in the plot, Hurston makes sure that readers understand not only familial connections but ethnic, racial, regional, and class connections as well. For example, if Yankees historically have been noted for their ability to hustle and move ahead in the world, Jim Meserve hustles and moves ahead. Moreover, the Southerner is quick to forge alliances with Yankee entrepreneurship. When Hatton marries Angie, he and his father-in-law go into real estate development by draining and clearing the swamp. Angie is from a higher economic class than Hatton, just as Jim had been from a higher social class than Arvay.

Jim and Arvay's son, Kenny, is the only Meserve child to attend college. In a subtly drawn psychological scene, Jim arranges for Felicia Corregio to be Kenny's date at a post-football dance at Florida State, a dance the whole Meserve family attends. Arvay, who has suspected Jim was too interested in the Corregio women, blames her husband and Felicia for Kenny's relationship with the girl. Blindly jealous, Arvay insists Jim take her home immediately. The college dance is followed by another rape when they get home; Jim rips off Arvay's dress and forces her to kiss him without any response from him. In this scene, Jim degrades Arvay, making sure that she follows each and every one of his commands. Clearly, Hurston expects us to see the connection between this scene and the earlier rape scene under the mulberry tree.

Arvay's dislike of Felicia—most likely because of prejudice and the association of the Corregio family with Earl's death—does nothing to dampen Kenny's feelings for the girl, although it does seem that he loves music more. He drops out of college to play his guitar and to lead a band, playing black music that he had learned from Joe Kelsey. As Kenny points out, white artists are playing the music now and soon will "take it all over." No longer are the music and dancing "darky"; "It's American, and belongs to everybody" (202).

One might expect the novel to end here, on a note of success and happiness, with both Angie and Kenny becoming rich in their individual ways. Jim, too, flourishes with a newfound interest in the shrimping industry on the coast. But Hurston extends the narrative, pushing it ever deeper into the romance between Jim and Arvay, and exploring, in particular, Arvay's capacity for love. Jim, showing off for Arvay, picks up a diamondback rattlesnake by the neck, and it begins to coil itself around Jim's arm. He looks at Arvay boastfully, much like Twain's Tom Sawyer, showing off in front of Becky Thatcher, looking for approval. But the snake quickly coils itself tighter around Jim's body, as it begins to free its head so that it can be in a strike position. Jim, who now notices his vulnerable position, calls to Arvay to help him, but she is paralyzed from fear. In her mind she imagines that she rescues Jim, but in fact she neither runs toward or away from him (255). Fortunately, Joe Kelsey's son, Jeff, who now works for Jim, saves him. Jim turns this dramatic snake encounter into a test of Arvay's love, one that she utterly fails in his eyes—as well as in Jeff's. As a result Jim leaves her to go to the coast to his shrimp business, but he says that he will be with her again if she ever becomes the woman he married her for (267).

Coincidentally, Arvay receives a telegram from her sister Larraine saying that their mother is dying (Brock Henson had died earlier). Arvay determines to go home to Sawley and to stay there. She erroneously perceives her home as a kind of edenic paradise, uncorrupted by greed and power. The illness of Arvay's mother provides an opportunity to be free of her married life with a man such as Jim, who always looked down upon her. Arvay thanks God for another chance at life (273).

Arvay's return home opens her eyes to the poverty of the place, to the smug narrowness and petty behavior of its people. She also discovers the meanness and hypocrisy of her sister and Carl, who have been abusing Arvay and Larraine's mother, Maria Henson, and stealing from her. Carl and Larraine attempt to intimidate Arvay as they try to extort money from her, but for once in her life Arvay stands up to them. Her dying mother leaves the Henson land and house (which is no more than a rat-infested shack, once Carl and Larraine have finished with it) to Arvay. Arvay not only gives her mother empathy but promises Maria to give her the sort of funeral she wants. The trip to Sawley allows Arvay to discover that although one may be born a cracker, one does not necessarily have to die a cracker. She gives up the faulty image of Carl she had as a young girl. And, for the first time, Arvay sees that she is not merely as good as Larraine; she is better. It is Arvay, not Larraine, who reaps the blessing of their mother, as well as the inheritance that Larraine so greedily desires. Arvay's final gesture in Sawley is to burn the Brock Henson house and give the land to the town as a park. The only condition is that the mulberry tree be preserved.

The fiery end to the Henson house is linked to the title of the novel. As Frank Slaughter noted in his 1948 review of *Seraph*, Arvay is the seraph: "One of an order of celestial beings conceived as fiery and purifying ministers of Jehovah" (in Gates and Appiah 34). In the Bible, Isaiah sees God on a throne, under hovering seraphim. Isaiah cries out that he is lost because he is a man of sin, and one of the seraphim flies to him and lays a live coal in Isaiah's mouth. At once his sin is taken away. Arguably, when Arvay sets fire to the Henson house, she repeats the action of the seraphim who eradicate evil with fire. By setting fire to the Henson house, Arvay eliminates Larraine and Carl's evil and at the same time purges herself of her own sense of guilt and unworthiness. She thus frees herself to return to Jim.

After her trip to Sawley, Arvay goes to New Smyrna on the coast of Florida. Here she joins Jim on his shrimp boat, which, she is surprised to learn, he has named for her, the *Arvay Henson*. When they set out to sea, Arvay again faces a test of her love. The ship must pass over a sandbar, dangerous and tricky to navigate. Jim's first mate fears the worst and cries out in terror that the bar is too rough to pass. When he grabs Jim's leg, Arvay pulls him off and the boat moves out to calm water. This test, of course, contrasts with the rattlesnake episode, in which Arvay stood immobilized. The episode on the boat, however, rings false with its forced and stilted language. The scene is not managed as well as the snake episode, in which the language, the actions of Jim, and the setting work together effectively. On the *Arvay Henson*, the scene is overwrought and melodramatic. The language seems not only artificial but staged, especially when the first mate holds on to Jim's leg, crying "Captain! My Captain! . . . Turn back," echoing Walt Whitman's poem of the same name. Equally incongruous are the numerous references to Alfred Lord Tennyson's "Crossing the Bar," in which God as the pilot is replaced with Jim Meserve (for a different reading, see Lowe 328, 330). We are told that any fear Arvay experiences while crossing the bar is like a birth pain, quickly "forgotten and gone" (331). All of her senses quicken as she stretches to become one with the sea, the rising sun, and the multiple colors on the horizon. As she says to Jim, it seems as if she has been on some journey and has just now arrived home (333). Arvay's sea change brings out her warmth and caring; she cooks for the crew and Jim, and she determines to win back Jim.

The narrative dissolves into the passion Jim and Arvay feel for each other; indeed, the ending is nearly *all* feeling. But Arvay is no fool. She recognizes that for all his male bluster and assertiveness, Jim Meserve is merely a "little boy," seeking the comfort of his mother. And she also recognizes her own capacity for nurturing love. Thus, like the hovering seraphim in Isaiah, she "hover[s]" over Jim (349).

Feminist critics understandably find the ending of *Seraph* difficult, if not impossible, to accept, but the ending follows the formula of a romance, with a conclusion neat and tidy. Arvay comes home to herself, she believes, to see that her job is "mothering" (351). Like the seraphim, Arvay discovers "exaltation," "peace," and "fullness" in her service to Jim (349–51). Did Hurston believe in this ending? We cannot know for certain; in her own life, she certainly did not live such an ending. In *Seraph*, Hurston seems to stand at some distance from Arvay and Jim as the ocean rocks them to sleep.

SETTING AND SYMBOLISM

Hurston uses setting in *Seraph* to comment generally on socioeconomic conditions in Florida in the early twentieth century and to delineate the psychological state of Arvay Henson in particular. There are three major settings: (1) Sawley and the Henson house, including the mulberry tree and the turpentine camp; (2) the Meserve house in Citrabelle and the Great Swamp; and (3) the *Arvay Henson* and the ocean.

Sawley is a hardscrabble backwoods town in west Florida, on the Suwanee River. The only reason for the town is the turpentine industry around which it developed, an industry that will disappear. At the end of the novel, tourism has replaced it as the major industry in Sawley. In the opening sentence of the novel, Hurston makes clear her ironic stance: the Suwanee became famous because of the popular song by Stephen Foster, a white man who never saw the river, or the "darkies" (as Foster refers to them) who sang, shuffled, and worked at the plantation "home." She thus deflects any criticism of a black author who writes about white folks since she knows them and the area first hand. If the life of Sawley revolves around turpentine and lumber, Hurston suggests that poverty, hookworm, ignorance, and fundamentalist religion seem to be by-products. Not only does the landscape look poor and stunted, so do the people. There were still men in Sawley who had fought in the Civil War, and the postwar reconstruction was still part of living memory. In Sawley, the races are clearly kept separate, even on Sunday when they worship. Girls married young—and someone like Arvay, who is twenty-one and still unmarried when the story opens, is looked upon as odd, to say the least.

Jim Meserve enters Sawley as an outsider because he was not born there and because his ancestors had owned plantations on the Alabama River before the Civil war. In contrast, the poor Whites or crackers who inhabit Sawley had never been around big estates and owned only small poor farms. Even though the war obliterated Jim's grandfather's fortune, Jim himself, because of his origins, is forever associated with good fortune. In short, Sawley remains in a narrow time warp, afraid to let go of the past because the present seems too much like it. Without a present, there can be no future.

Brock Henson bought his house on the small pay he earns as an overrider for the turpentine industry. The house itself is as ugly as the temperament of the man who owns it. It is a sorry-looking clapboard house that had started out ugly red and had turned rusty gray-brown. The only room with a ceiling is the parlor; the other rooms reveal the skinny rafters overhead. Water is drawn from a well, and a leaning privy is not far from the kitchen door. The garden remains uncared for; only a mulberry tree, associated with Arvay, offers any beauty on the Henson place. As the house and yard are grim, so too is family life, with little or no kindness, let alone love, either before or after Larraine marries Carl Middleton.

The furniture and interior décor of the house reveal the same tastelessness and poverty of the outside. The usual what-not shelves contain a collection of unrelated items that have no particular functional or aesthetic merit, such as seashells side by side with bits and pieces of crockery. The family Bible is on a shelf under the table centered in the room. The top of the table holds a number of objects: a kerosene lamp, a family album, and fancy cups and saucers, an indication of an effort to appear genteelly middle class. The walls have various pictures, with no order or connection; framed pictures rest on nails driven into the walls, with family pictures crowded next to a picture of Robert E. Lee at Manassas, astride his horse and looking down at Union soldiers. In Brock Henson's house, the Civil War is not forgotten, giving rise to or representing Henson's personal prejudices. Prints of the war are nailed next to images of Bible scenes, such as Peter, looking guiltily at Christ. Hurston uses these objects to poke fun at the class pretensions of such poor Whites as the Hensons who seek to emulate middle-class respectability.

Hurston also reveals the hollowness of such pretensions late in the novel, when Arvay returns home for a final time. She discovers the "museum-like" display of objects she and Jim sent Maria Henson over the years. Maria had kept money orders from Kenny, as well as photos of him with his band, under her mattress, along with things from Angie. Running around in the walls are rats, threatening to take over the house, just as Larraine and Carl try to do when they strip the house of nearly everything after Maria's death.

Arvay's burning of the house signifies the destruction of her illusions about her family; she realizes that there had never been any comfort—or virtue—in the Henson house. Instead, there had been a vain desire for acquisitions and a total lack of nurturing care. As far as Arvay is concerned, only the mulberry tree has any worth. It had provided her a secret place in which to find comfort when she was growing up, as well as a place of imaginative potential. Here she could indulge in games of pretend. The mulberry tree was also a place of sexual conflict and contradiction. Jim raped her under the mulberry tree, and Arvay both abhorred the act and felt guilty over it because of her own passionate response. Her ensuring that the mulberry tree survives when she destroys the Henson house marks Arvay's awareness that she had been blinded from "seeing and feeling" life (307). She looks at the tree as a "sacred symbol" from which she was able to win "a vivid way of life with love" (306). Indeed, she finally sees the mulberry tree as her "tree of life" (308).

The rape under the mulberry tree led directly to Arvay's marriage and life with Jim Meserve and to their first home at the turpentine camp. There is little description of the house they live in; it seems to serve as a way-station in their rise from poverty to material wealth. The camp reaffirms the racial segregation of Sawley. Jim, because he is white, has a better position than any black man, yet the Blacks are the real backbone of the turpentine industry. In addition, the camp provides Hurston an opportunity to demonstrate the energy and vibrancy of Blacks compared to the lives of such poor Whites as the Hensons. For example, Blacks have a celebration in honor of the Meserve marriage and sing and play music for Arvay and Jim.

Joe and Dessie Kelsey prove also to be far more loyal and helpful to the Meserve couple than anyone in Arvay's family. The camp is not far enough removed from Sawley and the Hensons to be much more than an adjunct location. Larraine can and does intrude on Arvay's home territory. The bleakness of the turpentine camp seems to be reflected in the birth of the deformed Earl David. Because of Carl and Larraine's numerous visits, Arvay is only too eager to go start a new life elsewhere, away from Sawley.

Citrabelle is the exact opposite of Sawley and the turpentine camp. To Arvay, Citrabelle seems like heaven, with its bright flowers and well-kept, painted houses. In fact, the bright pleasantness of the town worries Arvay. From her religious point of view, the people who live in Citrabelle must be lazy, unworthy of God's attention since they are not bowed down by arduous work: "It was the duty of man to suffer in this world," and Arvay sees the people of south Florida "plainly shirking their duty" (73). She never realizes that work in Citrabelle is seasonal; during the off-months people had either to live on far less money or find other work. Again, Hurston makes it clear that the productivity of the citrus groves is due in large measure to the hard-working black people who live in Colored Town. Although Jim is an overseer in the groves, it is the Blacks who "actually knew how things were done," who taught him (74).

Even though Arvay and Jim share a house in Citrabelle, they do not share a life. Arvay does not ask, and Jim does not offer any information, about how Jim earns his money, nor what it costs him in terms of his energy and hard work. Thus Citrabelle may seem much more pleasant than Sawley, but it further emphasizes the lack of communication between Arvay and Jim. Paradoxically, although their emotional lives seem to dwindle, their material lives flourish. Jim is able to acquire his own citrus grove and to build a new house on the land. This rise to wealth seems matched by the birth of two healthy children, Angie and Kenny. The growth of the house—its screened-in porch, for example, which is Arvay's joyful pride—reveals Jim's meteoric rise to wealth. Part of that wealth comes from the whiskey still that Jim and Joe Kelsey run; once Arvay discovers the devil's work (in liquor), both the still and Joe and Dessie disappear. The Corregios replace the Kelseys, much to Arvay's dismay. The substitution of the Portuguese family for the black family, Hurston suggests, demonstrates that Whites cannot sustain themselves without the assistance of minority people. Jim may not "own" the Kelseys or the Corregios, but he cannot seem to get along without them. They seem to be as much a part of the property as the citrus trees.

No matter how financially successful Jim Meserve becomes, their home outside of Citrabelle is no paradise. It borders on the Great Swamp: dark, unknown, and therefore dangerous. Arvay fears that Earl will become lost in it and die. Her fears prove prophetic. What she does not know is that Earl goes into the swamp many times and perhaps feels at home there. Earl himself is akin to the unknown darkness of the swamp. Even his own mother does not realize the dangerous aspects of her son; she denies his sexual assault on Lucy Ann Corregio and even his violent attempts to kill his mother.

The swamp obviously represents more than the dark deformity of poor Earl; it also represents the darkness in Arvay: in her mean-spiritedness, in her desire to inflict pain—even death—on her sister Larraine, and in her narrow focus on herself. The swamp signifies perhaps the unknown in all of us, the darkness within that we fear to explore. Later, after Earl is killed in the swamp, Hatton, Angie's husband, and Jim have the swamp drained. Hatton's real estate company develops the land, turning it into a kind of suburb of Citrabelle.

Even though the swamp is converted from loss to financial gain, from some sort of evil to human habitation, it does not mean that Jim and Arvay's home suddenly becomes paradise. There is still a snake—literally and metaphorically—in the garden. Jim, out of his own pride, does battle with the snake and almost loses his life. If the snake represents his pride, it also represents, strangely, Arvay's pride as well—in her own unworthiness, in her inability to overcome her fears ingrained in her cracker background. Although Jeff Kelsey, Joe's son, kills the snake, it remains very much alive as a kind of twisted evil in Arvay. Her pride in her origins dies only when she returns home to Sawley for the last time.

The ending of *Seraph* takes place on the *Arvay Henson*, Jim's shrimp boat, berthed in New Smyrna. On the boat, Arvay seemingly breaks free of her largely self-made prison. The imagery of this section of the novel depicts a far different world than that of Sawley and the turpentine camp, or even of Citrabelle, with its swamp and snakes. On the shrimp boats, white and black captains confer with each other; integrated crews run the boats. Alfredo Corregio captains the *Angeline* and a Black commands the *Kenny M*. The ocean on which these boats make their shrimp runs carries both danger and triumph; in short the ocean embraces life—and death. On the ocean, Arvay believes she has come home to herself. In forgetting herself when she comes to Jim's aid, she rescues not only him but herself. As she says, "Seems like I been off somewhere on a journey and just got home" (333). Jim reminds her that her life is like water, after all, which is on a journey back to the sea, to home. The water flowing to the sea originally came from the sea. Arvay tells Jim that if the water comes from the sea, it returns "to its real self at last" (335).

The imagery at the end of the novel, with its emphasis on the gentle rocking of the ocean, with the splendor of the sun as a new day dawns, reminds us of the ending of *Their Eyes Were Watching God*. However, in Hurston's earlier novel, plot, character, and setting all work together to prepare us for the magnificent mythic apotheosis of its ending. *Seraph* does not prepare us for such an ending, and although the language soars, we are not at all sure the lives of Arvay and Jim Meserve do the same.

CHARACTER DEVELOPMENT

The protagonist in *Seraph* is Arvay Henson. Her story is the most significant, and we perceive it primarily through her consciousness. Hurston takes a risk, however, in making Arvay the central character because she is not particularly likeable in a number of ways. Her narrow, constrained religious view of God's justice, her self-righteousness, and her sense of her own unworthiness threaten to become tiresome. Arvay's God is not the God of laughter and love we find in *Jonah's Gourd Vine* nor the God of majesty and awe we find in *Moses, Man of the Mountain*. Neither is Arvay's God one of nature as in *Their Eyes Were Watching God*. Arvay's God is one of punishment, one that is watching and waiting for her to make a mistake. Arvay lacks the imagination of either Lucy Potts in *Jonah* or of Janie in *Their Eyes*. In her mind she thinks of how much time she spent under the mulberry tree, a secret place for her imagination to run free, but we never see any evidence of her imagination at work throughout the novel. Arvay takes life as deadly serious; even her use of language is seriously literal. At the same time, however, Arvay has music in her; as a girl she played the organ in church without study, that is, naturally. In addition, she played with passion, a passion that later imbues her soul and body for Jim Meserve.

Arvay suffers from a deprived childhood. Both her mother and father seemed to have had little use for her when she was growing up. They constantly compared her unfavorably to her sister Larraine, who conformed to the "norm" for females in Sawley. Even Larraine's physical being—her stocky, buxom body and thick legs—is more in line with the other young women in Sawley. Arvay seems incongruously misplaced, with her golden hair, slim body, and shapely long legs. Larraine married early; when the novel opens, Arvay is twenty-one and still unmarried. This oddity links her to another, her religious declaration to become a missionary in India or some other distant nation. Both Maria and Brock find Arvay dumb and not quite right mentally in comparison to Larraine, and so they either ignored or damned her.

Arvay's resulting envy of Larraine colors her every thought of her sister. She hates her sister for stealing and marrying the Rev. Carl Middleton, who had initially courted Arvay; at least he led her to believe so. In her mind and heart, Arvay lusts for her sister's husband, committing what she believes to be mental sexual crimes with him. Later she believes Earl is a punishment for her "adultery" with Carl. The envy Arvay feels for Larraine finds its way even into her dreams. When Arvay and Jim live in the turpentine camp, Larraine pays a great deal of attention to Jim. Arvay fears two things: that her sister may steal Jim away, just as she did Carl, or that her sister will tell Jim of Arvay's love for Carl. These fears trigger Arvay to dream that she slits the throat of Larraine. Arvay realizes she has hated Larraine for many years. Hate, in this instance, may be too mild a word; Arvay wishes her sister dead—indeed she would like to kill Larraine. Arvay's dream leads her to believe she is like the biblical Cain who slew his sibling Abel. Because she is afraid that she may physically hurt Larraine, Arvay begs Jim to take her away from the Sawley area.

Only when Arvay returns to Sawley to see her dying mother does she resolve her jealousy of Larraine. Arvay finally sees her sister—as well as Carl—for what they are: greedy, unprincipled, and ignorant. Larraine and Carl, both lazy and fat, have produced ugly replicas of themselves in their children. They steal from the dying Maria, who has left everything to Arvay. It is not difficult to see in this scenario that the least favored child in the family becomes the most favored and receives the blessing of the parent; Arvay, who was always last in her mother's eyes, is now first. Carl nastily tries to extort money from Arvay because he fell on the porch of her newly inherited house. When she refuses to pay him anything, he and Larraine strip the house of everything of value, even ripping up floorboards. Before her death, Maria understands how much she misjudged Arvay and overrated Larraine. Maria's acknowledgment in large part empowers Arvay to free herself from the shadow of Larraine and to recognize her own worth.

But this reconciliation with her mother comes almost too late for Arvay. There is little doubt that Arvay's formative years spent under Brock Henson's roof mark her adulthood. Because she feels that her parents did not love her and that Larraine took Carl from her, Arvay fears any sort of intimacy that might lead to additional losses. Hence her hysterical "fits" to discourage would-be suitors, who, she thinks, will make her look like a fool, as Carl did. Despite her passion for Jim Meserve, she is always afraid to show it, believing she will lose him too. She cannot believe that Jim chooses to court her and desires her to marry him. She is ambivalent about his rape of her because she feels guilty of having caused it; moreover, she seems incapable of not responding to him with physical passion of her own. She clings to him after the rape because she does not want to lose him, once more appearing to be a fool in the eyes of her parents and the community.

Arvay's body—her own sensuality and passion—betrays her over and over with Jim. In the rape scene, she holds onto him for dear life, afraid that he will disappear from her. She expresses her need of him through her body, as she tries to "absorb him within herself" (54). Doing so would mean never having to lose him. Yet she is unable to articulate her desires—or fears—to Jim. What she feels and thinks stays buried within her, while what she says often becomes bitter and accusatory.

Although Arvay loves her children—all three of them—she also fails to articulate her love and hope for them as well. She lavishes attention on Earl, her firstborn, because she recognizes herself in him. In her mind Earl embodies—literally—her cracker origins; he is like her mother's brother Chester. Just as Arvay was, Earl is the least favored child in the family. If Arvay dreams of cutting her sister's throat, Earl attempts to kill his own mother and father.

Arvay's daughter Angeline dismays her mother probably because they are alike in many ways. Angeline is beautiful like her mother and "strange," at least to Arvay, in her headstrong desire to go her own way and to live her own life. Arvay is also jealous of her daughter because she resents Jim's attention to Angeline. As far as Arvay is concerned, Jim spoils Angeline and thus holds her in higher esteem than he does his own wife. In a sense Arvay revisits upon her daughter the old rivalry she felt for Larraine.

However, Arvay revisits more than sibling rivalry; she also relives her rape through Angeline. When Arvay overhears Hatton say he will rape Angeline, it seems to be a replay of Jim's rape of her. Not coincidentally, she gets Jim's revolver to shoot Hatton. Only Jim's arrival stops Arvay from killing the boy, but her deadly seriousness contrasts mightily with Jim's response, who says it is Angeline who is more apt to rape Hatton. Because Arvay recognizes in her daughter a passion and sensuality similar to her own, she determines to prevent Angeline from entering a relationship with a dominating man like Jim Meserve.

Yet Arvay mistakes the kind of young woman Angeline is. To be sure she has her mother's passion and sensuality. She is willful and demanding, but Angeline is also much more sure of herself than her mother. As Arvay had eloped with Jim, Angeline elopes with Hatton. Although Arvay is deeply disappointed with her daughter for giving up college for marriage, she prepares a wedding celebration for Angeline and Hatton, just as Maria Henson had done for Arvay and Jim. Unlike Arvay who never inquires about her husband's business dealings, Angeline becomes an equal partner in Hatton's real estate ventures. Angeline has the confidence that a comfortable upper-middle-class background and loving parents gave her; Arvay lacks such confidence until near the end of the novel.

Arvay's relationship with her son Kenny is also complex. She sees in him the same dashing good looks and devil-may-care attitude as in Jim. At the same time, she half resents Kenny because of his marked contrast to Earl. As Kenny grows older, Arvay fears losing him to another woman just as she fears losing Jim. The Oedipal implications here are unmistakable as Arvay views father and son as alike and desires to keep both of them in her life.

Through Arvay's three children, three facets of her are revealed. Earl represents the dark side of his mother. His mental, physical, and emotional deformities are linked to Arvay in subtle and complex ways. Mentally, Earl has a narrow range of focus; he does not have the capacity to explore or imagine any world different from his own. In a way, Arvay is similar, not because she lacks the mental capability but because she believes what her parents—and Jim—told her: that she had no sense at all. Physically, Earl lacks the strength to do many things; because of this, for example, he fails to kill his mother. Arvay can cook and clean, but she cannot move to free Jim of the snake that entwines him. Earl lacks the capacity for emotional intimacy, and thus he does not think twice of trying to kill his mother and father. Arvay's vulnerability and fear of losing those she loves prevents intimacy with Jim; only at the end of the novel does she open up herself to him, and even then one might question how much she has changed at that point. Angeline's beauty, her passionate ability for love, and her sensuality are all qualities that Arvay has. Even the feistiness and willfulness of Angeline come to her from her mother, although Arvay expresses these qualities differently. Kenny may be very much his father's son, but the music in him comes from his mother. Like Arvay, Kenny plays without study, naturally. Unlike his mother, Kenny is able to venture forth in the world with his music and become successful. For all of Arvay's faults, she is a caring individual. She cares deeply about her mother and helped her survive by having Jim send her money throughout the years. Arvay goes home when her mother is dying to offer her solace. There she discovers that her children also had sent presents to their grandmother; Kenny had even sent money. In addition, they sent their love in the form of notes and photos of themselves. If Arvay's view of the world was rather narrow, she nonetheless made it possible for her children to venture forth into a wider world—and to do so with love, caring, and even music.

If Arvay is complex, Jim Meserve is charming. An outsider in Sawley, he must have seemed to Arvay like an exotic Prince Charming looking to awaken some Sleeping Beauty—as, in a way, he does with her. The people in Sawley find evidence in him of his upper-class origins, as if the plantation money of his ancestors imprinted native intelligence and fine manners in him. Jim's good looks, wit, and charm seem to come from his Irish ancestors, but so too, he says, come his fighting and his drinking. And of course, as he also says, fighting and drinking are part of being a man.

Jim's ability as an entrepreneur to move ahead and to better himself financially represents what Hurston sees Whites doing all around her in Florida during the first half of the twentieth century. Hurston admires Jim's can-do attitude and his perseverance, perhaps in contrast to Joe Kelsey, who spends, but does not replenish, his money on good times. At the same time, Hurston points out how necessary Blacks—and later Portuguese—workers are to Jim's success. They are the ones who show Jim how the various industries work, from turpentine, to citrus groves, to shrimp boats. Joe Kelsey and later Alfredo Corregio run the whiskey still, not without risk, that enables Jim to run and expand his legitimate businesses.

Throughout Jim's rise in the business world, he seems able to charm and cajole blacks and other minorities to work their hardest for him. Hurston stops short of stating outright that Jim manipulates the people who work for him, but she is certainly satiric in her comments about Joe Kelsey as Jim's pet negro. The satire, however, cuts in two directions: towards the white man who keeps a pet and the black man who so willingly fills that role.

The Kelseys, although peripheral characters, are interesting because they are crucial to the lives of the Meserves, much more so than the Corregios, who eventually replace them. Joe Kelsey is the one who gives Jim the advice that women are to be treated like horses; they need to be broken and then rode hard. Yet, we never see Joe mistreat his wife. Dessie is the trusted midwife when Earl is born and continues to help Arvay. In fact, Dessie is much more of a sister to Arvay than Larraine ever is. In addition, Joe helps to bring up Kenny; he teaches the boy black music. When Kenny leaves to go North, Arvay tearfully asks Joe to go with him, to look after him, and to make sure he lives a moral life. Joe promises to do this, and says "we" Meserves have to stick together. Joe and Dessie's son Jeff, and his wife, eventually replace their parents with Jim and Arvay. In some ways, this smacks of the plantation system, and it is unclear what Hurston's position is. Is she being ironic, or does she believe this system works fine? Clearly Jim Meserve could not function as well as he does without the Kelseys—or later, the Corregios—but it is also clear that they never attain the social status of the Meserves.

Jim, with his charm and good looks, is attractive to both men and women; indeed, women, including Larraine, flirt with him but to no avail. With the exception of Arvay, Jim is primarily a man's man. That is, he seems most comfortable around men, doing business with them, telling them tall stories, drinking, and fighting with them. The "Battle of the Horse's Behind" (89–94) demonstrates Jim's quick wit, his love of the tall tale, and his cameradrie with men. When Hawley Pitts, a huge man, badgers the much smaller Pearly Snead, Jim immediately comes to the aid of the underdog. The episode, humorous as it is, also, in a rather offhand way demonstrates how Jim uses his wife. Jim pretends he must fight Hawley because he has had the temerity to show his ugly face around Jim's wife and thus frighten her. After both men beat on each other, the scene ends with jovial backslapping and drinks all around.

There is little doubt that Jim loves Arvay passionately, but his notion of love has to do with power and possession. For all of Jim's joking, drinking, and fighting, he is basically insecure as a man and thus constantly feels the need to assert his manhood. Hurston seems to ask the question of what makes the man: Is it his ability to manipulate other men and at the same time to maintain loyal friendships with them? Is it his ability to confront and control nature—draining swamps, clearing land, fighting rattlesnakes, conquering the ocean? Is it also to provide and care for one's family? And, especially, is it to possess and control love through the body of a woman?

Jim Meserve would answer yes to all of the above. And within the context of the novel, he would seem to be right, as a number of critics believe. For example, in Jim's eyes, his rape of Arvay is no real rape; it is a man's assertion of his rightful place over a woman. And, as he points out to Arvay, he plans to keep on doing it. According to Jim, women cannot think, and thus men have to do their thinking for them. Women exist to "hover and to feel" (105). Joe Kelsey agrees and advises Jim that the only way for men to make women love them is to force them to "knuckle under" (46). Kelsey's image of women as horses to be broken may be chilling to readers but not to Jim Meserve (46). Jim's rape of Arvay is swift, cruel, and violent. Although she feels pain that may be "sweet" (51), she struggles during the rape and tries to scream. Moreover, she is afraid.

The language surrounding Meserve's actions lets us know that Hurston does not take this scene lightly. Jim grits his teeth like an animal; there is "tearing" as he rips Arvay's underpants "ruthlessly" (51). There is little in this rape scene that makes it any different from his son Earl's assault on Lucy Ann Corregio except that Earl is hunted down like a wild animal and shot. After Jim's rape of Arvay, as they ride to the courthouse to be married, Jim makes light of the rape, saying that he has done it right and plans to keep on doing it—right, one supposes. In fact, he does rape her again after they are married (215–19).

Jim's use of rape to subdue Arvay always ends in his "happy arrogance" (219), a superiority he seems able only to claim by physically dominating his wife. Repeatedly, however, Jim is compared to a little boy, fleeing the dark to the comforting arms of his mother (349). After sex with Arvay, Jim always snuggles his head on her breast and falls instantly to sleep, as Arvay runs her fingers through his hair. She does "hover" over him as a mother would do, and it is precisely this hovering quality of Arvay's that attracts Jim. To be sure he admires her beauty, as well as her passion as evidenced in her eyes, but Arvay's ability to mother him mysteriously holds him. As Arvay notes again and again, Jim is like a "helpless" child (219). This man, who is like a god to her, trembles in her presence, mortally afraid he may lose her.

Hurston develops her central characters, Arvay and Jim, with lacings of irony and psychology. It may be too easy, for example, to say that Jim suffers from a mother fixation, ever yearning to return to the lost mother's embrace. In life—and in Hurston's fiction—the psyche is never as simple as that. Yet it is not coincidental that Jim finds in Angeline the beauty of his mother. Through Arvay and his daughter, Jim can regain his lost, dead mother and thus his sense of peace in himself. At the same time, that sense of peace is regressive; it is the peace of the child sleeping at his mother's breast.

If Arvay's relationship with her children helps us to understand her character, so too do we better understand Jim through his role as a father. Arvay is the parent who seems to have most of the care of the children, particularly in terms of their character and moral values (however, even though Arvay seems dedicatedly religious, there is never any mention of the family going to church). Jim generally is the parent who laughs with his children but rarely disciplines them. He totally ignores Earl David. To be sure, he feeds and clothes him; as Earl grows older, he wants to institutionalize him. The most attention he gives Earl is after the boy's attack on Lucy Ann, when it is far too late to do anything for him. Angeline pays her father great attention, far greater than to her mother, and reaps Jim's devotion. Jim is not upset about Angeline marrying Hatton because when he looks at Hatton, he sees himself. Hatton seems to be a clone of Jim Meserve, and thus Jim does not really "lose" his daughter to another man. Indeed, unknown to Arvay, Jim not only signs the papers allowing the seventeen-year-old girl to marry Hatton, he attends their wedding, facts Arvay discovers only well after the marriage. Jim continues to lavish attention on Angeline through Hatton, capitalizing his ventures in real estate. Kenny is in many ways like his father in wit and charm. Jim shucks off the care of Kenny to Joe Kelsey, the pet Negro Jim never really gives up. But Jim manages to control Kenny to a large extent. Even Kenny's big moment at Florida State, when he leads the band at the game, and again at the postgame dance, is orchestrated by Jim. Unknown to Arvay again, and it appears, to Kenny as well, Jim arranges for Felicia Corregio to be his son's date. Jim even provides the money for Felicia to dress stunningly, thus drawing attention not so much to Kenny but to himself. In fact, Jim uses his whole family at this event to ingratiate himself with a number of businessmen. Power over his family is a trump card he plays to win power in the business world.

At the end of the novel, the expectation remains that the two major characters have changed in some way. It is possible, perhaps, to see that Arvay has changed, insofar as she has left her Sawley origins behind her for good. And certainly on the *Arvay Henson*, she acts more audaciously; she dresses in male clothes (although Jim buys them for her to wear), and she initiates sex with Jim. Yet Jim Meserve seems not to have changed at all; he still tells Arvay not to make a sound and to hug his neck, a refrain he uses throughout the novel. The posture of the couple, finally, is the same one we have seen before: Jim sleeps blissfully at Arvay's breast, as she runs her fingers through his hair.

Perhaps Hurston's ambivalence about Jim Meserve can be summed up in the name she gave him: Meserve or Me-serve. Does the name imply that they serve each other? Certainly Jim does serve Arvay in providing her with material wealth and comfort, just as she serves him with love and devotion. Or does the name imply the egotistical selfishness and neediness of each character? Quite possibly Hurston meant the name to encompass both egoism and service.

THEMATIC ISSUES

In *Seraph on the Suwanee*, Hurston gathers many of the themes she explored in her other novels and in her autobiography: class, race, and gender. That she addresses these themes through the predominant use of white characters makes this perhaps her riskiest novel.

The Hensons are "crackers," as Hurston takes pains to delineate. As such they belong to that class of poor Whites who work hard but have few pleasures. They do have more than enough prejudice and ignorance to go around. Their religion tends to focus on hellfire and damnation, and repentance for sin is matched by an equal amount of backsliding into it (4). Girls marry young; Larraine marries Carl Middleton before she is sixteen; people consider Arvay, who is younger than Larraine, strange because she remains unmarried at twenty-one. What sets Arvay apart from her class are her religious fervor and her musical ability, as well as her slender beauty.

Crackers, Hurston suggests, form their prejudices early and hold on to them tenaciously. Blacks are strictly segregated, right down to the churches and to the types of jobs they hold. Black men do not/can not have the position of an overrider, a position reserved for someone like Brock Henson. Arvay continues to carry the prejudices of her class until the end of the novel, and even then she must make a determined effort to push them underground. She wonders, for example, how black women manage to straighten their hair. Earlier in the novel, even though Dessie Kelsey helps to birth Arvay's first child, and Joe Kelsey helps to make her life more comfortable, the Kelseys are expendable when Arvay learns about the whiskey still. Similarly, Arvay despises the Corregios, who are Portuguese ("no foreigners were ever quite white to Arvay" [120]). Arvay thinks of Mrs. Corregio, who was born in Georgia, as a traitor to her race and class for marrying anybody named Alfredo Corregio. Yankees fare no better. Arvay finds them foreign and therefore suspect. She dislikes Hatton

Howland and his mother, viewing them as unknown and therefore a threat to Arvay's way of life.

Throughout her married life, Arvay views Jim as someone above her, from a higher class. Indeed, his ancestors had owned plantations (and thus presumably slaves) before the Civil War. His family past, however, bears no resemblance to his present. Meserve's financial status is initially akin to the Hensons; he is broke. In fact, it is Brock Henson who gets Jim a job in the turpentine industry. Jim gets ahead financially because he moves easily among classes, races, and ethnic groups.

Hurston seems particularly ambivalent in those passages where Meserve makes friends with Blacks by visiting the jooks, those rowdy drinking and dancing establishments, exchanging stories and drinking with them. On the one hand, Hurston makes clear that without the help of Blacks—and later, of the Corregios—Jim Meserve would have remained as poor as the Hensons. Hurston walks a fine line between Meserve's learning from Blacks and his manipulation of them. Perhaps Me-serve means here that Jim will use those people who can be the most help to him. To be fair, however, he does not abuse any other class or race. As John Lowe points out, Jim Meserve puts his trust in Joe and Dessie Kelsey (Lowe 286). Jim sees them as two of the "nicest" people he has ever met. Late in the novel, Joe and Dessie's son and daughter-in-law, Jeff and Janie, also work for Jim. Arvay sees Joe, and later Jeff, as Jim's pet Negroes, and Jim does not disagree. "Kee-reck!" he says, and goes on to say how "damn fine" Joe is (60). Yet Arvay entrusts Joe Kelsey not only with her son's musical training but also with the care of his moral values. There is more than a touch of irony here, as Hurston draws a picture of the loyal family retainers handed down from one generation to another. Like his father, Jeff Kelsey also speaks of "us Meserves" (313).

If Jim Meserve is at home with those of lower class and other racial and ethnic groups, he is equally at home with bankers and businessmen. He spins out his humorous tales, and trots out his smart-looking family, all with his eyes on business. Jim is equally companionable with his Yankee son-in-law, Hatton, in whom he finds a kindred spirit. Both men draw no color or class lines when it comes to business, although we do not hear of Hatton and Jim building or promoting an integrated housing development.

The shrimping industry, however, provides Hurston with an opportunity to show integration at work. Here white and black boat captains cooperate; crews are sometimes "mixed." The common enemies are mechanical failures, the weather, and owners. Alfredo captains the *Angeline*, and the *Kenny M* has a black captain. On the shrimp boats, the requirements remain the same, no matter the class, ethnicity, or race: courage, intelligence, and strength.

As in her other novels, Hurston also deals with men's domination of women. If to be black, female, and poor is to be marginalized in a patriarchal world, what is it to be white, female (with blonde hair and blue eyes), and poor? To a large extent, in this novel, there appears to be little difference when it comes to how men view women. For example, there is almost a total lack of communication between Arvay and Jim from the day they meet. After they move to Citrabelle, Jim thinks, "There was not sufficient understanding" in their marriage (104), and is pained by the knowledge. However, Jim appears trapped in a double bind; on the one hand, he believes that as a woman, Arvay wasn't "given to thinking," and on the other, he expects her to "be awake enough to glimpse and see" what he desires and thinks (265). Arvay responds as any rational person would: "How could I, when you never let me know?" (265). Only at the end of the novel, do they "read" (understand) each other, presumably without talking. At the end, Jim says to her, "hush up!" and goes on to say he does not "need" (or want, apparently) any "long explanations."

At the beginning of the novel, Arvay, for all of her good looks, is suspect as a female because she is unmarried at twenty-one. Her fits can be cured, young men believe, by marriage; that is, through sex and the production of babies. Her body, minutely studied and talked about by the men in town, becomes a kind of joke, bandied about between the fantasized sheets in their minds. Tremendous emphasis is placed upon women's flesh in this novel and what men think of doing, as well as what they do. One recalls the episode of Kenny Meserve and Belinda Kelsey at the train station when they are children. Belinda's talent happens to be the somersault; her "shame," according to Arvay, is that she has on no underwear. When the train arrives, Kenny tells Belinda to show the passengers what she "has" in the way of a trick. When Belinda performs her somersault, the white women passengers are disgusted, but the white men pay money to see Belinda turn upside down again. This brief passage tells us a great deal about how white men view the female—even a very young girl.

When Jim courts Arvay, she believes that he wants her only for sex, and she continues to believe this during their married life. There is little that Jim does to prove her wrong. Hurston makes clear in this novel that the rape of women was very much a part of male-female relationships. Meserve rapes Arvay before their wedding and arrogantly continues to do so during their marriage. To a certain extent, Meserve reprises the role of Rhett Butler in Margaret Mitchell's *Gone with the Wind* (1939). In the movie of the same name, Butler carries Scarlett O'Hara up the stairs after they marry because she has refused to respond to him as he thinks she should; there is little doubt of Butler's intentions. Hurston, who hoped to sell *Seraph* as a movie (she had worked for Paramount pictures as a writer), certainly knew about Mitchell's novel (it won the Pulitzer Prize) and probably had read it and seen the movie (*Seraph*, "Foreward" x). Perhaps, in part, Hurston satirizes Mitchell's romantic characters Butler and O'Hara in the portraits of Jim and Arvay. At any rate, Meserve's rape of Arvay under the mulberry tree remains chilling, although laced with comic touches, such as Arvay's torn underpants flying like a flag from a branch in the tree.

The second rape we see contains no comedy (215–18). The rape is Arvay's punishment for making Jim leave the post-football game festivities as he conducts business. In this episode, Jim treats her like a slave, brought forward for a white master's enjoyment. Indeed, he tells her that his big mistake was in not beating her right from the beginning of their marriage (215). As he orders her to strip and she moves toward the closet, he tells her not to move: "You're my damn property" (216). If he wants her naked, she will be naked; if he wants her to move, he will tell her to do so. Jim stands over her "like a statue of authority" (217). Hurston replays here a scene of moral and physical degradation forced upon many black slave women by their white masters. She suggests in these powerful rape scenes the sickness and violence of slavery that continues in the sexual relations of men and women.

In the time frame of Hurston's novel, in the first half of the twentieth century, black men in untold numbers were lynched and mutilated for their supposed rape of white women. Hurston was surely aware of this, as she most likely was aware of the popular black blues singer, Billie Holiday, and her famous signature song, "Strange Fruit." This song, written and first performed by Holiday in 1939, depicts the horror of lynching: "southern trees bear a strange fruit," that of black bodies "swinging in the Southern breeze." In *Seraph*, clearly black men are not raping women. Instead, white men talk about and actually rape their own women, from Jim Meserve to Hatton Howland, and even to Earl's failed attempted rape of Lucy Ann. The vigilante posse that seeks out and destroys Earl in the swamp reminds us of all of those white posses tracking black men to their deaths because supposedly they had raped white women. Earl's attempt to kill both his mother and father speaks volumes against the sexual violence between the white men and women in this novel.

The end of the novel, when Arvay returns to Jim, papers over the gender issues raised in the rest of the novel. Although Arvay wears men's clothing when she is on the *Arvay Henson*, her role is decidedly that of mother and lover. Arvay says to herself that any woman would be happy to have a man like Jim (339), but as readers we may wonder whether this is true. For all of Jim's macho posturing, he remains a "little boy" (341). Readers may also wonder just why Arvay feels "good" to take care of him (341). In the final pages of the novel, Arvay must win Jim back, which she does; yet, Jim insists that he wants to hear no grumbling from her (349). Although Arvay may feel at home at the end of the novel, we—and Hurston—think at what cost.

A FORMULAIC READING

Hurston's last published novel may be classified as a romance. As such, the development of a relationship drives the narrative action of *Seraph*. Romance novels generally make use of formulas, or conventional structures or patterns found in a great number of works. For example, hot-tempered Irishmen, hard-drinking, fighting, and loving, is a formulaic representation, just as the virginal, "nice"-girl blonde is. Formulas also refer to plot types, such as the romance in which poor girl meets rich boy, they fall in love; poor girl loses rich boy, they find each other again; poor girl and rich boy marry to live happily ever after. This story pattern, of course, is that of "Cinderella," which also contains various cultural anxieties of class conflicts, as well as the fantasy that wealth resolves all problems and makes for happiness. In fact, the Cinderella pattern underlies Hurston's *Seraph*. Formulaic literature, however, should not be considered simplistic or superficial. Shakespeare used formulas, for example, while at the same time he transcended them.

To a large extent, any formulaic reading of a text owes a great deal to the Russian scholar Vladimir Propp, whose *Morphology of the Russian Folktale* was first published in 1928. Propp attempted to abstract from hundreds of folktales common elements (which he called "functions") or set pieces that performed in certain ways, such as the Cinderella element. Propp referred to elements that recur in a wide number of works as *formulae*. A formulaic reading—one that looks at the formulas in any work—is sometimes referred to as formalistic because critics rely on the work's form or structure of formulas to understand the work's meanings.

In recent years, the critic John Cawelti has used the term formula as a way of talking about characteristics of "large groups of individual works from certain combinations of cultural materials and archetypal story patterns" (Cawelti 7). These characteristics may be analyzed in individual works so that we better understand them. As Cawelti notes, in romance, "the defining characteristic is not that it [usually] stars a female"; what matters is *how* the love relationship she has with another develops (41). Most romances focus on the "overcoming of . . . social or psychological barriers" (Cawelti 42). In the Cinderella formula, for example, distinctions between social classes must be overcome, as well as sibling rivalry. Cinderella's wicked stepmother is merely a not-too-subtle code for the mother all daughters are in conflict with and must inevitably leave behind in growing up.

Seraph on the Suwanee follows the familiar formulaic pattern of the ideal (or Cinderella) romance, in which the hero and heroine function as the center of the novel, with more attention focused on the heroine. All other characters remain peripheral to these characters, although there are usually several characters who act as foils to the hero and heroine. In *Seraph*, Larraine and Carl Middleton function as foils to Arvay and Jim Meserve. Larraine seems to everyone, but especially to her parents, the ideal woman, wife, and mother. She is chatty, outgoing, with a physique desired by men. Carl is the "other" potential lover for Arvay. Even though Carl marries Larraine, he had flirted with and courted Arvay, with soft touches and longing looks. Arvay continues to desire him in her own mind, even while married to Jim, until the end of the novel. Carl, in contrast to the super-masculine Jim, is weak, vain, lazy, and immoral.

All romances raise issues of gender and *Seraph* is no exception. Maria and Brock Henson, for example, view Larraine as "normal," and Arvay as "queer," as long as she remains unmarried and proposes to be a missionary to foreign heathens. Brock Henson views Carl Middleton as somehow "soft," for not doing men's work, instead preaching (and that, not very well) every week. Jim Meserve's gender, on the other hand, is never in question, but the nature of his masculinity is something Arvay, like all romance heroines, must learn to understand and accept. *Seraph*, like other romances, begins with the female "push toward individuation and actualization of the self" (Radway 147). Such a move, in a society dominated by men, begins by separating from the mother; indeed, the step is often *against* the mother. In Arvay's case, she and Jim elope, to return to her parents' house after their marriage for the wedding reception. Angeline repeats the same pattern, much to Arvay's dismay, when she elopes with Hatton Howland, a Yankee replica of Jim Meserve. To a certain degree, most romances, including *Seraph*, chronicle the daughter's journey to female selfhood as an attempt to reject and then later reconcile with the mother. In effect, Arvay's journey follows this pattern, and it is only near the end of the novel, when she promises her mother that she will provide her with a proper funeral, that Arvay achieves a sense of self-integrity. The journey also involves Arvay's "taming" of Jim Meserve, which simply means claiming him for her own once she comes to understand him.

As with most romances, Arvay remains innocent of men until she meets Jim Meserve. Her fits when confronted by the boys in Sawley result not only from her fear of sexual experience but from a denial of her own sexuality. In spite of her innocence, or perhaps even because of it, Jim Meserve sees in her the potential of fully realized womanhood, which means to him, a sexually responsive wife who can give him children. Arvay's beauty captivates him, even as she remains oblivious to it. She fits the idea of the golden princess (which is how Jim thinks of her), with her blonde hair and gulf-blue eyes, with a tinge of green when she becomes her most passionate. As Jim says to her: "I saw you like a king's daughter out of a story-book" (263). Her beauty undermines Arvay's decision to have nothing to do with the opposite sex, and it undoes Jim, so that he aims to possess her.

Jim's wish to possess her leads to his rape of Arvay. For the most part, Hurston presents the rape scene in typical romance fashion. Jim penetrates her violently and forcibly, and Arvay, like Sleeping Beauty in the fairy tale, seems to be "awakened" by his probing of her body. Indeed, Arvay's own body betrays her, as evidenced by the greenishness of her blue eyes, and her grasping Jim tightly to her. The critic John Lowe, in his analysis of this scene, finds mutual desire in both characters and downplays—or even dismisses—the episode as rape (Lowe 282–85). But to take the scene lightly is to misread Hurston's use of rape as a convention in the romance novel.

To be sure, there is often a rape scene in popular romance novels. In *Seraph,* however, rape has unusual and heightened significance. Not only does Jim rape Arvay at the beginning of the novel, but he does so at least one more time in a way even more shocking than the first. And at the end of the novel, arguably Jim may not rape Arvay, but his language replicates that used by him in his earlier rape of her. Male rape of a woman is the ultimate weapon against her voice, and without a voice, the woman becomes an object, not a subject. In the first rape, when Arvay attempts to scream, Jim silences her by crushing her mouth with a kiss. In the second rape, he commands her to do his bidding, saying she cannot talk and kiss him at the same time: so "hush talking" (218). At the end of the novel, he warns her not to say "cheep" (348).

For a writer like Hurston, obsessed in all of her novels with issues of voice—and surely obsessed with the issue of her own writerly voice being heard—she would not design these scenes lightly, even while using conventional romance formulas. Hurston would have known very well the classic myth of Philomela, in which she is raped by her own brother-in-law and has her tongue cut out so that she cannot reveal to her sister Procne what has happened to her. Philomela reveals the rape, however, through the art of a weaving, which she sends to Procne, who avenges her sister. Arvay lacks any such recourse to art—she neither reads nor does she do any artistic sewing. But Hurston has art in her writing, and like Philomela, she forces us to look at what rape is and what it does to a woman.

The fact that it is Arvay's husband who rapes her does not make the action more acceptable—even Arvay knows that, although at the end of the novel, she accepts not saying "cheep." Nor are the rapes isolated events. Hatton threatens to rape Angeline, but she, unlike her mother, does not remain silent. She asserts that she will even help Hatton to rape her. Thus Angeline neutralizes Hatton's proposed act of rape, making it no rape at all. Arvay, who overhears the scene, takes Hatton's threat seriously and is appalled (she should; after all, she had been raped just before her wedding, with promise of more to come). Arvay goes for a gun to shoot Hatton. Jim hears from her about the proposed rape and laughs at it because he feels a male kinship with Hatton.

We also have Earl's sexual assault—a failed rape—upon Lucy Ann Corregio. Screams alert Arvay that something is terrible wrong, although she believes someone has hurt Earl. Although Arvay hears screams of terror, they are overtaken by a long howl, with yelps and growls, clearly Earl's voice. By the time she investigates, Earl has disappeared, leaving Lucy Ann traumatized on the ground. If Arvay was no victim of rape, as John Lowe believes, Lucy Ann is the picture of one. Spread-eagled on the ground, with her skirt up near her waist, she exhibits bloody wounds on her neck and thigh—both evidence of sexual violence intended to silence the victim. Lucy Ann remains so still that Arvay thinks she is dead. Indeed, at least for a time, Earl has succeeded in silencing this woman. Earl's attempted rape of Lucy Ann and Jim's rape of Arvay are different only in the results. The animal-like force of Jim's rape of Arvay finds bizarre repetition in the chewed, bloody fingers of Lucy Ann. Whereas Jim's rape of Arvay ends in their marriage, just as Hatton's proposed rape of Angeline does, Earl's attempted rape of Lucy Ann ends in his death.

Before Earl's death, however, he attempts to kill his mother with an axe and his father with a gun. Hurston may give us romance in this novel, but she forces readers to confront what is at its heart. Not only does she force us to pay attention to what rape is about, but she does not let us shrug off rape as an act of derangement, some sort of anomaly. Too many so-called "normal" men in the novel indulge themselves—or desire to, anyway—in rape. Earl is associated with Arvay's family in the novel, as if whatever he does is the result of Henson bad blood. But Earl recognizes himself as a product of both his parents, as his attempt to kill both his mother and father reveals. Earl's attempted parricide tells us, just as Sophocles' Oedipus's successful parricide does, that there is something wrong at the core of the family relationships.

Earl's death precipitates a widening gulf between Arvay and Jim. Their disengagement is a recurring formula in romance literatures. Arvay's failure to understand Earl's actions and subsequent death prevents her from understanding her relationship not only with her husband but with their remaining children. Once Angeline marries and Kenny departs for New York City, Arvay feels not only loss but at a loss. These feelings are compounded when she fails a test of courage; she does not rescue Jim in his own silly, macho battle with a rattlesnake (it is impossible to miss the phallic imagery here, as well as the association with the snake in the Garden of Eden). Instead, Jeff Kelsey saves his life. As a result of Jim misreading Arvay's inability to rescue him, they find themselves, as Hurston puts it, alone in a strange, yet "familiar" wood (259). Jim tells Arvay that he does not want a "stand-still" love but rather a "knowing" and "doing" love (262); in short, a love that satisfies him. Jim leaves her saying that as far as he is concerned, they have never been truly married. Jim tells her that two people are married only when they have the "same point of view" (266).

The separation of Arvay and Jim follows the usual romance formula in which traumatic events work against the lovers securing or maintaining any close relationship. Readers know this is no final separation, since Jim tells Arvay that if she comes to him as the potential woman he married, he will try again. Arvay's return to Sawley provides her with the impetus to change into what Jim desires. In fact, she discovers change everywhere—in Sawley, and in her mother, and her view of Carl and Larraine. Arvay's mother exhibits love for her daughter for the first time in her life. In the past, Larraine had always come first; now Arvay, the least favored, finds loving acceptance from her mother, who leaves her with both blessing and the Henson property, such as it is. Only when her mother dies can Arvay go on to be herself—a mother in her own right. As the psychologist Nancy Chodorow has written in her work on female personality development, the early mothering of a female child helps to solidify a daughter's identification with her mother. This strong identification later makes for difficulties in the daughter's individuation or ability to develop an individual and integrated self (Chodorow 109; 140). Throughout the novel, Arvay closely identifies herself with her mother, despite the fact that Maria Henson seemed to favor Larraine. Arvay continually refers to her mother as a moral and authoritative figure. Her mother's home, Arvay continues to believe, is where she can be most herself. Indeed, Arvay's whole sense of herself is in relation to her mother. Once her mother dies, Arvay can theoretically be most fully herself in relation to others, including Jim, not merely in relation to her mother.

Arvay must come to terms with herself not only in relation to her mother, but also with her sister Larraine, whom she has always hated, and with Carl, whom she thought she always loved. In a way, Larraine and Carl are the romance villains: they represent fat, slovenly indulgence, hypocrisy, and greed. They lack any moral values. It thus becomes easy for Arvay to reject them and to wonder why she ever concerned herself about them in the first place. Ironically, when she began her return journey to Sawley, she had believed that she was going *home* to what was good, honest, and simple, where greed for "money and power" (272) did not exist. Arvay discovers she was wrong.

The end of the novel, as most romances tend to do, seems to resolve all of its earlier tensions. Arvay realizes that her interpretation of Henson family life was wrong. More significantly, her interpretation of Jim Meserve was wrong. That is to say that Arvay's interpretation changes to coalesce with Jim's. She no longer worries about his behavior and attitude, for she has learned how to "read" him; as she says to him, she isn't as dumb as she used to be: "I can read your writing [now]" (347). Jim repeats these words to her (348), as he disrobes; he "shucked" his pants and "snatched" off his socks (348), and continues to tell her that he never wants to hear her complain against him again. She acquiesces by kissing him over and over.

In romance formulas, the heroine inevitably learns to read male behavior; in a patriarchal society, the romance suggests, women must be able to read male behavior in order to survive. Women learn that hardness, distance, and emotional (as well as physical) cruelty, often masked by jokes, hide the hero's intense longing for her. Hurston makes use of this formula at the end of *Seraph*. At the same time, she ratchets the ending to sublime heights that the novel can not sustain.

Despite the fact that Jim Meserve's language is that of the rapist—you'll do what I tell you and not resist (349)—underneath the macho bravado is the little boy fleeing to the arms of his mother. Arvay, ever striving to be the mother throughout the novel, is happy to *be* this figure. Indeed she looks at Jim as *her* little boy (349). What is Hurston's position at this point, when she dissolves everything into the mysteries of the flesh (350)? Arvay's "fullness" of being is given over in service to Jim, the little boy encased in the hard, super-masculine exterior that not only conquers the business world, but nature itself, clearing swamps and mastering the ocean. He also masters Arvay; she becomes the potential woman he married her for—she is good in bed and a good mother, who won't say "cheep."

Arvay not only reads Jim, she reads herself. Her job, she says, turns out to be "mothering" (351); she thinks of how she mothered everyone of importance to her. Her own mother had finally looked to Arvay for mothering. Even her father, Larraine, and Carl had "taken" from her because she had an excess of herself to give. The excess in Arvay seems also to spill over into Hurston's ending: in her use of biblical language, "exaltation," "resurrection" incongruously juxtaposed with Jim's grabbing Arvay's ears and "fretfully" shaking her head (348). The *Arvay Henson*—as well as Arvay herself—are in harmony with the wind and sea, bowing in "submission to the infinite" (349), which seems to be Jim Meserve himself who grips Arvay by the shoulders so hard that it hurts her. Such juxtapositions suggest that Hurston presents this scene with a double focus. The reader can interpret the ending as s/he will. Yes, Arvay faces the new day, the sun with confidence. She has learned her position: she was "meant to serve" (352). The phrase itself can be read two ways: fatalistically, as a woman she is supposed to serve, to bow in submission to infinite male power, and/or she has chosen to fulfill such a role.

Popular romances by their very nature are not only conventional—the Cinderella romance formula remains a favorite—but tend to be conservative, presenting to women a view of who they are in terms of the roles prescribed for them by a patriarchal culture. Arvay chooses to accept the roles necessary to maintain the current organization of society. Thus, Arvay's so-called "individuation" dovetails precisely with what patriarchal society not only expects but demands from women. Hurston makes it difficult for readers, however, to forget that at the heart of such a society are male misogyny and regression, played out in the violence of rape. Her novel purposefully undermines its own "happy" ending of Arvay's return to Jim by reminding us that the price of such a union is the absolute silence of the woman: she can not—and will not—say "cheep."

Bibliography

WORKS BY ZORA NEALE HURSTON

NOVELS

Jonah's Gourd Vine. New York: J.B. Lippincott, 1934. Reprint, New York: HarperPerennial, 1990.

Moses, Man of the Mountain. New York: J.B. Lippincott, 1939. Reprint, New York: HarperPerennial, 1991.

Seraph on the Suwanee. New York: Charles Scribner's Sons, 1948. Reprint, New York: HarperCollins, 1991.

Their Eyes Were Watching God. New York: J.B. Lippincott, 1937. Reprint, Urbana: University of Illinois Press, 1979.

COLLECTION: SHORT FICTION

"Drenched in Light" (1924), in *The Complete Stories*. New York: HarperCollins, 1995. 17–25.

"The Gilded Six-Bits" (1933), in *The Complete Stories*. New York: HarperCollins, 1995.

"Sweat" (1926), in *The Complete Stories*. New York: HarperCollins, 1995.

AUTOBIOGRAPHY

Dust Tracks on a Road. New York: J.B. Lippincott, 1943. Reprint, New York: HarperPerennial, 1995.

SELECTED NONFICTION

Mules and Men. New York: J.B. Lippincott, 1935.
Tell My Horse: Voodoo and Life in Haiti and Jamaica. New York: J.B. Lippincott, 1938.

WORKS ABOUT ZORA NEALE HURSTON

BIOGRAPHIES

Hemenway, Robert E. *Zora Neale Hurston: A Literary Biography.* Urbana: University of Illinois Press, 1980.
Howard, Lillie P. *Zora Neale Hurston.* Boston: Twayne, 1980.

REVIEWS AND CRITICISM

SHORT FICTION

Howard, Lillie P. *Zora Neale Hurston.* Boston: Twayne, 1980. 56–72.
Lowe, John. *Jump at the Sun: Hurston's Cosmic Comedy.* Urbana: University of Illinois Press, 1997. 62–82.

JONAH'S GOURD VINE

Beilke, Debra. " 'Yowin' and Jawin': Humor and the Performance of Identity in Zora Neale Hurston's *Jonah's Gourd Vine.*" *Southern Quarterly*, 36, 3 (Spring 1998), 21–33.
Burris, Andrew. Review. *The Crisis*, June 3, 1934. In *Zora Neale Hurston: Critical Perspectives Past and Present*, ed. Henry Louis Gates, Jr. and K.A. Appiah. New York: Amistad, 1993. 6–8.
Felton, Estelle. Review. *Opportunity.* August 1934. In *Zora Neale Hurston: Critical Perspectives Past and Present*, ed. Henry Louis Gates, Jr. and K.A. Appiah. 4–5.
Gruening, Martha. Review. *The New Republic.* July 11, 1934. In *Zora Neale Hurston: Critical Perspectives Past and Present*, ed. Henry Louis Gates, Jr. and K.A. Appiah. 3–4.
Hurston, Zora Neale. "Art and Such." Reprinted in *Reading Black: A Critical Anthology.* New York: Meridian, 1940. 22.
Lowe, John. *Jump at the Sun: Hurston's Cosmic Comedy.* Urbana: University of Illinois Press, 1997. 85–155.
Sundquist, Eric. "The Drum with the Man Skin: *Jonah's Gourd Vine.*" In *Zora Neale Hurston: Critical Perspectives Past and Present*, ed. Henry Louis Gates, Jr. and K.A. Appiah. New York: Amistad, 1993. 39–66.

Wallace, Margaret. *The New York Times Book Review*. May 6, 1934. In *Zora Neale Hurston: Critical Perspectives Past and Present*, ed. Henry Louis Gates, Jr. and K.A. Appiah. 8–9.

THEIR EYES WERE WATCHING GOD

Bond, Cynthia. "Language, Speech, and Difference in *Their Eyes Were Watching God*." In *Zora Neale Hurston: Critical Perspectives Past and Present*, ed. Henry Louis Gates, Jr. and K.A. Appiah. New York: Amistad, 1993. 204–17.

Brown, Sterling. Review. *The Nation*. October 16, 1937. In *Zora Neale Hurston: Critical Perspectives Past and Present*, ed. Henry Louis Gates, Jr. and K.A. Appiah. 20–21.

Callahan, John F. " 'Mah Tongue Is in Mah Friend's Mouf': The Rhetoric of Intimacy and Immensity in *Their Eyes Were Watching God*." In *In the African American Grain: The Pursuit of Voice in Twentieth-Century Black Fiction*. Urbana: University of Illinois Press, 1988. 115–49.

Davie, Sharon. "Free Mules, Talking Buzzards, and Cracked Plates: The Politics of Dislocation in *Their Eyes Were Watching God*." *Publications of the Modern Language Association of America* [PMLA] 108, 3 (May 1993), 446–59.

Ferguson, Otis. Review. *The New Republic*. October 13, 1937. In *Zora Neale Hurston: Critical Perspectives Past and Present*, ed. Henry Louis Gates, Jr. and K.A. Appiah. 22–23.

Gates, Henry Louis, Jr. "*Their Eyes Were Watching God*: Hurston and the Speakerly Text." In *Zora Neale Hurston: Critical Perspectives Past and Present*, ed. Henry Louis Gates, Jr. and K.A. Appiah. 154–203.

Hibben, Sheila. *The New York Herald Tribune Weekly Book Review*. September 26, 1937. 21–22.

Locke, Alain. Review. *Opportunity*. June 1, 1938. In *Zora Neale Hurston: Critical Perspectives Past and Present*, ed. Henry Louis Gates, Jr. and K.A. Appiah. 18.

Lowe, John. *Jump at the Sun: Zora Neale Hurston's Cosmic Comedy*. Urban: University of Illinois Press, 1997. 156–255.

Tomkins, Lucille. *The New York Times Book Review*. September 26, 1937. In *Zora Neale Hurston: Critical Perspectives Past and Present*, ed. Henry Louis Gates, Jr. and K.A. Appiah. 18–19.

Walker, Alice. "Dedication." In *I Love Myself When I Am Laughing . . . : A Zora Neale Hurston Reader*, ed. Alice Walker. New York: Feminist Press, 1979. 1–5.

Washington, Mary Helen. " 'I Love the Way Janie Crawford Left Her Husbands': Emergent Female Hero." In *Zora Neale Hurston: Critical Perspectives Past and Present*, ed. Henry Louis Gates, Jr. and K.A. Appiah. 98–109.

Wolff, Maria Tai. "Listening and Living: Reading and Experience in *Their Eyes Were Watching God*." In *Zora Neale Hurston: Critical Perspectives Past and Present*, ed. Henry Louis Gates, Jr. and K.A. Appiah. 218–29.

Wright, Richard. Review. *New Masses*. October 5, 1937. In *Zora Neale Hurston: Critical Perspectives Past and Present*, ed. Henry Louis Gates, Jr. and K.A. Appiah. 16–17.

MOSES, MAN OF THE MOUNTAIN

Caron, Timothy P. " 'Tell Ole Pharaoh to Let My People Go': Communal Deliverance in Zora Neale Hurston's *Moses Man of the Mountain*." *Southern Quarterly*, 36, 3 (Spring 1998), 47–60.

Ellison, Ralph. "Recent Negro Fiction." *New Masses* (August 5, 1941), 211.

Hemenway, Robert E. *Zora Neale Hurston: A Literary Biography*. Urbana: University of Illinois Press, 1980. 256–71.

Hurston, Zora Neale. "The Fire and the Cloud." *Challenge*, 1 (September 1934), 10–14.

Hutchison, Percy. *The New York Times Book Review*. November 19, 1939. In *Zora Neale Hurston: Critical Perspectives Past and Present*, ed. Henry Louis Gates, Jr. and K.A. Appiah. 27–29.

Locke, Alain. "Dry Fields and Green Pastures." *Opportunity*, 18 (January 1940), 7.

Lowe, John. *Jump at the Sun: Zora Neale Hurston's Cosmic Comedy*. Urbana: University of Illinois Press, 1997. 205–55.

McDowell, Deborah E. "Lines of Descent/Dissenting Lines." In *Zora Neale Hurston: Critical Perspectives Past and Present*, ed. Henry Louis Gates, Jr. and K.A. Appiah. 230–40.

Untermeyer, Louis. Review. *Saturday Review*. November 11, 1939. In *Zora Neale Hurston: Critical Perspectives Past and Present*, ed. Henry Louis Gates, Jr. and K.A. Appiah. 26–27.

DUST TRACKS ON A ROAD

Bontemps, Arna. "From Eatonville, Florida to Harlem." *New York Herald Tribune* (November 22, 1942), n.p.

Johnson, Barbara. "Thresholds of Difference: Structures of Address in Zora Neale Hurston." In *Zora Neale Hurston: Critical Perspectives Past and Present*, ed. Henry Louis Gates, Jr. and K.A. Appiah. 130–140.

Lionnet-McCumber, Francoise. "Autoethnography: The An-Archi Style of *Dust Tracks on a Road*." In *Zora Neale Hurston: Critical Perspectives Past and Present*, ed. Henry Louis Gates, Jr. and K.A. Appiah. 241–66.

Preece, Harold. "Dust Tracks on a Road." *Tomorrow* (February 1943), n.p.

Rayson, Ann. "*Dust Tracks on a Road*: Zora Neale Hurston and the Form of Black Autobiography," *Negro American Literature Forum*, 7 (Summer 1973), 39–ff.

Sherman, Beatrice. *The New York Times Book Review*. November 29, 1942. In *Zora Neale Hurston: Critical Perspectives Past and Present*, ed. Henry Louis Gates, Jr. and K.A. Appiah. 32–33.

Strong, Phil. Review. *Saturday Review*. November 28, 1942. In *Zora Neale Hurston: Critical Perspectives Past and Present*, ed. Henry Louis Gates, Jr. and K.A. Appiah. 30–32.

Trefzer, Annette. "Floating Homes and Signifiers in Hurston's and Rawlings's Autobiographies." *Southern Quarterly*, 36, 3 (Spring 1998), 68–76.

SERAPH ON THE SUWANEE

Carby, Hazel V. "Foreword." *Seraph on the Suwanee*, Zora Neale Hurston. New York: HarperCollins, 1991, viii–xviii.

Hedden, Worth Tuttle. *The New York Herald Tribune Weekly Review*. October 10, 1948. In *Zora Neale Hurston: Critical Perspectives Past and Present*, ed. Henry Louis Gates, Jr. and K.A. Appiah. 35–36.

Howard, Lillie P. *Zora Neale Hurston*. Boston: Twayne, 1980. 133–48.

Rayson, Ann. "The Novels of Zora Neale Hurston." *Studies in Black Literature*, 5 (Winter 1974), 1–11.

Slaughter, Frank G. *The New York Times Book Review*. October 31, 1948. In *Zora Neale Hurston: Critical Perspectives Past and Present*, ed. Henry Louis Gates, Jr. and K.A. Appiah. 34–35.

OTHER SECONDARY SOURCES

Abrahams, Roger D., ed. *Afro-American Folktales: Stories from Black Traditions in the New World*. New York: Pantheon, 1985.

Adell, Sandra. *Double-Consciousness/Double-bind: Theoretical Issues in Twentieth-Century Black Literature*. Urbana: University of Illinois Press, 1994.

Andrews, William L. *To Tell a Free Story: The First Century of Afro-American Autobiography, 1760–1865*. Urbana: University of Illinois Press, 1986.

Bakhtin, Mikhail. *The Dialogic Imagination: Four Essays*, ed. Michael Emerson. Trans. Caryl and Michael Holquist. Austin: University of Texas Press, 1981.

Barnes, Marian E. and Linda Goss, eds. *Talk That Talk: An Anthology of African-American Storytelling*. New York: Simon, 1989.

Bloom, Harold, ed. *Zora Neale Hurston: Modern Critical Views*. New York: Chelsea House, 1986.

Bone, Robert. *The Negro Novel in America*. New Haven: Yale University Press, 1958.

Bontemps, Arna, ed. *The Harlem Renaissance Remembered*. New York: Dodd, Mead, 1972.

Bordelon, Pamela, ed. *Go Gator and Muddy the Water: Writings by Zora Neale Hurston from the Federal Writers' Project*. New York: W.W. Norton, 1999.

Braxton, Joanne M. *Black Women Writing Autobiography: A Tradition Within a Tradition*. Philadelphia: Temple University Press, 1989.

Brueggemann, Walter. *Theology of the Old Testament: Testimony, Dispute, Advocacy.* Minneapolis: Fortress Press, 1977.

Callahan, John F. *In the African-American Grain: The Pursuit of Voice in Twentieth-Century Black Fiction.* Urbana: University of Illinois Press, 1988.

Campbell, Joseph. *The Hero with a Thousand Faces.* The Bollingen Series 14. Princeton: Princeton University Press, 1973.

Cawelti, John. *Adventure, Mystery, and Romance.* Chicago: University of Chicago Press, 1976.

Chodorow, Nancy. *The Reproduction of Mothering: Psychoanalysis and the Sociology of Gender.* Berkeley: University of California Press, 1978.

Christian, Barbara. *Black Women Novelists: The Development of a Tradition, 1892–1976.* Westport, CT: Greenwood Press, 1980.

Connor, Kimberly Rae. *Conversions and Visions in the Writings of African-American Women.* Knoxville: University of Tennessee Press, 1994.

Derrida, Jacques. *Of Grammatology.* Trans. Gayatri Spivak. Baltimore: Johns Hopkins University Press, 1974.

Du Bois, W.E.B. "Negro Writers." *The Crisis,* 19 (April 1920), 289–99.

———. *The Souls of Black Folks.* Chicago: McClurg, 1903.

Eakin, Paul John. *Fictions in Autobiography: Studies in the Art of Self-Invention.* Princeton: Princeton University Press, 1985.

Fanon, Frantz. *The Wretched of the Earth.* New York: Penguin, 1961.

Faulkner, William. "The Bear" in *Go Down, Moses and Other Stories.* New York: Vintage-Random, 1973.

Ferguson James. *Faulkner's Short Fiction.* Knoxville: University of Tennessee Press, 1991.

Fisher, Dexter and Robert B. Stepto. *Afro-American Literature: The Reconstruction of Instruction.* New York: Modern Language Association of America, 1979.

Gates, Henry Louis. *"Race," Writing, & Difference.* Chicago: University of Chicago Press, 1986.

Gates, Henry Louis, Jr. *Reading Black, Reading Feminist: A Critical Anthology.* New York: Meridian, 1990.

———. *The Signifying Monkey: A Theory of Afro-American Literary Criticism.* New York: Oxford University Press, 1988.

Gilson, Etienne. *The Spirit of Medieval Philosophy.* New York: Charles H. Scribner's Sons, 1940.

Hansberry, Lorraine. *A Raisin in the Sun.* New York: Signet, 1988.

Hawthorn, Jeremy. *A Concise Glossary of Contemporary Literary Theory.* London: Arnold, 1994. Reprinted, 1996.

Holloway, Karla F.C. *The Character of the Word: The Texts of Zora Neale Hurston.* Westport, CT: Greenwood Press, 1987.

hooks, bell. *remembered rapture: the writer at work.* New York: Henry Holt, 1999.

Ingarden, Roman. *The Literary Work of Art: An Investigation on the Borders of Ontology, Logic, and Theory of Literature.* Trans. By George G. Grabowicz. Evanston, IL: Northwestern University Press, 1973.

Iser, Wolfgang. *The Implied Reader: Patterns of Communication in Prose Fiction from Bunyan to Beckett*. London: Johns Hopkins University Press, 1974.

Johnson, Barbara. "Thresholds of Difference: Structures of Address in Zora Neale Hurston." In *"Race," Writing, and Difference*, ed. Henry Louis Gates. Chicago: University of Chicago Press, 1985. 317–28.

King James Version of the Holy Bible Containing the Old and the New Testaments Together with the Apocrypha. Translated out of the Original Tongues in the Year 1611. New York: Limited Edition Club, 1935–1936.

Kristeva, Julia. "Women's Time." *Signs* 7, 1 (Autumn 1981), 13–35.

Mitchell, Henry H. *Black Preaching: The Recovery of a Powerful Art*. Nashville: Abingdon Press, 1990.

Mitchell, Margaret. *Gone With the Wind*. New York: Macmillan, 1936.

Morrison, Toni. *Beloved*. New York: Plume, 1987.

———. *The Bluest Eye*. New York: Washington Square, 1972.

———. *Jazz*. New York: Alfred A. Knopf, 1992.

Olney, James, ed. *Autobiography: Essays, Theoretical and Critical*. Princeton, NJ: Princeton University Press, 1980.

Plant, Deborah G. *Every Tub Must Sit on Its Own Bottom: The Philosophy and Politics of Zora Neale Hurston*. Urbana: University of Illinois Press, 1995.

Propp, Vladimir. *Morphology of the Russian Folktale*. Trans. Laurence Scott. Austin: University of Texas Press, 1968.

Pryse, Marjorie and Hortense J. Spillers, eds. *Conjuring: Black Women, Fiction and Literary Tradition*. Bloomington: Indiana University Press, 1985.

Radway, Janice A. *Reading the Romance: Women, Patriarchy, and Popular Literature*. Chapel Hill: University of North Carolina Press, 1984.

Robinson, Beverly. "Historical Arenas of African American Storytelling." In *Talk That Talk: An Anthology of African-American Storytelling*, ed. Marian E. Barnes and Linda Goss. New York: Simon, 1989. 211–16.

Rodgers, Lawrence R. *Canaan Bound: The African-American Great Migration Novel*. Urbana: University of Illinois Press, 1997.

Rosenberg, Bruce A. *The Art of the American Folk Preacher*. New York: Oxford University Press, 1970.

Smitherman, Geneva. *Black Talk: Words and Phrases from the Hood to the Amen Corner*. Boston: Houghton Mifflin, 1994.

Speisman, Barbara. "From 'Spears' to *The Great Day*: Zora Hurston's Vision of a Real Negro Theater." *The Southern Quarterly* 36, 3 (Spring 1998), 34–46.

Stepto, Robert. *From Behind the Veil: A Study of Afro-American Narrative*, 2nd ed. Urbana: University of Illinois Press, 1991.

Sterne, Laurence. *Tristram Shandy*. London: Everyman's Library, 1956.

Trible, Phyllis. "The Book of Jonah." *The New Interpreter's Bible*. Vol. VII. Nashville: Abingdon Press, 1996. 463–529.

Walker, Alice. *The Color Purple*. New York: Pocket Books, 1985.

———. *Good Night Willie Lee, I'll See You in the Morning*. New York: Dial, 1975.

———. *The Third Life of Grange Copeland*. New York: Pocket Books, 1988.

Wall, Cheryl, ed. *Changing Our Own Words: Essays in Criticism, Theory, and Writing by Black Women.* New Brunswick, NJ: Rutgers University Press, 1989.

Washington, Mary Helen. *Invented Lives: Narratives of Black Women, 1860–1960.* Garden City, NY: Doubleday, 1987.

Watson, Steven. *The Harlem Renaissance: Hub of African-American Culture, 1920–1930.* New York: Pantheon Books, 1995.

Werner, Craig Hansen. *Playing the Changes: From Afro-Modernism to the Jazz Impulse.* Urbana: University of Illinois Press, 1994.

Wright, Richard. *Native Son.* New York: Harper & Brothers, 1940.

Index

About the Author

JOSIE P. CAMPBELL is Professor of English and Women's Studies at the University of Rhode Island. She is the author of *John Irving: A Critical Companion* (Greenwood, 1998) and *Popular Culture in the Middle Ages* (1986). She has written extensively on medieval and Renaissance drama, Canadian women's writing, and American Literature.